IMPORTANT NOTICE

The Forest Service has renumbered all of the forest roads in Western Washington.

The old numbering system was established more than thirty years ago, before road planners had any notion of the maze of roads that eventually would be developed. The new numbering system should make road directions easier to follow.

Unfortunately, most maps still use the old numbers. For many hikes we have listed the old and new numbers side by side, so that old maps and new road signs can be used together.

100 Hikes in the

North Cascades

Ira Spring and Harvey Manning

The Mountaineers
Seattle

THE MOUNTAINEERS: Organized 1906 "... to explore, study, preserve and enjoy the natural beauty of the Northwest."

Published by The Mountaineers, 306 Second Avenue West
Seattle, Washington 98119

Published simultaneously in Canada by Douglas & McIntyre, Ltd.
1615 Venables Street, Vancouver, British Columbia V5L 2H1

Manufactured in the United States of America

Edited by Barbara Chasan
Designed by Marge Mueller; maps by Helen Sherman, Gary Rands
    and Judith Siegel
Cover: Camping at the foot of Lyman Glacier, Glacier Peak Wilderness
Frontispiece: Cub Lake and Dome Peak from Bachelor Meadows trail

Library of Congress Cataloging in Publication Data

Spring, Ira.
    100 hikes in the North Cascades.

    Includes index.
    1. Hiking—Cascade Range—Guide-books.   2. Cascade
Range—Description and travel—Guide-books.
3. Hiking—Washington (State)—Guide-books.
4. Washington (State)—Description and travel—
1981–   —Guide-books.   I. Manning, Harvey.
II. Title.   III. Title: One hundred hikes in the
North Cascades.
GV199.42.C37S67   1985   917.97'5   85–18732
ISBN 0–89886–102–0

CONTENTS

*Hike lies partially in protected area.

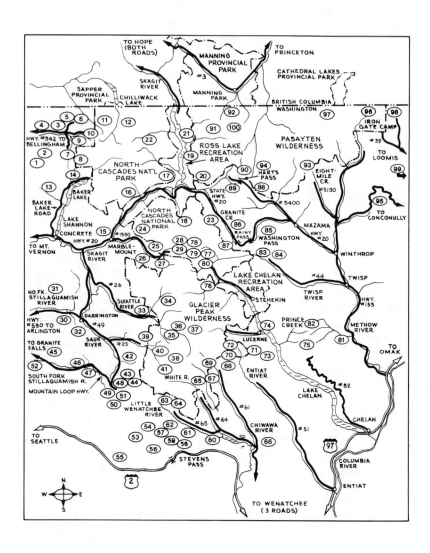

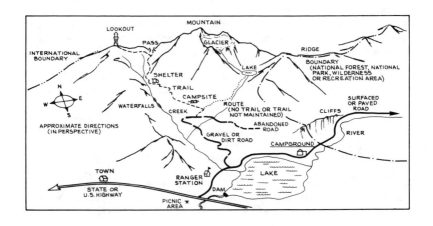

SAVING OUR TRAILS

Preservation Goals for the 1980s and Beyond

In the early 1960s The Mountaineers began publishing trail guides as another means of working "to preserve the natural beauty of Northwest America," through putting more feet on certain trails, in certain wildlands. We suffered no delusion that large numbers of boots improve trails or enhance wildness. However, we had learned to our rue that "you use it or lose it," that threatened areas could only be saved if they were more widely known and treasured. We were criticized in certain quarters for contributing to the deterioration of wilderness by publicizing it, and confessed the fault, but could only respond, "Which would you prefer? A hundred boots in a virgin forest? Or that many snarling wheels in a clearcut?"

As the numbers of wilderness lovers have grown so large as to endanger the qualities they love, the rules of "walking light" and "camping no trace" must be the more faithfully observed. Yet the ultimate menace to natural beauty is not hikers, no matter how destructive their great, vicious boots may be, nor even how polluting their millions of *Giardia* cysts, but doomsday, arriving on two or three or four or six or eight wheels, or on tractor treads, or on whirling wings—the total conquest of the land and water and sky by machinery.

Victories Past

Conceived in campfire conversations of the 1880s, Olympic National Park was established in 1938, the grandest accomplishment of our most conservation-minded president, Franklin D. Roosevelt. (Confined to a wheelchair and never himself able to know the trails with his own feet, FDR nevertheless saw the fallacy in the sneering definition of wilderness areas as "preserves for the aristocracy of the physically fit," knew the value of dreams that never could be personally attained.)

A renewal of the campaigns after World War II brought—regionally, in 1960—the Glacier Peak Wilderness and—nationally, in 1964—the Wilderness Act whereby existing and future wildernesses were placed beyond the fickleness of bureaucracies, guarded by Congress and the President against thoughtless tampering.

1968 was the year of the North Cascades Act, achieving another vision of the nineteenth century, the North Cascades National Park, plus the Lake Chelan and Ross Lake National Recreation Areas, Pasayten Wilderness, and additions to the Glacier Peak Wilderness.

In 1976 the legions of citizens laboring at the grass roots, aided by the matching dedication of certain of their Congressmen and Senators, obtained the Alpine Lakes Wilderness.

—And in 1984 the same alliance, working at the top and at the bottom and all through the middle, all across the state, won the Washington Wilderness Act encompassing more than 1,000,000 acres, including, in the purview of this volume, these new wildernesses—Boulder River, Henry M. Jackson, Lake Chelan-Sawtooth, Mt. Baker, and Noisy-

Diobsud; additions to the Glacier Peak and Pasayten Wildernesses; and a Mt. Baker National Recreation Area and a North Cascades Scenic Highway Corridor.

Is, therefore, the job done?

Goals Ahead

Absolutely not.

Had hikers been content with the victory of 1938 there never would have been those of 1960, 1968, 1976, and 1984. The American nation as a whole has a step or two yet to go before attaining that condition of flawless perfection where it fits seamlessly into the final mosaic of the Infinite Plan, and the same is true of the National Wilderness Preservation System. In the trail descriptions of this book we have expressed some of the more prominent discontents with the 1984 Act.

Among the omissions are the Alma-Copper and Hidden Lake areas, adjacent to the North Cascades National Park; Higgins Mountain, above the Stillaguamish River; Eagle Rock, near Skykomish; Nason Ridge, above Lake Wenatchee; and Beaver Meadows, Tiffany Mountain, and Chopaka Mountain, near the Okanogan.

There also are faults of omission from the newly created wildernesses: from the Boulder River Wilderness, Mt. Forgotten, Mt. Dickerman, Falls Creek, and Peek-a-boo Lake; from the Henry M. Jackson Wilderness, West Cady Creek, lower Troublesome and Lake Creeks, Lake Isabel-Ragged Ridge, Gothic Basin, and Big Four Mountain; from the Noisy-Diobsud Wilderness, the lower reaches of its two namesake creeks, the Upper Baker River, and Rocky and Thunder Creeks; from the Mt. Baker Wilderness, Damfino Creek, Church Mountain, Warm Creek, and Shuksan Lake; from the Lake Chelan-Sawtooth Wilderness, Foggy Dew, Safety Harbor, and Eagle Creeks on the south, and Cedar Creek on the north.

The additions to the existing Glacier Peak Wilderness failed to include, on the west, Falls Lake-Otter Creek, Circle Peak, and the White Chuck River, and on the east, the lower Entiat River, the North Fork of the Entiat, Mad River, Schaefer and Rock Creeks. The existing Pasayten Wilderness still does not enclose the upper Methow River, lower Lost River, South Twenty Mile Peak, and the Chewack River at Thirty Mile Campground.

The North Cascades Scenic Highway gives only modest protection; at that, it leaves out upper Canyon Creek, upper East Creek, and Driveway Butte.

As for the Mt. Baker National Recreation Area, it was specifically designed to permit snowmobiles to go to the very summit.

—And the above is only a very partial list of the remaining tasks. A very notable—and notorious—remaining problem is the management of the Lake Chelan National Recreation Area, and its failure, to date, to give the Stehekin Valley the care expected of the 1968 North Cascades Act.

It needs to be kept uppermost in mind that designation as "wilderness" or "national park" or "national recreation area" is a means, not the end.

The goals ahead are not words on a document or lines on a map but the protection of the land these symbols may signify. Any other symbols that do the job are satisfactory. The *protection* is the thing.

In contrast to the immediate past, the preservationist agenda of the immediate future is focused less on redrawing maps than employing any practical method to preserve roadless areas from further invasion by machinery. In fact, we are now at a stage where the saving of trails, important though that is, has a lower priority than the saving of fisheries and wildlife resources, scientific values, gene pools, and another contribution of wildland too long neglected, the provision of dependable and pure water for domestic and agricultural needs.

What in the World Happened to Us?

The wheel is more than the symbol. It is the fact. The National Wilderness Act so recognizes by banning "mechanized travel," including *but not limited to* motorized travel; bicycles—"mountain bikes"—are excluded too, for the simple reason that in appropriate terrain they really can go 5–10 miles per hour, an "unnatural" speed often incompatible with the "natural" 1–3 miles per hour of the traveler on foot.

Outside the boundaries of dedicated wilderness, many trails can be amicably shared by bicycles and pedestrians, both capable of being quiet and minimally destructive and disruptive of the backcountry scene. Attach a motor to the wheels, however, and the route no longer deserves to be called a "trail," it becomes a *road*.

In the past quarter-century conservationists have been busy saving Washington trails by creating a new national park and a bouquet of new wildernesses. Meanwhile, the U.S. Forest Service, without benefit of environmental impact statements, has been assiduously converting *true trails* (that is, paths suitable for speeds of perhaps up to 5 or so miles per hour, the pace of a horse) to *motorcycle roads* (that is, "trails" built to let off-road vehicles—the ORV—do 15–30 miles per hour).

In this quarter-century the concerted efforts of tens of thousands of conservationists protected large expanses of wildland from invasion by machines—but during the same period a comparative handful of ORVers have taken away more miles of trails, converted them to de facto roads, than the conservationists have saved. As the score stands in 1985, only 45 percent of Washington trails are machine-free by being in national parks and wildernesses; of the other 55 percent, half are open to motorcycles—and thus are not truly trails at all.

When automobiles arrived in America the citizenry and government were quick to see they should not be permitted on sidewalks. The Forest Service (and let it be added, the Washington State Department of Natural Resources, or DNR) are slower to recognize that whenever there are more than a few scattered travelers of either kind the difference in speed and purpose between motorized wheels and muscle-powered feet are irreconcilable.

Thinking to serve the laudable purpose of supplying "a wide spectrum of recreational opportunities," the Forest Service initially tolerated ORVs, then began encouraging them, widening and straightening and smoothing "multiple-use trails" to permit higher speeds, thus increasing the number of motors and discouraging hikers, in the end creating "single-purpose ORV trails"—in a word, roads.

Federal funds were employed for the conversion until that source dried up; since 1979 the Forest Service has relied heavily on money from the State of Washington Interagency for Outdoor Recreation (IAC), the subject of the following section of this book. Perhaps the most pernicious result is not the environmental damage, much of which can be repaired in time, but the appalling fact that when it accepts IAC funds the Forest Service signs a contract guaranteeing the trail or the equivalent to be kept open for ORVs in perpetuity. "Forever" surely is a major land-use decision, yet these conversations are made without environmental assessment, with only token public hearings, the notices tucked away in the fine print of small community newspapers.

Certainly, the Forest Service could not engage in such large-scale, long-term conversion of trails to roads if hikers were given the respect their numbers—overwhelming compared to the motorcyclists—deserve.

Hikers spoke up for the Washington Wilderness Act of 1984. By the many thousands they wrote letters to congressmen and senators. The pen is mightier than the wheel, and it must be taken up again, by those same tens of thousands, to write letters to congressmen and senators, with copies to the Regional Forester, Region 6, U.S.F.S., 319 S.W. Pine Street, P.O. Box 3623, Portland, Oregon 97208, asking that:

1. Trails be considered a valuable resource, treated as a separate category in all Forest Plans.
2. All trail users should be notified of public meetings concerning any Forest plan affecting trails; public meetings should be held in metropolitan areas as well as in small, remote communities near the trails.
3. To help reduce the conflict between hikers and ORVs, hikers on multiple-use trails (often with little children and heavy packs) shall have the right of way when meeting motors. For the safety of both parties, a speed limit of 7 mph shall be enforced on all multiple-use trails.

We do not concede that a "multiple-use trail" is a trail at all, but these measures can help ameliorate the present dangers, until philosophical retraining of land managers can be accomplished.

Harvey Manning

OF FEET AND WHEELS
AND CONFLICTS

There can be 10, 100, or even 1000 hikers in a given area, and except for those actually passed on the trail, they are unaware of one another. However, the noise of even one motorcycle bouncing off valley walls can disrupt those hikers' peace and quiet for miles around. Motorcyclists claim that when they drive to a nice spot they turn their motors off and enjoy the same peace and quiet that hikers do. This may be true, but it says nothing about how many people the machines disturbed before they were turned off.

On February 9, 1972, the President of the United States signed Executive Order 11644 stating "areas and trails [for ORVs] shall be located to minimize conflicts between off-road vehicle use and other existing or proposed recreational uses." Unfortunately, except where there is a serious safety problem, the Forest Service has given little consideration to the conflict between ORVs and hikers trying to get away from machines.

How do people feel about meeting other types of trail users? Because of their size, horses have "right of way" over motorcycles and hikers, even those hikers with heavy packs and small children, so most horse riders don't mind other users. Because of their speed, motorcycles have "right of way" over hikers. Furthermore, meeting horse riders and hikers makes cyclists think they are on a real trail and not a miniature motorcycle road, so most motorcyclists do not mind meeting other users.

To find out how hikers feel about sharing trails with motorcycles, the Washington Trails Association included at random 180 self-addressed postcards with a general mailing sent to 6000 people interested in hiking. The postcards asked five questions, and of the 180 cards mailed, 121 or 67 percent were returned, which is considered an extraordinary response. The tally is as follows:

    0 Enjoy meeting motorcycles while hiking
    6 Tolerate meeting a few motorcycles on trails
   41 Do not like meeting any motorcycles when hiking
   39 Will not hike on any trail used by motorcycles
   35 Hike only in wilderness where there are no machines

Four of the six who "tolerate a few motorcycles" added they didn't like meeting them. In addition to answering the questions, 46 squeezed in comments that were not complimentary to ORVs or the Forest Service for allowing machines on trails.

The survey may not be scientific but it shows overwhelmingly that 98 percent of the hikers who responded are opposed to motorcycles on trails. The policy of encouraging motor use on multiple-use trails turns hikers away, and eventually a multiple-use trail becomes a single-use ORV trail.

Forest Service trails originally were built for horses to carry personnel and equipment for fire protection and were adequate for the dozen or so pack strings that used them each year. The authors remember how we hiked for days in the 1930s without meeting either horses or other hikers. In the 1950s that changed. Fire patrols switched from horses to airplanes and trails became dominated by recreational users. The old trails in the main are still perfectly fine for hikers, but many are deteriorating with the increased horse and motorcycle use and require rebuilding, not because of hikers but for horses and ORVs.

Though horses represent less than 10 percent of trail use, the Forest Service tradition of building trails for them remains evident even now. The Rattlesnake Creek Trail fords the creek 14 times; two trails ford the Bumping River to reach the heart of the William O. Douglas Wilderness; and the Snowall Creek Trail in the Alpine Lakes Wilderness has two fords. By now, trail engineers with hikers in mind would have laid out different routings. Hikers, though, accepted their second-class citizenry with only a mumble. Then, suddenly, they became third-class citizens. With the advent of motorcycles came trail corners banked like a race track and 8-foot swaths cut through the forest that previously provided shade. The stepping stones a hiker yearns for were cleared from creeks to make speedy crossings for wheels.

The Forest Service estimates that hikers account for 85 percent[1] of trail use. So does 85 percent of the trail money go to hikers? I was told that all of the trail money goes for the benefit of hikers. Then I asked, "Just how much of the money is actually spent on hikers and how much money is used to correct problems caused by horses and machines?" Unfortunately, the Forest Service doesn't keep records that show this. Based on my 50 years of hiking, poring over Forest Service records, and talking with people, I estimated how much was spent on trails used primarily by hikers and how much was spent correcting the damage caused by horses and motorcycles on multiple-use trails. I figured that no more than one-third of all trail money was spent for the benefit of hikers, who represent 85 percent of the trail users, and that at least two-thirds of all trail money went to support horse riders and motorcyclists.

I hope this estimate prompts the Forest Service to check its figures and tell me if I'm wrong, and if so, where. Whether I'm right or not, in so doing it will have to analyze its trail expenditures and see how little is spent enhancing the hikers' experience.

Often I ponder "multiple use." In the 1930s, when Harvey Manning and my twin brother, Bob, and I started hiking, it meant horses and hikers. Even in the 1940s and 1950s and into the 1960s, that's what it meant. Then machines began to appear on our trails, and when we questioned the Forest Service, it justified its passive acceptance of the new user by saying, "This is multiple use." Hikers didn't speak up and the Forest Service assumed no one cared about this new addition to a growing company of backcountry travelers. If hikers had spoken, the problem never would have started, because the Forest Service would have received a resounding 98 percent[2] *"no never"* vote and found that the majority of hikers wouldn't even travel on trails that allowed motorcycles.

The Forest Service has held hearings on trail use and the ORV people made their views known and hikers didn't. With no statewide hiking organization to alert members, few hikers were even aware of the meetings. Without a real opportunity to discuss the impact on the environment with hikers or the conflict with other user groups, the Forest Service let the wheels run free on multiple use trails and thereby encouraged a market for trail bikes that never should have been manufactured.

Some Forest Service people, serious students of the forest, recognize that machines have no place on trails. A few years ago the Twisp Ranger District closed all of its trails leading to the Chelan Crest. The ranger was overwhelmed with complaints from motorcyclists, but didn't receive a single thank-you letter from hikers, and was forced to reopen four of the trails.

Other foresters, while not absolute fans of the wheels themselves, are what they consider "reasonable" compromisers, and I've had them tell me, "Hikers and motorcyclists are just going to have to learn to live with each other" and "Hikers are selfish not to share trails." But we can't. A major reason hikers go hiking is to get away from the world that is full up with wheels. Until the middle 1960s, once on the trail hikers were free of the noise and pollution in which we lived and worked. Now where can hikers escape? To the trails in national parks and wildernesses? Many are already so full of people fleeing from machines a person needs a permit to enter.

In the seven countries in the European Alps, all trails are closed to motorcycles. Even trails and roads used by farmers and foresters are closed to recreational use by motors. Even in Japan, where most of the machines come from, they are kept on a much tighter leash than here. But in America . . . .

But, only in America do letters to public officials accomplish so much. There are, in the state of Washington, approximately 350,000 self-propelled hikers and approximately 15,000 motorized trail users. With so overwhelming a 20 to 1 disproportion, why do hikers have any problem? The answer is simple. The ORV industry has spent millions advertising its way to the wilderness. ORV organizations, together with individual motorcyclists and lobbyists, have been active; hikers have not. Hikers must speak for themselves, must take up their pens—their pencils— their typewriters—their word-processors—their telephones. With whatever tool, hikers must speak! Give support to hiking organizations.[3] Urge the manufacturers of your sleeping bags, tents, and packs to protect trails and join organizations that support hikers. So *speak up.* Contact the Forest Service in your favorite hiking area, write your congressman and tell him how you think trails should be managed, then send a copy of the letter to the regional forester[4]—and don't forget what happened at Twisp—compliment the Forest Service when it makes a wise decision.

Ira Spring

---

1 Estimated by the Mt. Baker–Snoqualmie National Forest. The percentage may vary from forest to forest.
2 Washington Trails Association survey, March 1984.
3 American Hiking Society, 1701 18th Street N.W., Washington, D.C. 20009, and Washington Trails Association, 16812 36th West, Lynnwood, WA 98037.
4 Regional Forester, Region 6, USFS, 319 S.W. Pine Street, P.O. Box 3623, Portland OR 97208.

INTRODUCTION

Broad, smooth, well-marked, heavily-traveled, ranger-patroled paths safe and simple for little kids and elderly folks with no mountain training or equipment, or even for monomaniacs dashing from Canada to Mexico. Mean and cruel and mysterious routes through evil brush, over fierce rivers, up shifty screes and moraines to treacherous glaciers and appalling cliffs where none but the skilled and doughty should dare, or perhaps the deranged. Flower strolls for an afternoon, heroic adventures for a week.

A storm side (the west) where precipitation is heavy, winter long, snows deep, glaciers large, peaks sharply sculptured, vegetation lush, and high-country hiking doesn't get comfortably underway until late July. A lee side, a rainshadow side (the east) where clouds are mostly empties, summer is long, vegetation sparse, ridges round and gentle, and meadows melt free of the white by late June.

Places as thronged as a city park on Labor Day, places as lonesome as the South Pole that Scott knew. Scenes that remind of the High Sierra, scenes that remind of Alaska.

In summary, to generalize about the North Cascades: To generalize about the North Cascades is foolish.

Rules, Regulations, and Permits

Except for blocks of state (Department of Natural Resources) land around Chopaka Mountain and Mount Pilchuck-Sultan River, scattered enclaves of private lands mostly dating from mining and homestead days, and such miscellaneous bits as the Seattle City Light holdings on the Skagit River, the entirety of the North Cascades is federally administered. The U.S. Forest Service is the principal trustee, responsibility shared by Mt. Baker-Snoqualmie, Wenatchee, and Okanogan National Forests. Since 1968 the National Park Service has been on the scene in the North Cascades National Park and the accompanying Ross Lake and Lake Chelan National Recreation Areas, essentially parts of the park but permitting some activities, such as hunting, banned within the park proper.

Most of the national forest lands are under "multiple-use" administration, with roads, with logging, mining, and other economic exploitation, and with motorcycles allowed on (too) many trails. Some areas, however, have statutory protection within the National Wilderness Preservation System, where the Wilderness Act of 1964 guarantees that "the earth and its community of life are untrammeled by man, where man himself is a visitor who does not remain." The Glacier Peak Wilderness was established in 1960 and the Pasayten Wilderness in 1968. The Washington Wilderness Act of 1984 made additions to these two wildernesses and in the North Cascades established these new ones: Boulder River, Henry M. Jackson, Mt. Baker, Noisy-Diobsud, and Lake Chelan-Sawtooth. Within these, motorized travel is banned, as is any mechanized travel, such as "mountain bikes." Horse travel is carefully regulated, and though wilderness permits have been discontinued for hikers, they are subject to restrictions on party size and camping, and must acquaint themselves with the travel regulations before setting out.

The North Cascades National Park, established in 1968, was set aside, to use the words of the National Park Act of 1916, "to conserve the scenery and the natural and historic objects and the wildlife . . . " Each visitor therefore must enjoy the park "in such manner and by such means as will leave it unimpaired for the enjoyment of future generations." Most of the park is intended to be further covered by the Wilderness Act, giving a still higher degree of protection.

To help attain these goals, the Park Service requires each trail user to have a backcountry permit that must be shown on request to a backcountry ranger. Permits may be obtained by mail from the Park Service or in person from ranger stations on the major entry roads.

Maps

Each hike description in this book lists the appropriate topographic maps published by the U.S. Geological Survey. These can be purchased at map stores or mountaineering equipment shops or by writing the U.S. Geological Survey, Federal Center, Denver, Colorado 80225.

The national forests and the park publish recreation maps that are quite accurate and up-to-date and are inexpensive. Forest Service maps may be obtained at ranger stations or by writing:

Mt. Baker-Snoqualmie National Forest
1022 1st Avenue
Seattle, WA 98104

Wenatchee National Forest
P.O. Box 811
Wenatchee, WA 98801

Okanogan National Forest
P.O. Box 432
Okanogan, WA 98840

Park Service maps may be obtained, along with backcountry permits, at the ranger stations at Sedro Woolley, Marblemount, Chelan, and Stehekin.

In the National Forests a traveler not only must have a map published by the Forest Service but it must be a *current* map; the problem—and it is a distinct pain in the lower back—is that the Forest Service is engaged in renumbering roads, made necessary when the number of roads grew so large as to require the use of more than three digits. For instance, road No. 130 became road No. 1200830, and is perhaps shown as such on the new map, though the roadside sign may be simply "830." One ranger district is using parentheses, as 1200(830), another dashes, as 1200–830, and another commas, as 1200,830.

A traveler *must* know the right numbers because in many areas the Forest Service puts no names on signs, just numbers—the new ones. Your map, if it has the old numbers, will merely deepen your confusion. —And we hate to mention it, but many of the old signs remain, with the old numbers, so that even your *new* map compounds the difficulty. A word to the wise: never leave civilization without a full tank of gas, survival rations, and instructions to family or friends on when to call out the Logging Road Search and Rescue Team.

Clothing and Equipment

Many trails described in this book can be walked easily and safely, at least along the lower portions, by any person capable of getting out of a car and onto his feet, and without any special equipment whatever.

To such people we can only say, "welcome to walking—but beware!" Northwest mountain weather, especially on the ocean side of the ranges, is notoriously undependable. Cloudless morning skies can be followed by afternoon deluges of rain or fierce squalls of snow. Even without a storm a person can get mighty chilly on high ridges when—as often happens—a cold wind blows under a bright sun and pure blue sky.

No one should set out on a Cascade or Olympic trail, unless for a brief stroll, lacking warm long pants, wool (or the equivalent) shirt or sweater, and a windproof and rain-repellent parka, coat, or poncho. (All these in the rucksack, if not on the body during the hot hours.) And on the feet—sturdy shoes or boots plus two pair of wool socks and an extra pair in the rucksack.

As for that rucksack, it should also contain the Ten Essentials, found to be so by generations of members of The Mountaineers, often from sad experience:

1. Extra clothing—more than needed in good weather.
2. Extra food—enough so something is left over at the end of the trip.
3. Sunglasses—necessary for most alpine travel and indispensable on snow.
4. Knife—for first aid and emergency firebuilding (making kindling).
5. Firestarter—a candle or chemical fuel for starting a fire with wet wood.
6. First aid kit.
7. Matches—in a waterproof container.
8. Flashlight—with extra bulb and batteries.
9. Map—be sure it's the right one for the trip.
10. Compass—be sure to know the declination, east or west.

Camping and Fires

Indiscriminate camping blights alpine meadows. A single small party may trample grass, flowers, and heather so badly they don't recover from the shock for several years. If the same spot is used several or more times a summer, year after year, the greenery vanishes, replaced by bare dirt. The respectful traveler always aims to camp in the woods, or in rocky morainal areas. These alternatives lacking, it is better to use a meadow site already bare—in technical terminology, "hardened"—rather than extend the destruction into virginal places nearby.

Particularly to be avoided are camps on soft meadows (hard rock or bare-dirt sites may be quite all right) on the banks of streams and lakes. Delightful and scenic as such sites are, their use may endanger the water purity, as well as the health of delicate plants. Moreover, a camp on a

Pacific Crest Trail on side of Indian Head Peak

viewpoint makes the beauty unavailable to other hikers who simply want to come and look, or eat lunch, and then go camp in the woods.

Carry a collapsible water container to minimize the trips to the water supply that beat down a path. (As a bonus, the container lets you camp high on a dry ridge, where the solitude and the views are.)

Carry a lightweight pair of camp shoes, less destructive to plants and soils than trail boots.

As the age of laissez faire camping yields to the era of thoughtful management, different policies are being adopted in different places. For example, high-use spots may be designated "Day Use Only," forbidding camps. In others there is a blanket rule against camps within 100 feet of the water. However, in certain areas the rangers have inventoried existing camps, found 95 percent are within 100 feet of the water, and decided it is better to keep existing sites, where the vegetation long since has been gone, than to establish new "barrens" elsewhere. The rule in such places is "use established sites"; wilderness rangers on their rounds disestablish those sites judged unacceptable.

Few shelter cabins remain—most shown on maps aren't there anymore—so always carry a tent or tarp. *Never* ditch the sleeping area unless and until essential to avoid being flooded out—and afterward be sure to fill the ditches, carefully replacing any sod that may have been dug up.

Always carry a sleeping pad of some sort to keep your bag dry and your bones comfortable. *Do not* revert to the ancient bough bed of the frontier past.

The wood fire also is nearly obsolete in the high country. At best, dry firewood is hard to find at popular camps. What's left, the picturesque silver snags and logs, is part of the scenery, too valuable to be wasted cooking a pot of soup. It should be (but isn't quite, what with the survival of little hatchets and little folks who love to wield them) needless to say that green, living wood must never be cut; it doesn't burn anyway.

Both for reasons of convenience and conservation, the highland hiker should carry a lightweight stove for cooking (or not cook—though the food is cold, the inner man is hot) and depend on clothing and shelter (and sunset strolls) for evening warmth. The pleasures of a roaring blaze on a cold mountain night are indisputable, but a single party on a single night may use up ingredients of the scenery that were long decades in growing, dying, and silvering.

At remote backcountry camps, and in forests, fires perhaps may still be built with a clear conscience. Again, one should minimize impact by using only established fire pits and using only dead and down wood. When finished, be certain the fire is absolutely out—drown the coals and stir them with a stick and then drown the ashes until the smoking and steaming have stopped completely and a finger stuck in the slurry feels no heat. Embers can smoulder underground in dry duff for days, spreading gradually and burning out a wide pit—or kindling trees and starting a forest fire.

If you decide to build a fire, *do not make a new fire ring*—use an existing one. In popular areas patroled by rangers, its existence means this is an approved, "established" or "designated" campsite. If a fire ring has been heaped over with rocks, it means the site has been dis-established.

Litter and Garbage and Sanitation

Ours is a wasteful, throwaway civilization—and something is going to have to be done about that soon. Meanwhile, it is bad wildland manners to leave litter for others to worry about. The rule among considerate hikers is: *If you can carry it in full, you can carry it out empty.*

Thanks to a steady improvement in manners over recent decades, and the posting of wilderness rangers who glory in the name of garbage-collectors, American trails are cleaner than they have been since Columbus landed. Every hiker should learn to be a happy collector.

On a day hike, take back to the road (and garbage can) every last orange peel and gum wrapper.

On an overnight or longer hike, burn all paper (if a fire is built) but carry back all unburnables, including cans, metal foil, plastic, glass, and papers that won't burn.

Don't bury garbage. If fresh, animals will dig it up and scatter the remnants. Burning before burying is no answer either. Tin cans take as long as 40 years to disintegrate completely; aluminum and glass last for centuries. Further, digging pits to bury junk disturbs the ground cover, and iron eventually leaches from buried cans and "rusts" springs and creeks.

Don't leave leftover food for the next travelers; they will have their own supplies and won't be tempted by "gifts" spoiled by time or chewed by animals.

Especially don't cache plastic tarps. Weathering quickly ruins the fabric, little creatures nibble, and the result is a useless, miserable mess.

Keep the water pure. Don't wash dishes in streams or lakes, loosing food particles and detergent. Haul buckets of water off to the woods or rocks, and wash and rinse there. Eliminate body wastes in places well removed from watercourses; first dig a shallow hole in the "biological disposer layer," then touch a match to the toilet paper (or better, use leaves), and finally cover the evidence. So managed, the wastes are consumed in a matter of days. Where privies are provided, use them.

Party Size

One management technique used to minimize impact in popular areas is to limit the number of people in any one group to a dozen or fewer. Hikers with very large families (or outing groups from clubs or wherever) should check the rules when planning a trip.

Pets

The handwriting is on the wall for dog owners. Pets always have been forbidden on national park trails and now some parts of wildernesses are being closed. How fast the ban spreads will depend on the owners' sensitivity, training, acceptance of responsibility, and courtesy—and on the expressed wishes of non-owners.

Where pets are permitted, even a well-behaved dog can ruin someone else's trip. Some dogs noisily defend an ill-defined territory for their master, "guard" him on the trail, snitch enemy bacon, and are quite likely to defecate on the flat bit of ground the next hiker will want to sleep on.

For a long time to come there will be plenty of "empty" country for those who hunt upland game with dogs or who simply can't enjoy a family outing without ol' Rover. However, the family that wants to go where the crowds are must leave its best friend home.

Do not depend on friendly tolerance of wilderness neighbors. Some people are so harassed at home by loose dogs that a hound in the wilderness has the same effect on them as a motorcycle. They may holler at you and turn you in to the ranger.

Dogs belong to the same family as coyotes, and even if no wildlife is visible, a dog's presence is sensed by the small wild things into whose home it is intruding.

Horses

As backcountry population grows the trend is toward designating certain trails and camps "Hiker Only," because some ecosystems cannot withstand the impact of large animals and some trails are not safe for them. However, many wilderness trails will continue to be "Hiker and Horse" (no motorcycles, no "mountain bikes") and the two must learn to get along.

Most horse riders do their best to be good neighbors on the trail and know how to go about it. The typical hiker, though, is ignorant of the difficulties inherent in maneuvering a huge mass of flesh (containing a very small brain) along narrow paths on steep mountains.

The first rule is, the horse has the right of way. For his own safety as well as that of the rider, the hiker must get off the trail—on the downhill side, preferably, giving the clumsy animal and its perilously-perched rider the inside of the tread. If necessary—as, say, on the Goat Rocks Crest—retreat some distance to a safe passing point.

The second rule is, when you see the horse approaching, do not keep silent or stand still in a mistaken attempt to avoid frightening the beast. Continue normal motions and speak to it, so the creature will recognize you as just another human and not think you a silent and doubtless dangerous monster.

Finally, if you have a dog along, get a tight grip on its throat to stop the nipping and yapping, which may endanger the rider and, in the case of a surly horse, the dog as well.

Theft

A quarter-century ago theft from a car left at the trailhead was rare. Not now. Equipment has become so fancy and expensive, so much worth stealing, and hikers so numerous, their throngs creating large assemblages of valuables, that theft is a growing problem. Not even wilderness camps are entirely safe; a single raider hitting an unguarded camp may easily carry off several sleeping bags, a couple tents and assorted stoves, down booties, and freeze-dried strawberries—maybe $1000 worth of gear in one load! However, the professionals who do most of the stealing mainly concentrate on cars. Authorities are concerned but can't post guards at every trailhead.

Rangers have the following recommendations.

First and foremost, don't make crime profitable for the pros. If they break into a hundred cars and get nothing but moldy boots and tattered T-shirts they'll give up. The best bet is to arrive in a beat-up 1960 car with doors and windows that don't close and leave in it nothing of value. If you insist on driving a nice new car, at least don't have mag wheels, tape deck, and radio, and keep it empty of gear. Don't think locks help—pros can open your car door and trunk as fast with a picklock as you can with your key. Don't imagine you can hide anything from them—they know all the hiding spots. If the hike is part of an extended car trip, arrange to store your extra equipment at a nearby motel.

Be suspicious of anyone waiting at a trailhead. One of the tricks of the trade is to sit there with a pack as if waiting for a ride, watching new arrivals unpack—and hide their valuables—and maybe even striking up a conversation to determine how long the marks will be away.

The ultimate solution, of course, is for hikers to become as poor as they were in the olden days. No criminal would consider trailheads profitable if the loot consisted solely of shabby khaki war surplus.

Safety Considerations

The reason the Ten Essentials are advised is that hiking in the back-country entails unavoidable risk that every hiker assumes and must be aware of and respect. The fact that a trail is described in this book is not a representation that it will be safe for you. Trails vary greatly in difficulty and in the degree of conditioning and agility one needs to enjoy them safely. On some hikes routes may have changed or conditions may have deteriorated since the descriptions were written. Also, trail conditions can change even from day to day, owing to weather and other factors. A trail that is safe on a dry day or for a highly conditioned, agile, properly equipped hiker may be completely unsafe for someone else or unsafe under adverse weather conditions.

You can minimize your risks on the trail by being knowledgeable, prepared and alert. There is not space in this book for a general treatise on safety in the mountains, but there are a number of good books and public courses on the subject and you should take advantage of them to increase your knowledge. Just as important, you should always be aware of your own limitations and of conditions existing when and where you are hiking. If conditions are dangerous, or if you are not prepared to deal with them safely, choose a different hike! It's better to have a wasted drive than to be the subject of a mountain rescue.

These warnings are not intended to scare you off the trails. Hundreds of thousands of people have safe and enjoyable hikes every year. However, one element of the beauty, freedom and excitement of the wilderness is the presence of risks that do not confront us at home. When you hike you assume those risks. They can be met safely, but only if you exercise your own independent judgement and common sense.

Protect This Land, Your Land

The Cascade country is large and rugged and wild—but it is also, and particularly in the scenic climaxes favored by hikers, a fragile country. If man is to blend into the ecosystem, rather than dominate and destroy, he must walk lightly, respectfully, always striving to make his passage through the wilderness invisible.

The public servants entrusted with administration of the region have a complex and difficult job and they desperately need the cooperation of every wildland traveler. Here, the authors would like to express appreciation to these dedicated men for their advice on what trips to include in this book and for their detailed review of the text and maps. Thanks are due the Superintendent of North Cascades National Park, the Supervisors of the Mt. Baker-Snoqualmie and Wenatchee National Forests, and their district rangers and other staff members.

On behalf of the U.S. Forest Service and National Park Service and The Mountaineers, we invite Americans—and all citizens of Earth—to come and see and live in some of the world's finest wildlands, and to vow henceforth to share in the task of preserving the trails and ridges, lakes and rivers, forests and flower gardens for future generations, our children and grandchildren, who will need the wilderness experience at least as much as we do, and probably more.

Water

Hikers traditionally have drunk the water in wilderness in confidence, doing their utmost to avoid contaminating it so the next person also can safely drink. But there is no assurance your predecessor has been so careful.

No open water ever, nowadays, can be considered certainly safe for human consumption. Any reference in this book to "drinking water" is not a guarantee. It is entirely up to the individual to judge the situation and decide whether to take a chance.

In the late 1970s began a great epidemic of giardiasis, caused by a vicious little parasite that spends part of its life cycle swimming free in water, part in the intestinal tract of beavers and other wildlife, dogs, and people. Actually, the "epidemic" was solely in the press; *Giardia* were first identified in the 18th century and are present in the public water system of many cities of the world and many towns in America—including some in the foothills of the Cascades. Long before the "outbreak" of "beaver fever" there was the well-known malady, the "Boy Scout trots." This is not to make light of the disease; though most humans feel no ill effects (but become carriers), others have serious symptoms which include devastating diarrhea, and the treatment is nearly as unpleasant. The reason giardiasis has become "epidemic" is that there are more people in the backcountry—more people drinking water contaminated by animals—more people contaminating the water.

Whenever in doubt, boil the water 10 minutes. Keep in mind that *Giardia* can survive in water at or near freezing for weeks or months—a snow pond is not necessarily safe. Boiling is 100 percent effective against not only *Giardia* but the myriad other filthy little blighters that may upset your digestion or—as with some forms of hepatitis—destroy your liver.

If you cannot boil, use one of the several *iodine* treatments (chlorine compounds have been found untrustworthy in wildland circumstances), such as Potable Aqua or the more complicated method that employs iodine crystals. Rumor to the contrary, iodine treatments pose no threat to the health.

Be very wary of the filters sold in backpacking shops. One or two have been tested and found reliable (not against hepatitis) and new products are coming on the market but most filters presently available are useless or next to it.

HELIOTROPE RIDGE

Round trip to Heliotrope Ridge 6½
  miles
Hiking time 5 hours
High point 6000 feet
Elevation gain 2300 feet

Hikable August through
  September
One day or backpack
USGS Mt. Baker

A splendid forest walk leading to a ramble-and-scramble on flowery moraines below (and above) the ice chaos of the rampaging Coleman Glacier. See the mountain climbers—by the hundreds on many summer weekends, because this is the most popular route to the summit of Mt. Baker. They're a harmless and unobtrusive lot, boisterous in camp but sacking out early, rising somber and quiet in the middle of the night, and spending all day on the glaciers, out of sight and sound. Along the trail, hikers can enjoy the colorful displays of tents and axes and ropes and helmets and hardware.

Drive Highway 542 to the town of Glacier and about 1 mile beyond to Glacier Creek road, No. 39. Turn right some 8 miles to a parking lot at a sign, "Mt. Baker Trail," elevation 3700 feet.

Hike 2 miles, traversing and switchbacking through tree shadows, over cold little creeks, to Kulshan Cabin, built by the Mt. Baker Club and now maintained by the Western Washington Outdoor Club. (Respect the historic and deteriorating old cabin and the efforts of those who keep it going; don't use it unless necessary, and then only with care.)

The cabin is at 4700 feet, near but still below timberline, and camping inside and out is of the sort only a climber (his thoughts on high) can enjoy, so hike along and past. No reason to loiter.

The fun country is above. From the cabin the trail climbs crossing several streams which may be gushers from melting snowfields on a hot day. The way passes below steep flower-covered meadows, groves of alpine

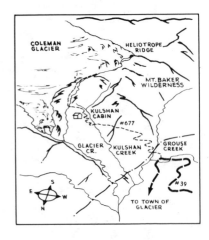

Avalanche lilies at edge of snowfield

Coleman Glacier from trail's end

trees, over a rocky moraine whistling with marmots to another moraine with a large glacier-scoured rock on the brink of a gravel precipice. Look down to the blue-white jumble of the Coleman Glacier and up to the gleaming ice-capped summit of Mt. Baker. Follow the moraine upward—stopping well short of the living glacier. Good camps below the trail in the timber.

Because of the enormous snowfall on Mt. Baker, and because this is the north side of the mountain, hikers who come earlier than August are liable to be surrounded by snow—and potential danger—above Kulshan Cabin. The crevasses, of course, are always there, visible or invisible.

Old road: 3904
New road: 39

Mount Baker from Skyline Ridge trail after a snowstorm

NOOKSACK RIVER
Mount Baker Wilderness

2 SKYLINE DIVIDE

Round trip to knoll 6 miles
Hiking time 4 hours
High point 6215 feet
Elevation gain 1700 feet

Hikable August through
**   September**
One day or backpack
USGS Mt. Baker

A large, green meadow. An enormous white volcano—pound for pound, the iciest in the Cascades. Views of forests and glaciers, rivers and mountains, sunsets and sunrises.

Drive Highway 542 to 1 mile beyond the town of Glacier. Turn right on Glacier Creek road No. 39 and in a hundred yards turn sharply left on Deadhorse road No. 37. Follow the south side of the Nooksack River some 4 level and pleasant miles. The road then climbs abruptly. At 7.5 miles pause to view a lovely waterfall splashing down a rock cleft, coming from the country where you're going. At 13 miles is the parking lot and trailhead, elevation 4500 feet.

The trail, moderate to steep, climbs 2 miles in silver firs and subalpine glades to an immense ridge-top meadow, the beginning of wide views. South are the sprawling glaciers of the north wall of Mt. Baker. North, beyond forests of the Nooksack Valley, are the greenery of Church Mountain and the rock towers of the Border Peaks and, across the border, the Cheam (Lucky Four) Range. On a clear day salt water can be seen, and the Vancouver Island Mountains, and the British Columbia Coast Range. Eastward is Mt. Shuksan and a gentler companion, little Table Mountain, above Heather Meadows.

The broadest views are atop the 6215-foot knoll to the south; from the meadow, it partly blocks out Baker. Follow the trail ¾ mile along the ridge and take the sidepath up the knoll. Sprawl and enjoy. (Note to photographers: The best pictures of Baker from here generally are taken before 10 a.m. and after 4 p.m.)

Beyond the knoll the trail follows the ridge another half-mile to a saddle at 6000 feet and then splits. The left contours a scant mile to a dead end in Chowder Basin, headwaters of Deadhorse Creek, and campsites with all-summer water. The right climbs a step in Skyline Divide to 6500 feet and proceeds along the tundra crest 2 miles to a 6300-foot saddle (and usually, a snowmelt pool) at the foot of the abrupt upward leap of Chowder Ridge, whose summit is accessible on a track suitable for goats, climbers, and life-weary hikers.

In early summer water is available for camping all along Skyline Divide, but later a party often must look for springs in Chowder and Smith Basins or snowfield dribbles on the ridge.

In benign weather the supreme overnight experience is atop the 6500-foot tundra, watching salt waterways turn gold in the setting sun and lights of farms and cities wink on, then awaking at dawn to watch Baker turn shocking pink. However, the tundra is tough enough to withstand sun and frost and storm but not human abuse. Do not build fires; if chilly, crawl in your sleeping bag. Do not sack out on soft turf; lay your sleeping pad and bag on a hard rock or bare dirt.

Old road: 3904   3907
New road: 39   37

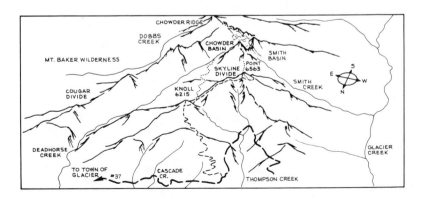

3

EXCELSIOR MOUNTAIN

**Round trip from Canyon Creek
  road 5½ miles
Hiking time 4 hours
High point 5699 feet
Elevation gain 1500 feet**

**Hikable mid-July through
  September
One day or backpack
USGS Mt. Baker**

Views from this meadow summit include Nooksack valley forests and
Puget Sound lowlands, Mt. Baker and the Border Peaks, the south-
ernmost portion of the British Columbia Coast Range, and more. Flowers
in July, berries and colors in September. Three trails lead to the site of a
long-gone lookout cabin; the easiest and most scenic is recommended
here, but take your pick.

Drive Highway 542 to the town of Glacier and 2 miles beyond to Canyon Creek road No. 31. Turn left 15 miles to the parking lot in a clearcut
at the start of trail No. 625; elevation, 4200 feet.

Climb gently through forest ½ mile to the junction with Canyon Ridge
trail No. 689 and a bit more to 4500-foot Damfino Lake, two small ponds
surrounded by acres of super-delicious blueberries (in season). Campsites
and running water near the smaller lake.

Climb another timbered mile, then go up a narrow draw and shortly
enter meadows. Cross a notch, sidehill forest, then broad meadows, rising
in ½ mile to 5300-foot Excelsior Pass, some 2½ miles from the road.
(Pleasant camps at and near the pass when there is snowfield water—
perhaps until early August.) Leave the main trail at the pass and climb a
way trail ¼ mile east to the 5699-foot peak.

Sit and look. See the glaciers of Mt. Baker across forests of the Nooksack. See more ice on Mt. Shuksan and other peaks east. See the steep-
walled Border Peaks and snowy ranges extending far north into Canada.
And see green meadows everywhere.

The summit is a magnificent place to stop overnight in good weather,

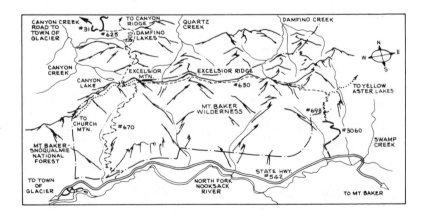

Mount Baker from Excelsior Mountain

watching a sunset and a dawn; no water, though, except possible snow-melt.

Two alternate trails can be used to vary the descent. (They can also be used to ascend the peak but for reasons that will be obvious are not the best choices.)

Alternate No. 1: From Excelsior Pass, descend trail No. 670 4 miles and 3500 feet to the highway, reached 8 miles east of Glacier at a small parking area (with trail sign on opposite side of road). The trail switch-backs steeply on south-facing slopes that melt free of snow relatively early in the season; an excellent hike from the highway in May or June, turning back when snowfields halt progress. In summer this route to high country is long and hot and dry.

Alternate No. 2: From the peak traverse High Divide trail No. 630 east 5 miles. At 4960-foot Welcome Pass find a steep trail dropping south 2 miles to an unmaintained logging road; descend the road 2 more miles to the highway, reached at a point some 13 miles east of Glacier.

Experienced off-trail roamers can extend their flower wanders west from Excelsior Pass toward Church Mountain and east from Welcome Pass to Yellow Aster Butte.

Old road: 400   4021
New road: 31   3060

4 CHURCH MOUNTAIN

Round trip 8½ miles
Hiking time 6 hours
High point 6100 feet
Elevation gain 4500 feet

Hikable late July through
September
One day
USGS Mt. Baker

The first thrilling view of emerald meadowland gained while driving east along Mt. Baker Highway is on Church Mountain. The view is

Mount Shuksan from side of Church Mountain

straight up, nearly a vertical mile, yet the green is so vivid and appears so close a person cannot but wish to go there. A person can readily do so but must be a sturdy person and carry much water because the climb is far longer than it looks and by midsummer is dry. However, the views back down to the valley and out to Mt. Baker and Shuksan are worth the sweat. In certain kinds of weather the problem is not heat. The viewpoint, on the east peak of Church, is a small platform atop a rocky pinnacle, just large enough to hold the lookout building that used to be here until it was abandoned because wind kept blowing the structure off its foundation.

Drive Highway 542 to the town of Glacier and 7.7 miles beyond. Turn left on road No. 3040, signed "East Church Road." (Avoid the unsigned road at about 7.2 miles.) Drive 2.6 miles to the road-end and trailhead, elevation 1600 feet.

The trail begins on an abandoned logging road, switchbacks up a clearcut to virgin forest, and ascends relentlessly, zigging and zagging. In a bit more than 3 miles the way opens out in heather and flowers and the trail cut can be seen switchbacking up the emerald meadowland to the rocky summit. Shortly below the top is an old storage shed, now a marmot condominium. From here the path, carved from rock, passes an odd-shaped outhouse to the lookout site.

Look down to bugs creeping along the concrete ribbon beside the silver ribbon of river. Look east into the North Cascades, north to Canada, south toward Mt. Rainier. To the west are frightful cliffs of 6315-foot Church Mountain, only 200 feet higher than the lookout peak. Below are the two little Kidney Lakes, snowbound much of the year.

Old road: 4015
New road: 3040

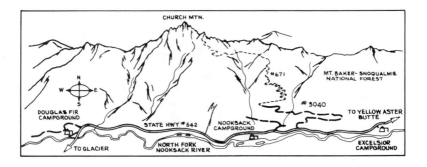

5   YELLOW ASTER LAKES

Round trip to Yellow Aster Butte
  6 miles
Hiking time 8 hours
High point 6100 feet
Elevation gain 3200 feet

Hikable mid-July through
  October
One day or backpack
USGS Mt. Shuksan

If views turn you on, there's plenty to exclaim about here—across the Nooksack valley to Mt. Baker and Mt. Shuksan, over the headwaters of Tomyhoi Creek to gaudy walls of the Border Peaks, and down to mile-long Tomyhoi Lake and out the valley to farms along the Fraser River. However, many a hiker never bothers to go to the summit of the butte or to lift eyes from the meadows and snowy-cold lakes and ponds set in pockets scooped from the rock by the glacier that appears to have left about a half-hour ago. Try the trip in late July for the flower show, in late August for the blueberry feast, and in October for autumn colors and winter frost.

Drive Highway 542 to Glacier and 13.5 miles beyond to highway maintenance sheds. Just past is a sign, "Tomyhoi Trail 5, Twin Lakes 7." Turn left up narrow, steep, rough road No. 3065 for 2.2 miles to the Keep Kool Trail No. 699, elevation 2960 feet.

The name, of course, is intended to mock the laboring hiker as he sets out on grown-over logging road of the 1940s, proceeds on straight-up cat track of the same era (high-grading the giant Douglas firs), and continues in virgin forest on a wall-climbing miners' trail, gaining 1200 feet in the first mile. It is nevertheless difficult to get overheated, what with the magnificent deep forest and the creeks to rest by. After the first mile the angle relents and at 4700 feet, about 2 miles, the way flattens to cross a delightful meadow shelf with grand views, bubbling creeks, and superb camps. A steep tilt up through parkland leads to the first tarn at 5200

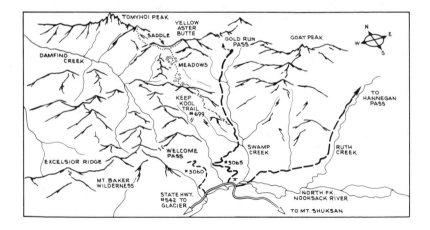

Upper Yellow Aster Lakes

feet, followed in quick succession by more tarns at 5400 feet and the beginning of holes and rusty junk left by the prospectors lest we forget them. At 5500 feet, some 2½ miles, the route (there is now no real trail, nor is one needed) enters the glory hole—a basin with lakes and ponds and pools almost beyond counting. (There are more tucked in pockets up on the ridge.)

An easy stroll leads to the summit of Yellow Aster Butte. A much longer walk climbs from lush herbaceous meadows to tundra to lichen-black felsenmeer very near the summit of 7451-foot Tomyhoi Peak, whose final hundred feet is for climbers only.

Now then: We have included this trip only after due thought, because the "yellow asters" (actually golden daisies) don't need any more human boots and fires. The area's crying need is better protection from all the boots that have gotten there unaided by guidebooks. It needs hikers who do not build fires in the flowers and campers who scatter themselves about on the ridge and off in secluded nooks. In summary, particularly tender care for the most beautiful spot on the entire Nooksack Crest.

Old road: 401
New road: 3065

6 WINCHESTER MOUNTAIN

Round trip from Twin Lakes 4 miles
Hiking time 3 hours
High point 6521 feet
Elevation gain 1300 feet
Hikable late July through September
One day
USGS Mt. Shuksan

Round trip from Tomyhoi trailhead 9 miles
Hiking time 6 hours
Elevation gain 3000 feet

An easy and popular trail through alpine meadows to a summit view of Baker, Shuksan, Border Peaks, and Tomyhoi, with looks far down to Tomyhoi Lake and forests of Silesia Creek. Especially beautiful in fall colors.

Drive Twin Lakes road No. 3065 (Hike 5) 2.2 miles to Keep Kool Trail and continue upward. At 3 miles is an intersection; go left. At 4.5 miles is the Tomyhoi Lake trail sign, elevation 3600 feet.

The Twin Lakes road is not the work of the Forest Service or built to its specifications. A "mine-to-market" road, it was constructed by the county and is maintained in the upper reaches solely by the miners, and then only when they are engaged in their sporadic activity, and then only minimally. The first 4.5 miles to the Tomyhoi Lake trail usually are in decent condition, but the final 2.5 miles to Twin Lakes are something else, culminating in five wickedly sharp switchbacks. Many people prefer to protect cars and nerves from damage by parking near the Tomyhoi Lake trail and walking to the lakes. Because road maintenance is so difficult, this last stretch is not open to automobiles until the middle of August, some years not at all; when the miners finally give up, the road will be abandoned, returning Twin Lakes to the realm of trail country—where they belong.

The two lakes, lovely alpine waters at an elevation of 5200 feet, often are frozen until early August, though surrounding parklands melt free earlier. Between the lakes is an undeveloped campsite with a classic view of Mt. Baker.

Find the Winchester Mountain trail at the road-end between the lakes.

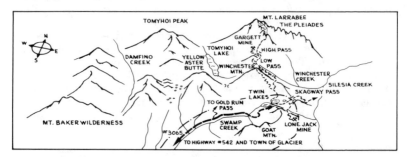

Goat Mountain from Winchester Mountain trail

Within ¼ mile is a junction with the High Pass (Gargett Mine) trail. Take the left fork and climb a series of switchbacks westerly through heather, alpine trees, and flowers. Near the top there may be a treacherous snow patch, steep with no runout, often lasting until late August. It may be possible to squirm between the upper edge of the snow and the rocks. Otherwise, drop below the snow and climb to the trail on the far side. Don't try the snow without an ice ax and experience in using it.

In 1½ miles the trail rounds a shoulder and levels off somewhat for the final ½ mile to the summit, site of an abandoned fire lookout cabin and a fine place to while away hours surveying horizons from Puget Sound lowlands to the Pickets and far north into Canada. The cabin is being restored by the Mt. Baker Hiking Club. Overnight stays are allowed. For free reservations contact Glacier Ranger Station.

Twin Lakes make a superb basecamp for days of roaming high gardens, prowling old mines, and grazing September blueberries. Even if the upper road must be walked, access is easy for backpacking families with short-legged members.

For one of the longer explorations of the many available, take the High Pass trail (see above). A steep snowfield near the beginning may stop all but trained climbers; if not, there is no further barrier to Low Pass (about 1½ miles) and 5900-foot High Pass (2½ miles). Follow an old miner's trail high on Mt. Larrabee to a close view of the rugged Pleiades. Investigate the junkyard of the Gargett Mine. Wander meadow basins and admire scenery close and distant.

Old road: 401
New road: 3065

7 CHAIN LAKES LOOP

Round trip 6 miles
Hiking time 4 hours
High point 5400 feet
Elevation gain 1500 feet

Hikable late July through
 October
One day
USGS Mt. Shuksan

Alpine meadows loaded with blueberries (in season), a half-dozen small lakes, and at every turn of the trail a changing view, dominated by "the magnificent pair," the white volcano of Mt. Baker and the massive architecture of Mt. Shuksan. The area is a wildlife sanctuary, so deer are frequently seen. All this on an easy hike circling the base of a high plateau guarded on every side by impressive lava cliffs.

Drive Highway 542 to closed-in-summer Mt. Baker Lodge (Heather Meadows Recreation Area). Continue on gravel road 3 miles upward to the 5200-foot road-end on Kulshan Ridge. The winter snowpack here is often 25 feet deep on the level, with much greater depths in drifts, so the road commonly is snowbound until late August. Drive as far as possible and walk the rest of the way.

Because the trailhead often is buried in deep snow until September, many hikers start on the wrong path. Look on the Mt. Baker side of the road-end Artist Point parking lot and spot the big, wide trail dropping a short way into forest. (Don't make the mistake of going uphill, toward Table Mountain—unless, of course, that's where you *want* to go.)

(The Table Mountain trail climbs 500 feet through lava cliffs to grand views atop the plateau; to here, the walk is easy and rewarding. The trail then continues over Table Mountain and descends cliffs to meet the Chain Lakes trail. However, on the way it crosses a steep and dangerous snowfield which has killed enough hikers that the summit traverse is not recommended.)

The Chain Lakes trail traverses almost on the level a short mile

Icebergs on Iceberg Lake

Mount Baker reflected in Iceberg Lake

around the south side of Table Mountain to a saddle between Table Mountain and Ptarmigan Ridge. At the junction here take the right fork, dropping 300 feet to the first of the four Chain Lakes, tiny Mazama Lake, reached about 1¾ miles from the road. A bit beyond is aptly named Iceberg Lake, which many years never melts out completely. Halfway around the shore one sees Hayes Lake on the left. A sidetrail follows the Hayes Lake shore and crosses a low rise to Arbuthnot Lake. Don't try to push the route farther; return the way you came.

The main trail now begins a 600-foot climb to 5400-foot Herman Saddle at about 3 miles. Cliffs of the narrow slot frame Baker west, Shuksan east. Spend some time sitting and looking from one to the other. Then descend amid boulders, heather, and waterfalls, dropping 1100 feet to meadow-surrounded Bagley Lakes. Pause to wander flower fields of the inlet stream. Look for skiers on the north side of Table Mountain; die-hards ski the permanent snowfields all summer and fall, until winter sends them to other slopes.

Between the Bagley Lakes find an unmaintained path (easy going even if the tread is lost) climbing to the Austin Pass Warming Hut and the Artist Point parking area, gaining 900 feet in 2 miles. If transportation can be arranged (by use of two cars, or by means of a helpful friend), this final ascent can be eliminated.

Curtis Glacier and Mount Shuksan from Lake Ann

NOOKSACK RIVER
Mount Baker Wilderness

LAKE ANN

Round trip to Lake Ann 8 miles
Hiking time 6–8 hours
High point (at the saddle) 4800 feet
Elevation gain about 1000 feet in,
    1000 feet out

Hikable August through
    September
One day or backpack
USGS Mt. Shuksan

When North Cascades climbers and hikers compare memories of favorite sitting-and-looking places, Lake Ann always gets fond mention. The Mt. Shuksan seen from here is quite different from the world-famous roadside view, yet the 4500-foot rise of glaciers and cliffs is at least as grand. And there is plenty to do. However, if taking the trip on a weekend, make it a day hike—you'll be hard-pressed to find an empty campsite.

Drive Highway 542 to the Mt. Baker ski area. Continue on gravel road about 1½ miles upward to the parking lot at Austin Pass, 4700 feet. Until August, snow blocks the road somewhere along the way, adding ½ mile or so of walking.

The trail begins by dropping 600 feet to a delightful headwater basin of Swift Creek. Brooks meander in grass and flowers. Marmots whistle from boulder-top perches. Pleasant picnicking.

From the basin the trail descends a bit more and traverses forest, swinging around the upper drainage of Swift Creek. At 2¼ miles is the lowest elevation (3900 feet) of the trip, an attractive camp in meadows by a rushing stream, and a junction with the Swift Creek trail. If camping beyond here, carry a stove; very little firewood is left at the lake.

Now starts a 900-foot ascent in 1½ miles, first in heather and clumps of Christmas trees, then over a granite rockslide into forest under a cliff, to a cold and open little valley. If the way is snow-covered, as it may be until mid-August, plod onward and upward to the obvious 4800-foot saddle, beyond which is Lake Ann. When whiteness melts away, the waterfalls and moraines and flowers and ice-plucked buttresses of the little valley demand a slow pace.

What to do next? First off, sit and watch the living wall of Shuksan. Then, perhaps, circumnavigate the lake, noting the contact between granitic rocks and complex metamorphics. In September, blueberry upward on the ridge of Mt. Ann. If time allows, go on longer wanders.

Recommended Wander No. 1: Follow the trail from Lake Ann as it dips into the headwater basin of Shuksan Creek, then switchbacks up and up toward Shuksan. At a rocky gully a climber's track branches steeply to the left. Just here the main trail may be nonexistent for a few yards; if so, scramble across gravel to regain the tread. Continue to a promontory a stone's throw from the snout of the Lower Curtis Glacier. Look up to the mountain. Look down forests to Baker Lake. Look beyond Swift Creek to the stupendous whiteness of Mt. Baker.

Recommended Wander No. 2: From the Lake Ann saddle climb the heathery spur to Shuksan Arm, with spectacular campsites (snowbanks for water) and views both of Baker and Shuksan.

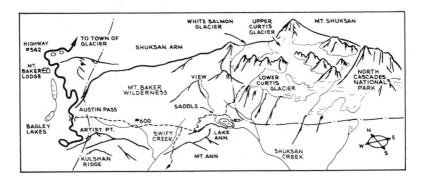

9 NOOKSACK CIRQUE

Round trip to end of gravel bars
  8½ miles
Hiking time 6–8 hours
High point 3100 feet
Elevation gain 600 feet
Hikable August and September

One day or backpack
USGS Mt. Shuksan
Park Service backcountry use
  permit required (obtained at the
  Glacier Public Service Center)

A wild, lonesome cirque, a wasteland of glacial violence, one of the most dramatic spots in the North Cascades. Icefalls, waterfalls, rockfalls, moraines, a raging river, the stark pinnacle of Nooksack Tower, and the 5000-foot northeast wall of Mt. Shuksan. But the way is only partly on trail, the rest being bushwhacking and cobble-hopping. The trip can only be recommended to rational people for late summer when the river is low enough to fully expose gravel bars.

Drive Highway 542 east from Glacier 13 miles to the Nooksack River bridge. Just before the bridge, turn left on Nooksack River road No. 32. In 1.3 miles take the right fork, road No. 34, and go another 3 miles to the road-end and trailhead, elevation about 2550 feet.

The way starts on a grown-over logging road of the 1950s, descending to the right and then climbing, at about ¾ mile reaching the end of the clearcut and the beginning of true trail, No. 680, at about 2800 feet. Constructed tread goes 1 mile through gorgeous big trees, an old-growth museum, to the end by the river. Cross a large tributary on logs (or an upstream footlog).

For the next ¾ mile there are two alternate ways. Depending on how high the river is and where its channel happens to be, airy and scenic

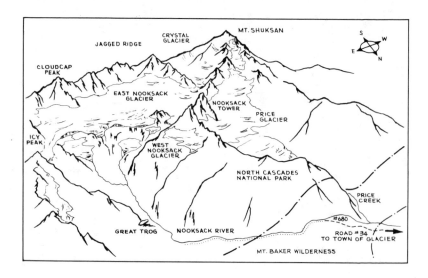

Nooksack River and Icy Peak

gravel bars may be continuous. Icy Peak appears, then the cirque itself, with hanging ice cliffs of the East Nooksack Glacier falling from Cloud-cap (Seahpo) Peak and Jagged Ridge. If the gravel won't go, the woods will. Find the boot-beaten path across some small sloughs, the start marked by a rock cairn. At several places the woods path and the gravel bars are connected by linking paths, permitting alternation.

At the end of this ¾ mile, about 2800 feet, the trail goes out on the gravel for good, a large cairn often marking the spot. The next 1 mile is on gravel bars (which may be under water) or on the riverbank terrace, partly in big timber but mostly in fierce brush, particularly nasty on an enormous alluvial fan issuing from a big gulch.

At the fan-maker creek, 2950 feet, are the last of the big trees. The next ¾ mile is easy, following mossy gravel on brushfree terraces well above high water.

At 3100 feet, about 4¼ miles from the road, the good times are over and the sensible hiker will make this the turnaround. The view of the cirque, "the deepest, darkest hole in the North Cascades," is superb. The camping (no fires allowed; bring a stove) is splendid.

Upstream from here the river gushes from a virtual tunnel through overhanging alder, with no gravel bars even in the lowest water. If you insist on persisting, dive into the slide alder, watching for cut branches and blazes and cairns. After about ¾ mile you'll attain the Great Trog (a large rock with an overhang), 3600 feet, formerly the grandest storm camp in the Cascades but now full of boulders. Exploring upward from here is tough going except in spring, when the moraines and cliffs and boulders are buried under fans of avalanche snow, and then it's danger-ous.

Old road: 402   404
New road: 32   34

10 HANNEGAN PASS AND PEAK

Round trip to Hannegan Pass 8 miles
Hiking time 6 hours
High point 5066 feet
Elevation gain 2000 feet
Hikable mid-July through September
One day or backpack
USGS Mt. Shuksan

Round trip to Hannegan Peak 10 miles
Hiking time 8 hours
High point 6186 feet
Elevation gain 3100 feet

A prime entry to the Chilliwack and Picket section of the North Cascades National Park. The walk begins in a delightful valley dominated by the white serenity of Ruth Mountain and concludes with a relaxed wander to a meadow summit offering a panorama of the north wall of Shuksan, the Pickets, and wildness high and low.

Drive Highway 542 east from Glacier 13 miles to the Nooksack River bridge. Just before the bridge turn left on Nooksack River road No. 32. In about 1.5 miles take the left fork, Ruth Creek road No. 32 and continue 4.5 miles to road-end at Hannegan Campground, 3000 feet.

The first trail mile ascends gently through trees and avalanche-path greenery near Ruth Creek, with looks upward to the waterfall-streaked cliffs and pocket ice fields of Mt. Sefrit and Nooksack (Ruth) Ridge. At a bit more than 1 mile the snow dome of Ruth Mountain comes in sight—a startling expanse of whiteness for so small a peak. Now the path steepens, climbing above the valley floor.

Rest stops grow long, there is so much to see. At 3½ miles, 4600 feet, trail swings to the forest edge beside a meadow babbling creek; across the creek is a parkland of heather benches and alpine trees. Splendid campsites, the best on the route; those least harmful to the terrain are designated by the Forest Service, which wishes campers would not build fires here. The final ½ mile switchbacks in forest to Hannegan Pass, 5066 feet.

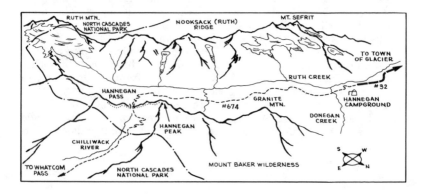

Looking north from side of Hannegan Peak

Views from the pass are restricted by trees; the camping is so poor (scarce wood, undependable water) and so damaging to the tiny meadow it is strongly discouraged and ought to be forbidden. Hikers who come only to the pass will feel richly rewarded by scenes along the way but may be disappointed by the lack of a climactic vista. A sidetrip is therefore recommended.

Visitors usually are drawn southward and upward on the climbers' track toward Ruth Mountain. This path leads to lovely meadows and broader views but dwindles to nothing before long, tempting the unwary onto steep and dangerous snow slopes. Leave Ruth to the climbers. There's a better and safer sidetrip.

From the pass, saunter westerly up open forest, following game traces when available. Emerge into a steep, lush meadow (slippery when wet), at the top break through a screen of trees to heather and flowers, and wander wide-eyed up the crest of a rounded ridge to the summit plateau of Hannegan Peak, 6186 feet. Roam the meadow flats, looking down into valley forests of Ruth and Silesia Creeks and Chilliwack River, looking out to glaciers and cliffs of Baker, Shuksan, Ruth, Triumph, Challenger, Redoubt, Slesse, and dozens of other grand peaks. Many of these peaks and valleys—including the entire route of this hike—have been omitted from the North Cascades National Park. This grievous error must be rectified.

In good weather a party can camp comfortably on the summit; carry a stove for cooking, collect water from snowfield trickles, and enjoy the panorama in sunset and dawn. Experienced highland travelers can run the open ridge north to connect with the Copper Mountain trail (Hike 11). The ridge running west to Granite Mountain is also inviting.

‖ COPPER MOUNTAIN

**Round trip to Copper Mountain
  Lookout 20 miles**
Allow 2–3 days
High point 6260 feet
**Elevation gain about 4800 feet in,
  1500 feet out**

**Hikable August through
  September**
**USGS Mt. Shuksan and Mt.
  Challenger**
**Park Service backcountry use
  permit required (obtain at
  Glacier Public Service Center)**

A remote meadow ridge on the west edge of the North Cascades National Park, offering a rare combination of easy-walking terrain and panoramas of rough-and-cold wilderness. Views across far-below forests of the Chilliwack River to the Picket Range—and views west to other superb peaks and valleys proposed for addition to the park. However, hikers planning a visit should be aware of severe restrictions on use of the area. The Park Service currently permits only "nine tents" to camp at any given time on the entire 6-mile length of the ridge. No fires allowed anywhere; carry a stove.

Drive to Hannegan Campground and hike 4 miles, gaining 2000 feet, to Hannegan Pass (Hike 10). Descend forest switchbacks into avalanche-swept headwaters of the Chilliwack River, then sidehill along talus and stream outwash patched with grass and flowers. Note chunks of volcanic breccia in the debris and look up to their source in colorful cliffs—remnants of ancient volcanoes.

At 1 mile and 650 feet below Hannegan Pass is a 4400-foot junction and a nice riverside campsite, Boundary Camp. The Chilliwack River

Mount Shuksan from Copper Ridge

trail goes right, descending. The Copper Mountain trail goes left and up, entering forest and climbing steadily, switchbacking some, crossing the upper portion of Hells Gorge (sliced into volcanic rocks), and emerging into parkland.

At 7 miles the trail attains the 5500-foot ridge crest between Silesia Creek and the Chilliwack River. A memorable look back to Hannegan Pass, Ruth Mountain, and Shuksan—and the beginning of miles of constant views.

(From this point, experienced hikers can make an off-trail ridge-running return to Hannegan Peak and Pass; also, a short sidetrip leads to a tiny cirque lake.)

The trail continues along the open crest, up a bit and down a bit, then climbs around a knob to a wide, grassy swale at 8 miles. Some 300 feet and a few minutes below the swale is little Egg Lake, 5200 feet, set in rocks and flowers. Two "tents" permitted at the lake, two others on Knob 5689, Silesia Camp.

The way goes up and down another knob to a broad meadow at 9 miles. Now comes the final mile, gaining 1100 feet to 6260-foot Copper Mountain Lookout, the climax. Beyond the green deeps of Silesia Creek are the Border Peaks and the incredible fang of Slesse—and far-off in haze, ice giants of the British Columbia Coast Range. Look down and down to the white thread of the Chilliwack River and beyond its forest valley to Redoubt and Bear and Indian and the magnificent Pickets. Also see Shuksan and Baker. And more peaks and streams, an infinity of wildland.

Beyond the lookout the trail descends about 1½ miles to the last two "tents" at 5200-foot Copper Lake (blue waters under steep cliffs), then traverses and descends about 7 more miles (views much of the way) to the Chilliwack River trail at 2300 feet; this junction is 15 miles from Hannegan Pass. A 34-mile loop trip using this return route adds low-valley forests to the high-ridge wander.

For another exploration leave the trail before the steep descent to Copper Lake and investigate ridges and basins toward the 7142-foot summit of Copper Mountain.

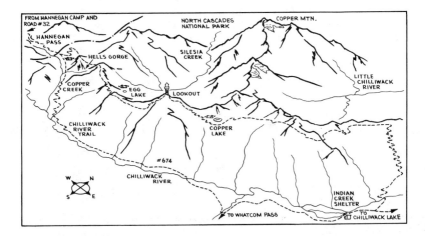

12   WHATCOM PASS

Round trip 34 miles
Allow 3–5 days
High point 5200 feet
Elevation gain 4600 feet in, 2600 feet out

Hikable late July through September
USGS Mt. Shuksan and Mt. Challenger
Park Service backcountry use permit required (obtain at Glacier Public Service Center)

A long hike on an old miners' route to the Caribou goldfields in Canada, entering the heart of the most spectacular wilderness remaining in the contiguous 48 states. Virgin forests in a U-shaped valley carved by ancient glaciers; rushing rivers; mountain meadows; and a sidetrip to lovely Tapto Lakes, the ultimate blend of gentle beauty and rough grandeur. Whatcom Pass is the high point on the increasingly popular walk across the North Cascades National Park from the Mt. Baker region to Ross Lake. However, hikers planning a trip should be aware the Park Service has banned camping between Tapto Camp and Twin Rocks Camp; they thus must be prepared to cover 5 miles in one day, gaining about 800 feet and losing 2200, a distinct discouragement of lengthy sidetrips.

Drive to Hannegan Campground and hike 4 miles, gaining 2000 feet, to Hannegan Pass (Hike 10). Descend the Chilliwack River trail, which drops rapidly at first and then gentles out in delightful forest, reaching the U.S. Cabin shelter (camping) at 10 miles.

At about 11 miles, elevation 2468 feet (2600 feet down from Hannegan Pass), the trail crosses the Chilliwack River on a cablecar. The way now climbs moderately to the crossing of Brush Creek at about 12 miles. Here is a junction.

The Chilliwack trail goes north 9 miles to the Canadian border and about 1 mile more to Chilliwack Lake. The forest walk to the border is worth taking in its own right; parties visiting the region during early summer when the high country is full of snow may prefer pleasures of the low, green world. (See note on border crossing in hike 100.)

From the 2600-foot junction the Brush Creek trail climbs steadily,

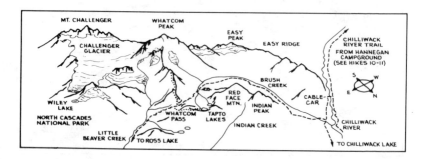

Mount Challenger from Whatcom Pass

gaining 2600 feet in the 5 miles to Whatcom Pass. At 15 miles is Tapto Camp, and at 17 miles 5200-foot Whatcom Pass.

Views from the meadowy pass are superb, but there is vastly more to see. Plan to spend at least a full day touring the area; Tapto makes the best base. The first thing to do is ramble the easy ridge south of the pass to a knoll overlooking the mind-boggling gleam of Challenger Glacier.

Tapto Lakes are next. (However, don't bother if snow is still deep around the pass; the lakes will then be frozen and their basins solid white.) Climb steep slopes north from the pass, following a boot-built path in alpine forest. When the hillside levels off continue left in meadows to rocky ground above the lakes. Enjoy the waters and flowers, the stupendous view of Challenger.

The classic "across the national park" hike from Hannegan Campground to Big Beaver Landing on Ross Lake covers 38½ up-and-down miles on easy trail beside wild rivers, through gorgeous forests, over three passes. Total elevation gain on the way, 5400 feet. To have time for sidetrips a party should allow 7–9 days. From Whatcom Pass drop abruptly (56 switchbacks!) into headwaters of Little Beaver Creek, an enchanting place where waterfalls tumble from cliffs all around. Camping here at Twin Rocks Camp, 3000 feet. At 6 miles from Whatcom Pass is Stillwell Camp and the 2400-foot junction with the Beaver Pass trail. To conclude the cross-park journey, see Hike 22.

Old road: 402
New road: 32

13

PARK BUTTE— RAILROAD GRADE

Round trip to Park Butte 7 miles
Hiking time 6–8 hours
High point 5450 feet
Elevation gain 2250 feet

Hikable mid-July through
October
One day or backpack
USGS Hamilton and Mt. Baker

Recommending any one hike in the parklands of Mt. Baker's southwest flank is like praising a single painting in a museum of masterpieces. There are days of wandering here, exploring meadows and moraines, waterfalls and lakes, listening to marmots and watching for mountain goats. The trail to Morovitz Meadow gives a good sampling of the country, with impressive near views of the glaciers of Baker, the towering Black Buttes (core of an ancient volcano), the Twin Sisters, and far horizons.

Drive Highway 20 east from Sedro Wooley 14.5 miles and turn left on the Baker Lake–Grandy Lake road. In 12.5 miles, just past Rocky Creek bridge, turn left on Loomis–Nooksack road No. 12, go 3 miles to Sulphur Creek road No. 13, and follow it 6 miles to the end in a logging patch (inside the Mt. Baker Recreation Area!) at about 3200 feet. Find the trail west of the road, near Sulphur Creek.

The trail immediately crosses Sulphur Creek into the heather and blueberries (in season) of Schreibers Meadow, passes frog ponds and a dilapidated shelter cabin, then enters forest. In 1 mile is an interesting area where meltwater from the Easton Glacier has torn wide avenues through the trees. The drainage pattern changes from time to time; generally three torrents must be crossed by footlog or boulder hopping.

Beyond the boulder-and-gravel area the trail enters cool forest and switchbacks steeply a long mile to lower Morovitz Meadow. The grade gentles in heather fields leading to upper Morovitz Meadow, 4500 feet. Pleasant campsites here, some in alpine trees, some in open gardens beside snowmelt streams.

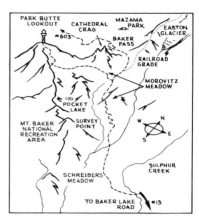

Snout of Easton Glacier

Mount Baker lost in clouds from Park Butte trail

At the trail junction in the upper meadow, go left to Park Butte, climbing to a ridge and in a mile reaching the 5450-foot summit. Views of Mt. Baker glaciers (and much more) are magnificent. Parties with spare time and energy may well be tempted to descend to the delightful basin of Pocket Lake or roam the ridge to 6100-foot Survey Point.

There is another direction to go from Morovitz Meadow. Leave the trail near the junction and ramble upward to the intriguing crest of Railroad Grade, a moraine built by the Easton Glacier in more ambitious days. Look down the unstable wall of gravel and boulders to the naked wasteland below the ice. Walk the narrow crest higher and yet higher, closer and closer to the gleaming volcano. In late summer hikers can scramble moraine rubble and polished slabs to about 7000 feet before being forced to halt at the edge of the glacier.

From either Railroad Grade or Baker Pass, inventive walkers can pick private ways through waterfall-and-flower country to the edge of a startling chasm. Look down to the chaotic front of the Deming Glacier, across to stark walls of the Black Buttes. All through the wide sprawl of Mazama Park are secluded campsites, beauty spots to explore. Don't forget little Mazama Lake or nearby Meadow Point.

Old road: 3725   372
New road: 12   13

14   LITTLE SHUKSAN LAKE

Round trip 3 miles
Hiking time 4 hours
High point 4500 feet
Elevation gain 1700 feet in, 300
  feet out

Hikable mid-July through
  September
One day
USGS Mt. Shuksan

The hike to this beauty spot and grand views is short, but the same can be said for climbing the stairs to the top of Seattle's Smith Tower—twice. The boot-beaten path is as steep as a trail can get and not require climbing ropes and pitons. Indeed, at spots it's nothing but a scramble route, wickedly treacherous on the descent.

Drive the Baker Lake road (Hike 13) to Koma Kulshan Guard Station and 10 miles beyond. Turn left on road No. 1160, sign-described as "limited maintenance," so you won't be too surprised by a rockslide (1983) at about 2 miles that a passenger car may refuse to cross. At a bit more than 4 switchbacking miles the road makes a final zig to climb around a cliff on a narrow roadbed blasted from solid rock; the view of Mt. Baker above is spectacular and so is that of Baker Lake, a swan dive below. At 4.7 miles the road abruptly ends in a space just big enough for a couple of cars to park and latecomers to turn around to go someplace else. Please don't block that turnaround; backing down this cliff-hanger would be no picnic. The road-end is the trailhead, elevation 2800 feet.

Trail No. 608 is unmarked but obvious, starting in a huckleberry-covered clearcut. Sawn logs show that fishermen's boots have occasional help in maintenance. The path quickly enters virgin forest and climbs steeply, and more steeply, gaining 1700 feet in a scant mile up a narrow ridge that gives a few views down to Baker River, 3000 feet below below below.

At 4500 feet the way tops the ridge and Mt. Shuksan is framed by foreground trees. The Sulphide Glacier is on the left of the Summit Pyramid, Crystal Glacier and Ragged Ridge on the right. For views of Mt. Baker follow the ridge ¼ mile farther to its highest point, a heather meadow.

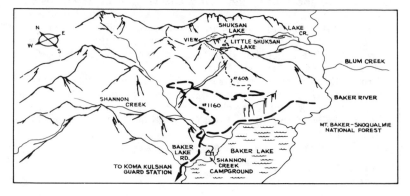

Little Shuksan Lake and Mount Blum

The trail drops 300 feet to Little Shuksan Lake, 4200 feet. The fishermen's trail continues down to 3800-foot Shuksan Lake, with fish (it darn well better have *something* to justify getting there) but few views.

The "Little" is ringed by clumps of trees, fields of heather, and acres of blueberries. Though shallow, the lake has interesting bays and a picturesque island. Campsites are numerous. By midsummer the outlet dries up and the water warms up (enough for swimming).

Old road: 3817
New road: 1160

Skagit valley from Cow Heaven. Whitehorse Mountain in distance

SKAGIT RIVER—ROSS LAKE
Unprotected area

15   COW HEAVEN

Round trip 11 miles
Hiking time 8 hours
High point 4400 feet
Elevation gain 4000 feet

Hikable July through October
One day
USGS Marblemount and Lake
   Shannon

Years ago, Skagit ranchers chased cows way up here to chew the alpine salads. Now only the occasional horse gobbles the flowers, so it's a heaven for hikers, with views from the Skagit Valley to the Pickets, Eldorado, Whitehorse, and countless peaks between. But the route to heaven lies through purgatory—gaining 4000 feet in 5½ miles. Moreover, from August on a water shortage just about forces the trip to be done in a single grueling day, though in early summer snowmelt permits camping.

Drive Highway 20 to Marblemount. At the town edge turn north .7 mile to the North Cascades National Park ranger station. Directly opposite the station take an unmarked road passing the information office. Go by a barn and small house and at 1.2 miles from the highway, where the road dead-ends at Olson Creek, spot the well-signed trailhead, elevation a meager, low-down 400 feet. The final ¼ mile of road often is washed out and must be walked.

The route is signed "Cow Heaven Trail 763, 4 miles." Don't believe it—the best views are at least 5½ miles. Eager to get the job done, the path wastes no time flirting, but starts steep and stays steep. The initial 2 miles are in fine shape, the tread wide and edged by soft moss, cooled by deep shadows of virgin forest. A creek is crossed at 1 mile and recrossed at 1½ miles—the last for-sure water. At about 2¼ miles the tread dips into a shallow ravine and for the next ½ mile often is gullied to naught. Just beyond 3 miles the way passes above an all-summer (usually) stream. Tall trees yield to short ones and at 4 miles to a dense tangle of mountain ash, white rhododendron, and huckleberry. At 4½ miles, about 3600 feet, a brief flat with bits of heather invites camping—but provides no lake, pond, river, creek, dribble, or spring for the purpose, only (through July?) a snowfield.

Maintained trail ends here, but a sketchy path, beaten out mainly by hunters, heads over the knoll on the skyline, climbing to the 4400-foot viewpoint. If aggrieved leg muscles and swollen tongue permit, continue up the alpine ridge to steadily broader views.

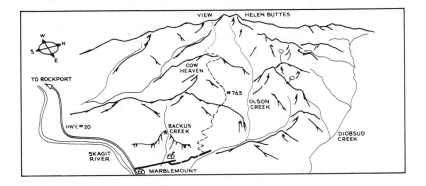

16 THORNTON LAKES— TRAPPERS PEAK

Round trip to lower Thornton
  Lake 9½ miles
Hiking time 6–8 hours
High point 4900 feet
Elevation gain 2100 feet in, 400
  feet out

Hikable mid-July through
  October
One day or backpack
USGS Marblemount
Park Service backcountry use
  permit required

Three deep lakes in rock basins gouged by a long-gone glacier. Close by are living glaciers, still gouging. All around are icy peaks on the west edge of the North Cascades National Park. From a summit above the lakes, a splendid view of Triumph and Despair and the Picket Range. Not realizing they are in a national park, many hikers come here with dogs and guns and without a permit, and sometimes go away with tickets. The camping is unpleasant to miserable, and not recommended unless you're there for the fishing (which also is poor). Make it a day hike.

Drive Highway 20 to Marblemount and 11 miles beyond to Thornton Creek road, which is unmarked—spot it between mileposts 117 and 118. Turn left 5 steep miles to a parking area, elevation about 2800 feet.

The first 2 miles are on an abandoned logging road. Then begins the trail, which was never really "built" in a formal sense but just grew; it's very steep in places and mucky in others. Except for the abandoned road across clearcuts, most of the way lies in forest. At a bit more than 1 mile from the abandoned road is an opening and a small creek to jump. The trail then switchbacks up a forested slope to the ridge crest.

Recuperate atop the 4900-foot ridge crest. Look down to the lake basin and out to Mt. Triumph. Then drop 400 feet to the lowest and largest Thornton Lake. Across the outlet stream are campsites designated by posts; no fires allowed.

To reach the middle and upper lakes, traverse slopes west of the lower lake. The middle lake usually has some ice until the end of July; the upper lake, at 5000 feet in a steep-walled cirque, ordinarily is frozen until mid-August.

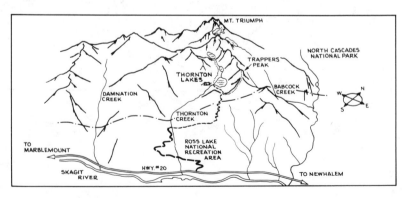

Middle Thornton Lake and Mount Triumph

If views are the goal, don't drop to the lakes. Leave the trail at the 4900-foot crest and follow a faint climbers' track up the ridge to the 5964-foot summit of Trappers Peak. See the fantastic Pickets. And see, too, the little village of Newhalem, far below in the Skagit Valley. The route is steep in places and requires use of the hands, but is not really tough. Early in the season there may be dangerous snow patches; go above or below them. Turn around content when the way gets too scary for plain-and-simple hikers.

Diablo Lake from Sourdough Mountain

SKAGIT RIVER—ROSS LAKE
Ross Lake National Recreation Area

17 SOURDOUGH MOUNTAIN

Round trip to TV tower 7 miles
Hiking time 7 hours
High point 4800 feet
Elevation gain 3900 feet
Hikable May through October
One day or backpack
USGS Diablo Dam and Ross Dam
Park Service backcountry use
** permit required**

Loop trip 14 miles
Allow 2 days
High point 5985 feet
Elevation gain 4500 feet
Hikable July through October

No other hike from the Skagit River can match these views of the North Cascades National Park. Look down to Diablo Lake and Ross Lake and out to forests of Thunder Creek. Look south to the ice of Colonial and Snowfield, and southeast to Buckner and the sprawling Boston Glacier. Look east to the king of the Skagit, Jack Mountain, and north to Canada, and northwest and west to the Pickets.

There are two routes to Sourdough Mountain. One is an extremely steep trail—a strenuous day trip and even with an overnight camp not an easy weekend. The other is a loop which can be done in an arduous 2 days.

Drive Highway 20 to the Seattle City Light town of Diablo, at the base of Diablo Dam. Park in the main lot; elevation 900 feet.

Direct trail: Walk back from the parking lot past the powerhouse and tennis court and find the signed trail behind the covered swimming pool. The trail starts steep and stays steep; countless short switchbacks gain 3000 feet in the first 2½ miles before the way "levels off" to an ascent of 2000 feet in the final 4 miles to the summit.

After 1½ miles of zigzags from the road up a forested hillside, an opening gives a sample of panoramas to come. At 3 miles is an unmarked junction. The left fork climbs a steep ½ mile to a TV antenna serving Diablo. For most day hikers this 4800-foot viewpoint is far enough, adding northern vistas to the southern. The way to this turnaround point often is free of snow in May, offering a spectacular springtime hike.

The main trail climbs from the junction, on a gentler grade than before, reaching a designated campsite at Sourdough Creek, 4 miles, elevation 5000 feet. (Water can be found at several places before this point, but it's thirsty travel at best.) In another 1½ miles the summit and fire lookout cabin are attained, with all the previous views plus additional ones north up Ross Lake and west to the Pickets.

Loop trail: From the parking lot, hike the unmarked ½-mile trail to the top of Diablo Dam and take the Diablo Lake passenger boat to the base of Ross Dam. Climb the road 400 feet in 1 mile to the top of Ross Dam, cross the dam, and find the Big Beaver trail. In 3 miles is a junction. Turn left on the Sourdough Mountain trail and climb 3000 feet in 4 miles to a designated campsite in Pierce Mountain saddle, and 1000 feet more in 1 mile to the 5985-foot lookout. Tread is indistinct or absent in the final rocky mile to the summit; watch for cairns. Descend to the parking lot via the "direct trail."

If two cars or a helper are available, a party can shortcut the loop by hiking from Highway 20 the 1 mile down to Ross Dam (Hike 21) and exiting to a pickup at Diablo.

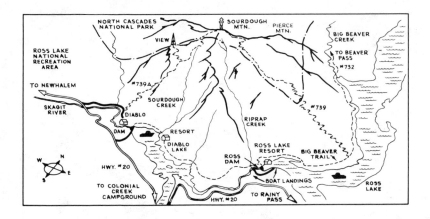

18 THUNDER CREEK

Round trip to McAllister Creek 11
miles
Hiking time 5–7 hours
High point 1800 feet
Elevation gain 600 feet
Hikable April through November
One day or backpack
USGS Ross Dam and Forbidden
Peak
Park Service backcountry use
permit required

Round trip to Park Creek Pass 36
miles
Allow 3–5 days
High point 6040 feet
Elevation gain 6000 feet
Hikable late July through
October
USGS Ross Dam, Forbidden Peak,
Mt. Logan, Goode Mountain

One of the master streams of the North Cascades, draining meltwater
from an empire of glaciers. The first portion of the trail, easy walking, is
nearly flat for miles, passing through groves of big firs, cedars, and hemlocks, with views of giant peaks. The route continues to a high pass amid
these peaks; for experienced wilderness travelers, the trip from Thunder
Creek over Park Creek Pass to the Stehekin River is a classic crossing of
the range. Designated camps are scattered along the way, permitting
travel by easy stages.

Thunder Creek trail

Drive Highway 20 to Diablo Dam and 4 miles beyond to Colonial Creek Campground, where the trail begins, elevation 1200 feet.

The trail follows Thunder Arm of Diablo Lake about 1 mile, then crosses Thunder Creek on a bridge, and in another ½ mile comes to a junction with a trail climbing to Fourth of July Pass and Panther Creek. The Thunder Creek trail continues straight ahead on the sidehill, going up and down a little, mainly in big trees except at 3½ miles, in a burn meadow from a lightning fire in 1971, and at 5 miles, in another from a 1970 fire; the openings give neck-stretching looks to the summits of Snowfield and Colonial. At about 1¼ and 2 miles respectively are Thunder and Neve Camps.

At 5½ miles is the site of long-gone Middle Cabin, signed "Miners Rest Stop," and ¼ mile farther is the bridge to the McAllister Creek Camp, a good turnaround for a day or weekend trip. The trail to here offers one of the best forest hikes in the North Cascades and is open to travel early in the season and late.

At 6 miles the way goes from national recreation area to national park; dogs must stop. At 7 miles past Tricouni Camp, the trail crosses Fisher Creek and follows it, climbing 1000 feet above the valley floor, which here is a vast marshland. At 9 miles are Junction Camp, 3000 feet, and a junction with Fisher Creek trail (Hike 23). Off the trail a bit are grand views down to the valley and across to glaciers of Tricouni and Primus Peaks. Shortly thereafter an obscure spur trail descends 1000 feet in 1 mile to the two Meadows Cabins, at the edge of the marsh. The main trail passes stunning viewpoints of the enormous Boston Glacier, Buckner and Boston and Forbidden thrusting above, drops steeply to the valley bottom at 2200 feet, and climbs to Skagit Queen Camp, 13 miles, 3000 feet, near where Skagit Queen Creek joins Thunder Creek. The way climbs steeply, gentles out somewhat in a hanging valley; at 15½ miles, 4300 feet, is the last designated campsite, Thunder Basin Camp. No fires. From here the trail ascends steadily up and around the meadow flanks of Mt. Logan to 6040-foot Park Creek Pass, 18 miles, a narrow rock cleft usually full of snow. To continue down to the Stehekin River, see Hike 80.

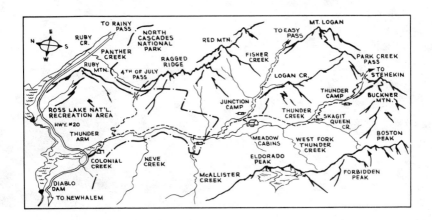

19   EAST BANK TRAIL

One-way trip from Panther Creek
  to Hozomeen 31 miles
Allow 3–5 days
High point about 3500 feet
Elevation gain about 5000 feet
Hikable mid-June through
  October
USGS Ross Dam, Pumpkin
  Mountain, Skagit Peak,
  Hozomeen Mountain
Park Service backcountry use
  permit required

Round trip from Panther Creek to
  Rainbow Camp 15 miles
High point 2600 feet
Elevation gain 900 feet in, 1250
  feet out
Hikable May through October

When full, the reservoir known as Ross Lake simulates nature and is, indeed, a veritable inland fjord. Unfortunately, draw-downs of water for power production expose dreary wastelands of mud and stumps. Because of the low elevation, the hike along the lake is especially attractive in

Lightning Creek bridge and Ross Lake

spring, when most mountain trails are deep in snow—sorry to say, that's when the lake is at its visual worst. Generally the reservoir is full from late June to October and at a lower level other months, the maximum draw-down of as much as 150 feet usually coming in March or April.

However, even when stumps are showing there still are grand views across the waters to high peaks. To learn the valley in all its moods, to enjoy the panoramas from end to end, hike the East Bank Trail, mostly through forest, a little along the shore, and finally detouring inland to reach Hozomeen Campground. The complete trip can be done in several days or any portion selected for a shorter walk.

If only a portion of the trail is to be hiked, travel to Ross Dam and arrange with Ross Lake Resort for water-taxi service to the chosen beginning point and a pickup at trip's end (Hike 21).

To do the entire route, drive Highway 20 the 8 miles from Colonial Creek Campground to Panther Creek Bridge and find the trailhead in the large parking area, elevation 2000 feet.

The trail drops 200 feet to the crossing of Ruby Creek and a junction beyond. Go left to Ruby Creek Barn, a scant 3 miles from the highway. The way leaves the water's edge to climb 900 feet over Hidden Hand Pass, returning to the lake near Roland Point Camp, 7½ miles.

The next 7½ miles to Lightning Creek are always near and in sight of the lake. Some stretches are blasted in cliffs; when the reservoir is full the tread is only a few feet above the waves, but when the level is down the walking is very airy. There are frequent boat-oriented camps, including the one at Lightning Creek, 15 miles from the highway.

Here the trail forks. The left continues 3 more miles up the lake, ending at the Desolation Peak trailhead (Hike 21).

For Hozomeen, take the right fork, switchback up 1000 feet to a glorious view of the lake, then lose all that elevation descending to a camp at Deer Lick Cabin (locked), 4 miles from the lake. The trail bridges Lightning Creek to a junction with the Three Fools Trail (Hike 91). Go left 7 miles to the junction with the abandoned Freezeout trail; go left on a bridge over Lightning Creek to Nightmare Camp, in a spooky cedar grove. The way leaves Lightning Creek and climbs to Willow Lake at 2853 feet, 10 miles. Another 5 miles of some ups but mostly downs lead by a sidetrail to Hozomeen Lake and at last to the road-end at Ross Lake, 31 miles from the trailhead at Panther Creek.

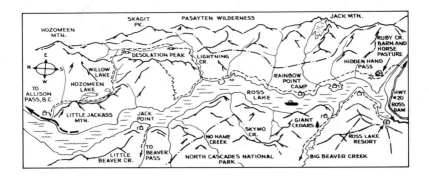

Crater Mountain

20 CRATER–DEVILS LOOP

One-way trip to Devils Dome
  Landing 27 miles; complete loop
  43 miles
Allow 5–9 days
High point 6982 feet
Elevation gain about 7500 feet
Hikable mid-July through
  October

USGS Crater Mountain, Azurite
  Peak, Shull Mountain, Jack
  Mountain, Pumpkin Mountain
Park Service backcountry permit
  required for camping at Ross
  Lake

Hoist packs and wander meadow ridges east of Ross Lake, encircling the far-below forests of Devils Creek and the cliffs and glaciers of 8928-foot Jack Mountain, "King of the Skagit," looking to peaks and valleys from Canada to Cascade Pass, the Pickets to the Pasayten. The trip is recommended as a loop but for shorter hikes the climaxes can be reached from either end.

Drive Highway 20 eastward from Colonial Creek Campground, in 8 miles passing the Panther Creek trailhead; at 11 miles is the unmarked parking area along the riverbank at the junction of Canyon and Granite Creeks, which here unite to become Ruby Creek. Elevation, 1900 feet.

The trailhead is directly across both creeks—but you probably won't be able to get there from here. A signed trail leads to a bridge over Granite Creek 300 yards upstream from the confluence, and some years Canyon Creek has a handy log jam, and you're off and away. However, if Canyon Creek must be forded, better forget it—this is not the place for a novice to learn how to wade cold, swift North Cascades rivers.

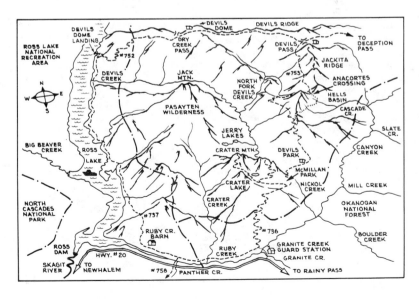

Probably, therefore, your trip must start westward 3 miles, at the Panther Creek trailhead, and begin by walking the trail up the north side of Ruby Creek to the Crater Mountain trailhead. If the complete loop is contemplated, this is the logical beginning anyhow—and in any event it's a delightful river-and-forest walk.

Once the trailhead is reached the work begins—the trail gains 3400 feet in 4 miles. Fortunately, the labor is mostly shaded by big trees and there is water at several well-spaced points and ultimately glimpses of peaks. At 4 miles, 5280 feet, is a junction.

For a compulsory sidetrip, go left ¾ mile to the impressive cirque and shallow waters of 5800-foot Crater Lake. Just before the meadow-and-cliff-surrounded lake, a 2-mile trail climbs eastward to a lookout site on the broad, 7054-foot easternmost summit of Crater Mountain. From the lake a 2½-mile trail climbs westward to another lookout site on the 8128-foot main summit of Crater; the final ½ mile is for trained climbers only, but the panoramas are glorious long before difficulties begin. When this higher lookout was manned, the final cliff was scaled with the help of wooden ladders and fixed ropes. Maintenance proved too difficult and summit clouds too persistent, causing installation of the lower lookout. Now both cabins are long gone.

From the 4-mile junction the trail descends the gently sloping table of McMillan Park to Nickol Creek, 4900 feet, then climbs an old burn, loaded with blueberries in season, to Devils Park Shelter, 7 miles, 5600 feet. (This and the other shelters are not maintained but will be left as they are until too dangerous, then demolished.) One can roam for hours in this plateau of meadows, clumps of alpine trees, and bleached snags.

The way now climbs northward along Jackita Ridge into a larch-dotted basin. At 8¾ miles, some 6200 feet, is a junction of sorts. The well-maintained Jackita Ridge trail No. 753, the main route, continues up across the basin. The long-abandoned alternate Hells Basin trail, un-signed and with no tread at first, climbs to the 6700-foot ridge crest, drops more than 1000 feet into stark Hells Basin, regains the elevation to climb over Anacortes Crossing, and loses it again to rejoin the Jackita Ridge trail.

From the unmarked junction at 8¾ miles the main route ascends a shoulder, switchbacks 800 feet down a slate scree to a rocky basin, rounds another shoulder and drops 300 feet into another open basin, climbs 500 feet to a third shoulder, drops 1000 feet through meadows and forest to the North Fork Devils Creek, and ascends very steeply up-stream ½ mile to the 5500-foot junction with the trail to Anacortes Crossing—which is some 1500 feet and 1 mile from here, and another compulsory sidetrip. Main-route distance to this junction, 13¼ miles.

The trail traverses sweeping gardens of Jackita Ridge, up some and down more, to Devils Pass, 15¼ miles, 5800 feet. The best camping is at Devils Pass Shelter, several hundred feet and ½ mile below the pass in a pretty meadow with a year-round spring, reached via the Deception Pass trail and then a sidetrail.

From Devils Pass the way turns west on the Devils Ridge trail, going through open woods near and on the ridge top, then climbing a lush basin to Skyline Camp, 18 miles, 6300 feet—a lovely spot for a campfire and a star-bright sleep, but with no water after the snows are gone. (In fact,

Crater Lake

there is no dependable water between North Fork Devils Creek and Dry Creek Pass.)

A flower-and-blueberry traverse and a short ridge-crest ascent lead, at 20 miles, to the 6982-foot site of the demolished Devils Dome Lookout, the highest elevation of the main-route trail.

Now down into a basin of waterfalls and boulders and blossoms and around the flowery slopes of Devils Dome, with time out for a compulsory, easy-walking, off-trail roaming to the 7400-foot summit and wide horizons. At 21½ miles is a ¼-mile sidetrail to 6000-foot Bear Skull Shelter, the first possible camp if the loop is being done in the reverse direction and a long day—5½ miles and 4500 feet—above Ross Lake.

At last the highlands must be left. The trail goes down the crest a short bit to Dry Creek Pass, descends forests and burn meadows to the only dependable creek at 28 miles, enters young trees (hot and grueling to climb in sunny weather) of an old burn, crosses the East Bank Trail, and ¼ mile later, at 27 miles, ends at the lakeside camp of Devils Dome Landing.

To return to the start, either hike the East Bank Trail (Hike 19) or, by prearranged pickup, ride back in a boat of Ross Lake Resort (Hike 21).

21   DESOLATION PEAK

Round trip from Desolation Landing 9 miles	**Hikable mid-June through August**
Hiking time 7 hours	**One day (from the lake) or**
High point 6085 feet	**backpack**
Elevation gain 4400 feet	**USGS Hozomeen Mountain**
	Park Service backcountry use permit required

A forest fire swept the slopes bare in 1926, giving the peak its name. The lookout cabin on the summit gained fame in literary circles after being manned for a summer by the late Jack Kerouac, "beat generation" novelist and sometime Forest Service employee. Some of his best writing describes the day-and-night, sunshine-and-storm panorama from the Methow to Mt. Baker to Canada, and especially the dramatic close-up of Hozomeen Peak, often seen from a distance but rarely from so near. Since Kerouac, the lookout frequently has been manned by poets. The steep trail is a scorcher in sunny weather; carry lots of water.

The start of the Desolation Peak trail can be reached by walking 18 miles on the East Bank Trail (Hike 19) or by riding the water taxi. For the latter, drive Highway 20 eastward from Colonial Creek Campground 3.8 miles to the parking lot of the Ross Dam trailhead, elevation 1800 feet. But before this, from home or while driving up the Skagit Valley, telephone Ross Lake Resort. (There is no direct telephone service to the resort, but contact can be made. Dial "Operator," ask for "Everett Operator," give the number 397-7735, and make arrangements. Bring cash—the taxi man will not accept checks or credit cards.) Then, from the trailhead, drop 200 feet to the dam and boat dock opposite the resort; here the resort boat will ferry you to your destination and return to pick you up at a prearranged time.

The trail starts steep and stays steep, climbing 1000 feet a mile. For such a desolate-appearing hillside there is a surprising amount of shade, the way often tunneling through dense thickets of young trees. This is

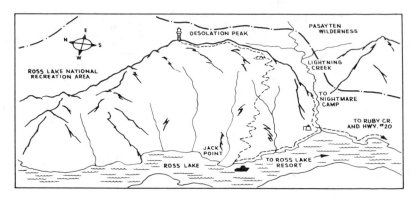

Jack Mountain on left and Ross Lake from Desolation Peak

fortunate, because the sun can be unmerciful on the occasional barren bluffs.

Views come with every rocky knoll. In ½ mile see a small grove of birch trees. In 2 miles, there is a spring—which may, however, dry up in a rainless summer. At 3 miles the trail enters steep, open meadows and at 4 miles is the ridge crest. A high bump remains to be climbed over before the lookout is sighted. The flower fields include some species that properly "belong" on the east slopes of the Cascades.

The horizons are broad and rich. Only Mt. Baker stands out distinctly among the distant peaks, though those who know them can single out Shuksan, the Pickets, Colonial, Snowfield, Eldorado, and scores of other great mountains. Closer in, the spectacular glacier of 8928-foot Jack Mountain dominates the south. To the north rise the vertical walls of Hozomeen, the south peak so far climbed by but a single route, with many virgin cliffs remaining to tempt the experts. West across Ross Lake are the deep valleys of No Name Creek, Arctic Creek, and Little Beaver Creek. East are the high, meadow-roaming ridges of the Cascade Crest and the Pasayten country.

The fjordlike Ross Lake reservoir, dotted by tiny boats of fishermen, is the feature of the scene. Unfortunately, from fall to spring miles of dreary mud flats are exposed as the reservoir is drawn down; plan the trip for summer, when the full reservoir adorns rather than desecrates the Ross Lake National Recreation Area.

There is a designated campsite (no fires) in the trees just below the high meadows; water is from snowfields only and usually rare or nonexistent by late July. Because of the time spent getting to the trailhead, the best plan for a weekend trip is to travel the first day to Lightning Creek Camp, stay there overnight, and do the climb the second day.

22 BEAVER LOOP

Loop trip 26½ miles
Allow 3–5 days
High point 3620 feet
Elevation gain about 3500 feet
  including ups and downs
Hikable June through October

USGS Hozomeen Mountain, Mt.
  Spickard, Mt. Challenger, Mt.
  Prophet, Pumpkin Mountain
Park Service backcountry use
  permit required

This loop hike from Ross Lake to close views of the Picket Range and back to Ross Lake offers perhaps the supreme days-long forest experience in the North Cascades. The 27-mile trip up the Little Beaver valley and down the Big Beaver passes through groves of enormous cedars, old and huge Douglas firs and hemlocks, glimmery-ghostly silver fir, lush alder, young firs recently established after a fire (in 1926 enormous portions of the Skagit country burned), and many more species and ages of trees as well. And there are brawling rivers, marshes teeming with wildlife, and awesome looks at Picket glaciers and walls.

Travel by car and trail to Ross Lake Resort (Hike 21) and arrange for taxi service up the lake and a pickup at trip's end. The loop (or day or weekend hikes) can begin at either end; the Little Beaver start is described here.

After a scenic ride up Ross Lake, debark at Little Beaver Landing; a campground here, elevation 1600 feet. The trail starts by switchbacking 800 feet to get above a canyon, then loses most of the hard-won elevation. At 4½ miles is Perry Creek Shelter, an easy ford-or-footlog crossing of

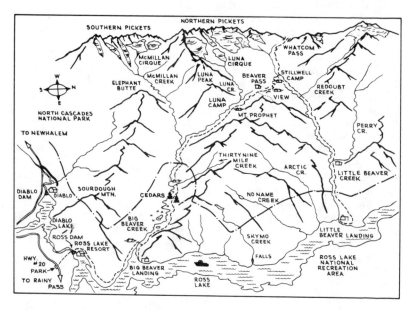

Big Beaver valley

several branches of the creek, and a passage along the edge of a lovely marsh. At 9 miles is Redoubt Creek; scout around for a footlog. At 11½ miles, 2450 feet, is a junction.

The Little Beaver trail goes upstream 6 miles and 2800 feet to Whatcom Pass (Hike 12). Take the Big Beaver trail, which crosses Little Beaver Creek, passes a sidetrail to Stillwell Camp, and climbs a steep mile to Beaver Pass, 3620 feet. The trail goes nearly on the level a mile to designated campsites at Beaver Pass Shelter (emergency use only), the midpoint of the loop, 13½ miles from Little Beaver Landing and 13 miles from Big Beaver Landing.

An hour or three should be allowed here for an easy off-trail sidetrip. Pick a way easterly and upward from the shelter, gaining 500–1000 feet through forest and brush to any of several open slopes that give a staggering look into rough-and-icy Luna Cirque; the higher the climb the better the view.

Passing Luna Camp on the way, descend steeply from Beaver Pass into the head of Big Beaver Creek; two spots on the trail offer impressive glimpses of Luna Cirque. At 6 miles from Beaver Pass Shelter (7 miles from Big Beaver Landing on Ross Lake) the Big Beaver tumbles down a 200-foot-deep gorge; a good view here of Elephant Butte and up McMillan Creek toward McMillan Cirque. The moderately up-and-down trail crosses recent avalanches which have torn avenues through forest, passes enormous boulders fallen from cliffs above, and goes by a marsh.

At 8 miles from Beaver Pass (5½ from Ross Lake) cross Thirtynine

Canadian dogwood, or bunchberry, growing in Big Beaver valley

Cedar grove and Big Beaver valley trail

Mile Creek; campsite. The way now enters the glorious lower reaches of Big Beaver Creek, a broad valley of marshes and ancient trees, including the largest stand of western red cedar (some an estimated 1000 years old) remaining in the United States. Seattle City Light planned to flood the lower 6 miles of the valley by raising Ross Dam, but after an epic 15-year battle, in 1983 the plans were permanently dropped.

Passing one superb marsh after another, one grove of giant cedars after another, at 3 miles from Ross Lake the trail for the first time touches the banks of Big Beaver Creek, milky-green water running over golden pebbles. Finally the trail reaches Big Beaver Landing, from which a ¼-mile trail leads left to Big Beaver Camp. (This is a boaters' camp. Hikers should use Pumpkin Mountain Camp, 100 yards south of the bridge over Big Beaver Creek on the Ross Lake trail.)

There are two ways to return to Ross Dam. One is by hiking the 6-mile Ross Lake trail, which branches right from the Big Beaver trail at a junction ¼ mile before the landing. The second is to arrange in advance with Ross Lake Resort to be picked up at Big Beaver Landing.

23 EASY PASS—FISHER CREEK

Round trip to Easy Pass 7 miles
Hiking time 7 hours
High point 6500 feet
Elevation gain 2800 feet
Hikable mid-July through
September
One day or backpack
USGS Mt. Arriva and Mt. Logan
Park Service backcountry use
permit required

One-way trip from Easy Pass to
Colonial Creek Campground 19
miles
Allow 3–4 days
Elevation gain 5300 feet

Dramatic are the views, but the trail definitely is not easy. Prospectors found this the easiest (maybe the only) pass across Ragged Ridge, and thus the name. However, the tread is rough, at times very steep, and in spots muddy. Finally, the pass area is very small, extremely fragile, and camping is not allowed.

Drive the North Cascades Highway 21.5 miles east from Colonial Creek Campground or 6.2 miles west from Rainy Pass to an unmarked spur road and parking area, elevation 3700 feet.

In a short ¼ mile the trail crosses swift, cold Granite Creek, hopefully on a footlog, and then climbs 2 miles in woods to the edge of a huge avalanche fan, 5200 feet, under the rugged peaks of Ragged Ridge. The trail now may become elusive, buried in snow or greenery. (Make very

Elephanthead growing below Easy Pass

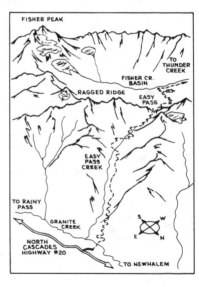

Fisher Creek Basin and Fisher Peak

sure not to lose the path; cross-country exploration here is agonizing.) The way goes over the avalanche fan and Easy Pass Creek and begins a long, steep ascent along the south side of the valley to the pass. Flower gardens. Small groves of trees. Watercourses. Boulder fields. Up, always up. The route crosses Easy Pass Creek twice more and at about 6100 feet comes within a few feet of a gushing spring, the source of the creek. Tread shoveled from a steep talus slope leads to the 6500-foot pass, a narrow, larch-covered saddle.

For the best views wander meadows up the ridge above the pass and look down 1300 feet into Fisher Creek Basin and out to glaciers and walls of 9080-foot Mt. Logan.

To continue to Diablo Lake, descend 1½ miles to a designated no-fire camp in Fisher Basin, 5200 feet. At 5½ miles is Cosho Camp and, just beyond, a footlog crossing of Fisher Creek. At 10½ miles is Junction Camp, where is met the Thunder Creek trail (Hike 18), which leads to Colonial Creek Campground at 19 miles from the pass.

Lookout Mountain and Eldorado Peak

CASCADE RIVER
Partially in North Cascades National Park

24 LOOKOUT MOUNTAIN– MONOGRAM LAKE

**Round trip to Lookout Mountain
8½ miles
Hiking time 9 hours
High point 5719 feet
Elevation gain 4500 feet
Hikable mid-July through
October
One day or backpack
USGS Marblemount**

**Round trip to Monogram Lake 7½
miles
Hiking time 9 hours
High point 5400 feet
Elevation gain 4200 feet in, 600
feet out
Park Service backcountry use
permit required**

Take your pick: a fire lookout with a commanding view of North Cascades peaks and valleys, or a cirque lake, a fine basecamp for roaming, nestled in the side of a heather-covered ridge.

Drive Highway 20 to Marblemount and continue east 7 miles on the Cascade River road to the 1200-foot trailhead between Lookout and Monogram Creeks.

The trail climbs steeply in a series of short switchbacks along the spine of the forested ridge between the two creeks, gaining 2400 feet in the 2½ miles to a campsite at the first dependable water, a branch of Lookout Creek at 3600 feet. At 2¾ miles is a junction, elevation 4200 feet.

Lookout Mountain: Go left from the junction, shortly emerging into meadow and switchbacking relentlessly upward. The tread here may be hard to find and difficult to walk. In 1½ miles from the junction, gaining 1500 feet, the 5719-foot summit is attained.

Flowers all around—and views. Look north and west to the Skagit River Valley, southeast and below to the Cascade River. Mountains everywhere, dominated by giant Eldorado Peak. About ¼ mile below the summit, in a small flat, is a spring that runs most of the summer. Magnificent camps here for enjoyment of the scenery in sunset and dawn—but disaster camps in a storm.

Monogram Lake: Traverse right from the junction on a steep, lightly timbered hillside. The trail leaves trees for meadow and in a mile crosses a creek, climbs to a 5400-foot crest with broad views, and descends to 4800-foot Monogram Lake, usually snowbound through July. Designated no-fire campsites around the meadow shores.

The lake is a superb base for wanderings. For one, climb open slopes to the southeast and then follow the ridge northerly to a 5607-foot knoll looking down into Marble Creek and across to the splendor of 8868-foot Eldorado—a closer and even better view of the peak than that from Lookout Mountain. Continue on the ridge for more flowers, then drop through gardens to the lake. For a more ambitious tour, ascend meadows on the southern extension of Teebone Ridge and ramble to the 6844-foot south summit of Little Devil Peak, with looks down to small glaciers. Climbers can continue on and on along the rocky-and-snowy ridge, but hikers must stop when the terrain gets too rough for party experience.

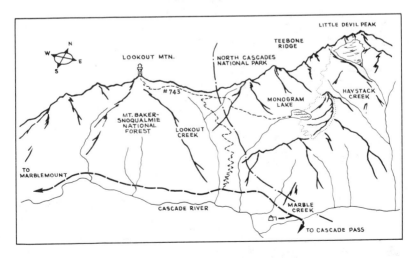

25 HIDDEN LAKE PEAKS

Round trip to Sibley Creek Pass 6
  miles
Hiking time 5 hours
High point 6100 feet
Elevation gain 2700 feet
Hikable mid-July through
  October
One day or backpack
USGS Eldorado Peak and Sonny
  Boy Lakes
Park Service backcountry use
  permit required at Hidden Lake

Round trip to Hidden Lake
  Lookout 8 miles
Hiking time 8 hours
High point 6890 feet
Elevation gain 3500 feet
Hikable August through October

Flower fields, heather meadows, ice-carved rocks, and snow-fed water-falls on an alpine ridge jutting into an angle of the Cascade River Valley, providing an easy-to-reach viewpoint of the wilderness North Cascades from Eldorado on the north through the Ptarmigan Traverse to Dome Peak on the south.

Drive Highway 20 to Marblemount and continue east on the Cascade River road 9.5 miles (2 miles past the Marble Creek bridge) to Sibley Creek road No. 1540. Turn left 4.7 miles to road-end (the way rough but passable to suitably small and spry cars) in a logging patch, elevation 3400 feet.

Trail No. 745 begins in a clearcut, entering forest in ¼ mile and switchbacking upward 1 mile. The way then emerges from trees into lush brush and crosses Sibley Creek. (Some years avalanche snow may linger in the creek bottom all summer, in which case look for obvious trail cut through very steep sidehill greenery.) The trail switchbacks up alder clumps and deep grass and flowers to a recrossing of Sibley Creek at 2½ miles, 5200 feet. Note, here, the abrupt and striking transition from metamorphic to granitic rocks, the first supporting richly green herbaceous flora, the other dominated by heather. Just past the crossing is a minimal campsite.

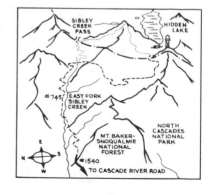

Ptarmigan in summer plumage

Ice covered Hidden Lake and Sahale Peak, center

Sibley Creek Pass: Leave the trail at the second crossing and follow your nose upward, scrambling very steep and slippery, then easy meadows ½ mile to 6100-foot Sibley Creek Pass on the exact boundary of the North Cascades National Park. The view is down to Cascade River forests and up the valley to Cascade Pass and out everywhere to alpine magnificence.

The pass is the recommended destination for short-trippers and hikers lacking experience in snow travel. The views are at least as glorious as those elsewhere on the ridge and the route is free of tricky snowfields much earlier in the summer. From the pass a moderate rock scramble leads to the 7088-foot highest summit of the Hidden Lake Peaks.

Hidden Lake Lookout: From the second crossing the trail traverses wide-open heather-and-waterfall slopes (several nice good-weather camps), then rounds a corner and climbs. One snow-filled gully may be too treacherous for hikers lacking ice axes. If so, don't attempt to cross, but instead go straight uphill to find a safe detour, or turn back and visit Sibley Creek Pass. The trail may be snow-covered at other points but by proceeding straight ahead the tread can be picked up. At 3½ miles is a tiny basin, a lovely nonstorm campsite. The abandoned lookout cabin can now be seen atop cliffs. Continue a short way, usually on a gentle snowfield, to the 6600-foot saddle and look down to Hidden Lake and out to a world of wild peaks.

Though it's only ½ mile and 300 feet from the saddle to the broader views of the 6890-foot lookout, parts of the trail may be lost in extremely dangerous snow, suited only for trained climbers. Even without snow the final section of trail is airy.

From the saddle an easy walk over loose boulders leads to the 7088-foot peak. Or descend rough talus to the 5733-foot lake, ordinarily snowbound through most of the summer. Designated no-fire campsites above the lake.

26 KINDY RIDGE— FOUND LAKE

**Round trip from slide to Kindy
  Ridge viewpoint about 10 miles
Hiking time 11 hours
High point 5791 feet
Elevation gain 4700 feet in, 300
  feet out
Hikable July through October
One day
USGS Sonny Boy Lakes and
  Snowking Mountain**

**Round trip to Found Lake about
  14 miles
Allow two days
High point 4800 feet
Elevation gain 3600 feet in, 1100
  feet out
Hikable mid-July through
  October**

A close view of seldom-approached Snowking Mountain, high meadows to explore, and six alpine lakes for camping and prowling. *However, this is a poor trail, at times hard to find,* recommended only for experienced cross-country travelers.

Drive Highway 20 to Marblemount and continue east 14.5 miles on the Cascade River road. Turn right on Kindy Creek road No. 1570 over the Cascade River to an unnumbered road. In 1979, this was blocked by slides at an elevation of 1500 feet. If and when it's reopened, drive on, but until then walk some 4 miles to the road-end in the clearcut of the salvage logging after a 1950s fire. Elevation, 2200 feet.

Follow the road grade across the clearcut; look carefully for a trail angling back to the left toward the corner of the uncut timber. This trail follows, then crosses a creek before starting ever steepening switchbacks up the ridge. Be prepared for a very steep scramble near the ridge top.

Memorize the trail intersection on the ridge in order to find the way when returning. Don't clutter up the forest with plastic markers. Daniel Boone got around without them.

The trail follows the ridge crest to the top of a 5116-foot wooded knoll. From the knoll drop down on the trail 300 feet to the saddle, leave the trail, and climb 1000 feet to the 5791-foot viewpoint. Trees are few so the way is obvious; generally trend right for the easiest grade.

To see all the view, move about the broad summit—being careful of fis-

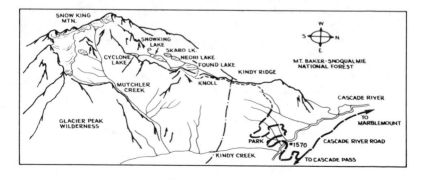

Snowking Mountain and Snowking Lake from Kindy Ridge

sures, some of them deep, that split the rock. Snowking Mountain and its glaciers are the big reward but there are dividends in all directions— Eldorado, Boston, Formidable, and Resplendent. Five beautiful lakes lie below. Two of them—Neori, the lower, and Skaro, the upper—are clear, blue water. Snowking Lake, the largest, and a nameless pond above it are a striking turquoise. The other two lakes, Found and Cyclone, are out of sight.

Kindy Ridge is a splendid day hike but waterless and thus campless. For basecamps, since the country is of the kind that cries out for exploration, pick up the Found Creek trail at the 4800-foot saddle between the two knolls and descend 1 mile to 4000-foot Found Lake, gateway to the other lakes and the slopes of Snowking Mountain.

Old road: 354   354A
New road: 1570   no number

27 MIDDLE AND SOUTH FORKS CASCADE RIVER

Round trip to South Fork
  trail-end 6 miles
Hiking time 3 hours
High point 2200 feet
Elevation gain 500 feet
Hikable June through October
One day or backpack
USGS Sonny Boy Lakes and
  Cascade Pass

Round trip to Spaulding Mine
  Trail end 7 miles
Hiking time 5 hours
High point 3200 feet
Elevation gain 1500 feet

Standing on a high summit, looking out to horizons and down to valleys, expands the spirit. Standing in a low valley, looking up from forests to summits, gives humility. To know the North Cascades a person must

Middle Fork Cascade River crossing

walk low as well as high. The Middle Fork Cascade valley is one of the "great holes" of the range, an excellent place to learn respect. The companion South Fork is one of the grandest wilderness valleys in the range, giant trees rising high—but not so high as the giant, glaciered peaks all around.

Drive Highway 20 to Marblemount and continue east 16.5 miles on the Cascade River road. Turn right on South Fork Cascade River road No. 1590, extremely rough; some people prefer to walk the 1.5 miles to the start of South Cascade River trail No. 769, elevation 1800 feet.

The first ½ mile is up and down along the river bottom to a junction. The South Fork trail goes straight ahead, crosses the Middle Fork, climbs a bit, and enters Glacier Peak Wilderness. With modest ups and downs the way proceeds through magnificent forest to the end of maintained trail at 3 miles from the road, at about 2200 feet. Good camps along the path. An extremely arduous climbers' route continues another 6 miles to Mertensia Pass, 5000 feet.

Back at the junction, the left fork, the Spaulding Mine trail No. 767 climbs as steeply up along the Middle Fork as its cascades are falling down, sometimes seen and always heard. At the 2400-foot lip of the hanging valley the way gentles out in a superb stand of big trees. At 2 miles is a small creek; leave the trail here and walk several hundred feet down to the riverbank for a look up avalanche-swept Cleve Creek to a glacier on the west ridge of Mt. Formidable. Back on the trail, continue upstream in sometimes forest, sometimes avalanche greenery to the trail end somewhere around 3 miles, 3200 feet. By following gravel bars of the river upstream, or gravel washes of tributary torrents up the slopes of Johannesburg, enlarged views can be obtained of the Middle Cascade Glacier, cliffs of Formidable, and the summits of Magic, Hurry-up, and Spider. Camps abound along the river.

Old road: 3404
New road: 1590

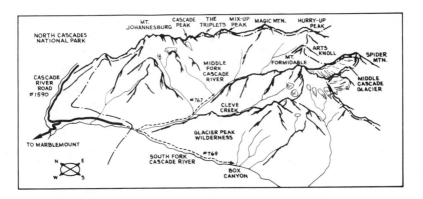

28   BOSTON BASIN

Round trip to first high moraine
  7 miles
Hiking time 8 hours
High point 6200 feet
Elevation gain 3000 feet
Hikable July through October

One day or backpack
USGS Cascade Pass and
  Forbidden Peak
Park Service backcountry use
  permit required

After Forbidden Peak was described in a book as one of the "50 classic climbs in North America," the meadowlands of Boston Basin began to be infested by climbers from all over North America seeking the 50 Peak Pin. Since a normal hiker—finding himself amid the nowadays usual throng of 60 or 70 peakbaggers busy clicking carabiners—is liable to start screaming uncontrollably, and since the trail is unmaintained and poor, and since the camping is lousy, why go? Well, on a Tuesday or Thursday in late October, when the classicists are back in school, a person might just sneak up to the basin for a day and find the solitude proper for savoring the contrast of yellowing meadows and gray moraines and white glaciers.

Drive Highway 20 to Marblemount and continue east on the Cascade River road 23.5 miles to the Diamond Mine junction. Park here, elevation 3200 feet.

Begin by walking 1 steep mile on abandoned road to the Diamond Mine, which didn't dig for diamonds or much of anything else except the cash that could be extracted from investors and ultimately settled for the cash extracted from the National Park Service. Continue upward on a climbers' scramble-path that intersects an ancient miners' trail. Miners of old did better work than modern climbers, so things improve. Vintage tread leads through a short bit of woods and then across a ½-mile-wide

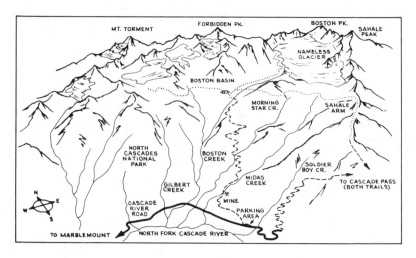

Mount Johannesburg from Boston Basin

swath of avalanche greenery, down which roar Midas Creek and Morning Star Creek. Next come switchbacks in deep forest to a broken-down mine cabin; bad-weather campsites here, no scenery.

About ¼ mile from the wrecked cabin the trail emerges from timber and swings around the foot of an open moraine to a raging torrent; boulder-hop across (the best crossing is upstream from where the trail meets the creek) and climb to a viewpoint atop the moraine. Look up to the fearsome cliffs and spires of Forbidden Peak and Mt. Torment, and to the nameless glacier falling from Boston and Sahale Peaks, and across the valley to the mile-high wall of Johannesburg and its fingerlike hanging glaciers.

For one exploration of Boston Basin, traverse and climb westward over moraines and creeks to rich-green, marmot-whistling flower fields and beyond to waterfalls pouring down ice-polished buttresses under Mt. Torment.

For another exploration, look for intermittent tread of an old miners' trail that ascends a moraine crest to tunnels and artifacts close under Sharkfin Tower, right next to the glacier falling from Boston Peak.

A spectacular for the experienced highland rambler only: Climb moraines and meadows to Sahale Arm and descend to Cascade Pass; those capable of doing the tour need no further clues.

To conclude, there's a world of wandering in Boston Basin, if you can get there when the place isn't up to the scuppers in ropes and hard hats. However, absolutely no camping is allowed in the meadows. You must stay at the 5800-foot "climbers' camp," between the forks of Boston Creek, or up high on the snow or rock; if in doubt, go with the latter.

29 CASCADE PASS— SAHALE ARM

Round trip to Cascade Pass
7 miles
Hiking time 5 hours
High point 5400 feet
Elevation gain 1800 feet
Hikable mid-July through
October
One day
USGS Cascade Pass

Round trip to Sahale Arm 11 miles
Hiking time 10 hours
High point 7600 feet
Elevation gain 4000 feet
Hikable mid-July through
October
One day or backpack
Park Service backcountry use
permit required

An historic pass, crossed by Indians from time immemorial, by explorers and prospectors for a century, and recently become famous as one of the most rewarding easy hikes in the North Cascades. But the beauty of the pass is only the beginning. An idyllic ridge climbs toward the sky amid flowers and creeklets of sparkling water and views that expand with every step.

Drive Highway 20 to Marblemount and continue east 25 miles on the Cascade River road to road-end parking lot and trailhead, 3600 feet.

In some 33 switchbacks the 10-percent grade "highway" climbs forest about 2 miles, then makes a long, gently ascending traverse through parkland and meadows to Cascade Pass, 3½ miles, 5400 feet. Spectacular as the scenery is from road-end, the hikers runs out of superlatives before reaching the pass. The 8200-foot mass of Johannesburg dominates: Hardly an hour goes by that a large or small avalanche doesn't break loose from its hanging glacier; several times a summer a huge section of ice roars all the way to the valley floor.

Cascade Pass retains its famous vistas, but during years of overuse the meadows were loved nearly to death. The Park Service is seeking to rehabilitate the flower gardens and thus camping and fires are forbidden at the pass. However, a few campsites are available below the pass to the east, in Pelton Basin, enabling a longer stay for extended sidetrips.

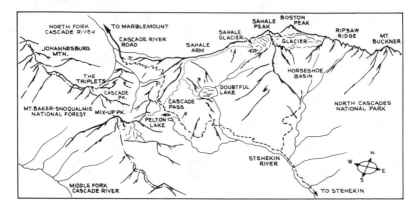

Cascade Pass and Eldorado Peak

One sidetrip from the pass, easy and quick, is the wandering way south up the meadow crest of Mixup Arm.

To explore the sky, climb north on a steep and narrow trail through meadows; find the start a few feet over the east side of the pass below a rock outcrop. In 1 mile and 800 feet the trail reaches the ridge crest and a junction. The right fork descends heather 800 feet in 1 mile to 5385-foot Doubtful Lake, a great hike in its own right.

However, Sahale Arm calls. Walk the old prospectors' trail up and along the gentle ridge of flowers, and up some more. Look down to the waterfall-loud cirque of Doubtful Lake and east into the Stehekin River valley. Look west to Forbidden Peak and the huge Inspiration Glacier on Eldorado. Look south to nine small glaciers on the first line of peaks beyond Cascade Pass. Walking higher, see range upon range of ice and spires, finally including the volcano of Glacier Peak. To see all this in sunset and starlight and dawn, camp in the rocks at the toe of the Sahale Glacier—this is permitted.

30 BOULDER RIVER

Round trip 9 miles
Hiking time 3 hours
High point 1600 feet
Elevation gain 700 feet

Hikable almost all year
One day or backpack
USGS Granite Falls

See for yourself the only long, lowland, virgin-forested valley left in the Mt. Baker–Snoqualmie National Forest. The Boulder River trail once was part of the Forest Service trail over Tupso Pass and down Canyon Creek to the South Fork Stillaguamish road. It was also the shortest trail to the fire lookout on top of Three Fingers. However, the Tupso Pass area was clearcut in the 1960s so the trail between Boulder Ford and the pass was abandoned.

The walk is especially good in late spring when the high country is still buried in snow or in late fall when the maple trees have turned yellow. There are no views of mountains so a cloudy day is as good as a sunny one.

Drive Highway 530 east from Arlington 19.8 miles (to just beyond milepost 41) and turn right on forest road No. 2010 toward French Creek Campground (sign was missing in 1985). Drive past the campground and at 3.6 miles, where the road makes a switchback, find the Boulder River trailhead, elevation 950 feet.

Trail No. 734 follows a long-abandoned railroad logging grade ¾ mile to the virgin forest. At 1¼ miles the way passes a double waterfall that plunges directly into the river—a favorite picnic spot. In ¼ mile is another lovely waterfall. With more ups than downs the trail proceeds along the valley, always in splendid forest and always within sound of the river, though it's mostly hidden in a deep canyon. At 4½ miles, 1600 feet, the trail ends abruptly at Boulder Ford. A campsite here and others a few feet downstream.

Old road: 320
New road: 2010

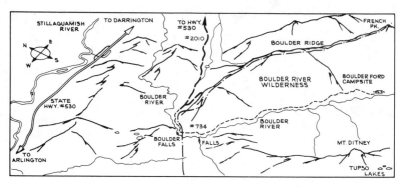

Waterfall plunging into Boulder River

31 ROUND MOUNTAIN

Round trip 4 miles
Hiking time 4 hours
High point 5400 feet
Elevation gain 1900 feet

Hikable early June through
October
One day or backpack
USGS Round Mountain and
Fortson

Not what you'd call a pristine wilderness experience, not with clear-cuts all around and close, but a charming Swiss-type view of the Still-aguamish valley. Look down on farm pastures which from this distance seem as tiny as any in the Alps. Watch ant-sized cars creep along the highway. Trace meanders of the Stillaguamish River beneath the towering, glacier-hung peaks of Whitehorse and Three Fingers. The trail will be kept in a primitive condition with minimum maintenance as a hikers-only route.

Drive Highway 530 east from Arlington to 5 miles west of Darrington. Turn north on Swede Heaven Road (387th N.E.), cross the river, and go downvalley a short bit. Turn right on the first forest road angling upward, road No. 18, and continue 12.5 miles to a junction with spur road No. 1850. Find (perhaps with difficulty) the unmarked trailhead in a short ½ mile, elevation 3500 feet.

The trail contours through woods, passing above several logging patches, and comes to Coney Pass, a saddle in a ridge with an old clearcut on the north slope. The way follows the fire line along the narrow ridge crest to a high point, drops a few feet, goes by some ancient trail signs, and starts up a steep hillside. In some places the path is completely overgrown with huckleberry and young fir trees. If tread is lost, return to the

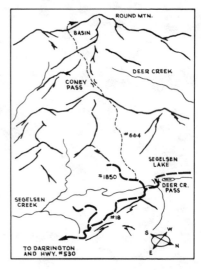

Rosy twisted stalk

Glacier Peak, in distance, from Round Mountain

last for-sure spot and try again—once off the route, progress becomes hopeless.

After traversing the high-angle mountainside from east to west, climbing steadily, at about 1 mile the way heads sharply up, gaining a tough 300 feet; open meadows close above offer inspiration. With an abrupt transition from steep forest to rolling heather slopes, the trail enters a large basin and disappears beside a small creek and possible campsite, 4900 feet.

Some hikers will be content with a picnic by the stream and a good viewpoint at the basin edge. Others will want to scramble the last ½ mile and 500 feet to the summit. Just about any line of ascent works, but be careful of small cliffs. The best route is up the creek bed, then left to the skyline, and on to the approximately 5400-foot summit.

Views, views, views: Darrington and farms of the Stillaguamish, Whitehorse Mountain, Three Fingers Mountain, Glacier Peak, Dome Peak, Mt. Baker, and countless more.

Old road: 3403   3403E
New road: 18   1850

32   SQUIRE CREEK PASS

Round trip to pass 9 miles
Hiking time 6 hours
High point 4000 feet
Elevation gain 2400 feet

Hikable July through October
One day or backpack
USGS Silverton

Hike through lovely forest to a 4000-foot pass with a dramatic view of seldom-seen cliffs of Whitehorse, Three Fingers, and Bullon—some of the steepest and grandest walls in the western reaches of the Cascades.

From the business section of Darrington drive west 5 miles on Squire Creek road No. 2040. The road is paved in the city but quickly turns to dirt and ends in 5 miles at a washout, elevation about 1600 feet.

Walk the abandoned road ½ mile and pick up trail No. 654. The first mile traverses a lovely valley-bottom stand of virgin forest and then the way switchbacks steeply upward on rough tread. Whitehorse and Three Fingers tantalize through the trees until approximately 3 miles, at the foot of a huge boulder field, when views open wide and grow more dramatic with each step. At 4½ miles, 4000 feet, the pass is attained. Secluded campsites are scattered about the pretty meadows, but after the snowfields melt the water is chancy and dubious.

A shorter route to the pass—a steep 2-mile trail gaining 2200 feet—misses the fine forest and has no exciting views along the way. From the business district of Darrington drive east to the edge of town, turn right, and follow the paved road up the south side of the Sauk River, the city road becoming road No. 20. In about 2 miles turn right on Clear Creek road No. 2060 about 5 miles to the trailhead, elevation 1800 feet.

Old road: 3203   3211   3210
New road: 2040   20   2060

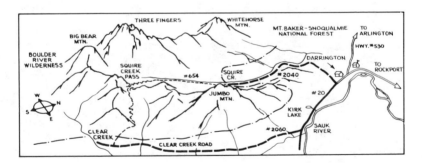

Three Fingers from Squire Creek Pass trail

33 GREEN MOUNTAIN

Round trip 8 miles
Hiking time 6 hours
High point 6500 feet
Elevation gain 3000 feet

Hikable late June through
October
One day or backpack
USGS Downey Mountain

The name of the peak may seen banal, but probably no one has ever looked up its slopes from the Suiattle River valley without exclaiming, "What a *green* mountain!" The trail climbs through these remarkable meadows to a lookout summit with magnificent views to every point of the compass.

Drive north from Darrington or south from Rockport to Suiattle River road No. 26 and continue 19 miles to Green Mountain road No. 2680. Turn left 5 miles to road-end in a logging patch, elevation about 3500 feet. Find the trail sign above the road several hundred yards before the road-end.

The trail climbs a rather steep mile in mossy forest to a grubby hunters' camp with a year-round spring, then enters the vast meadow system admired from below. First are fields of bracken fern and subalpine plants, then, on higher switchbacks, a feast (in season) of blueberries. Views begin—down to Suiattle forests and out to White Chuck Mountain and Glacier Peak. More meadows, and views of Mt. Pugh and Sloan Peak, seen beyond the intervening ridge of Lime Mountain.

At 2 miles, 5300 feet, the trail rounds a shoulder and in ½ mile traverses and drops 100 feet to a pair of shallow ponds amid gardens. Pleasant camps here, and all-summer water. Wood is scarce so carry a stove.

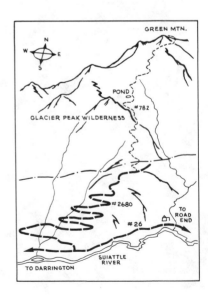

Columbine

Glacier Peak from the Green Mountain trail

A short way above the pond basin the trail enters a larger, wide-open basin (great camps, but no water in late summer). The summit can now be seen directly above, and also Glacier Peak. Climb in flowers to the ridge and along the crest to the 6500-foot summit, 4 miles. A few yards below the ridge on the east is a small rocky-and-snowy basin; delightful and scenic good-weather camps with water but no wood.

Look north along the ridge to the nearby cliffs and glaciers of 7311-foot Buckindy (experienced highland travelers can wander there). Look up Downey Creek to peaks of the Ptarmigan Traverse from Dome north to Formidable. Look up Milk Creek to the Ptarmigan Glacier on Glacier Peak. Look to other peaks in all directions, too many to name.

Old road: 345   3227
New road: 26   2680

34 BACHELOR MEADOWS

Round trip to Bachelor Meadows
23½ miles
Allow 2–3 days
High point 6000 feet
Elevation gain 4600 feet

Hikable mid-July through
September
USGS Downey Mountain and
Dome Peak

A pleasant hike through virgin forest along Downey Creek to Sixmile Camp. For those with the energy and ambition, and experience in traveling rough wilderness, it's a tough climb some 5½ miles farther to meadows under 8264-foot Spire Point, with views of deep and blue Cub and Itswoot Lakes, Dome Peak, Glacier Peak, and other icy mountains.

Drive Suiattle River road No. 26 (Hike 33) 19.5 miles to Downey Creek Campground and the trailhead, elevation 1450 feet.

The first mile climbs steadily, then the way levels into easy ups and downs amid tall firs, hemlocks, and cedars, crossing small streams, sometimes coming close to the river. At 6¼ miles, 2400 feet, the trail crosses Bachelor Creek. If an overnight stop is wanted here, cross Downey to Sixmile Camp.

For Bachelor Meadows, proceed onward, and now upward, initially on well-graded trail and then, at 7½ miles, on a route trampled out by boots, climbing over roots and plunging through gooey bogs. The worst windfalls have been cut but there are plenty of problems. In about 2 miles cross Bachelor Creek. The track becomes hard to follow through a boulder-strewn meadow deep in ferns and flowers. Views appear of Spire Point at the head of the valley. At about 3½ miles are a succession of good campsites; choose one under trees, away from fragile heather.

Now the trail climbs a short but steep mile and at 5400 feet abruptly leaves forest and enters an improbable little valley at a right angle to the main valley and just under Spire Point. Water and flat campsites here in a scenic meadow.

For broader views continue up the trail ½ mile through heather, following the small valley south to a 6000-foot pass. The trial drops ½ mile to 5338-foot Cub Lake and on down to 5015-foot Itswoot Lake.

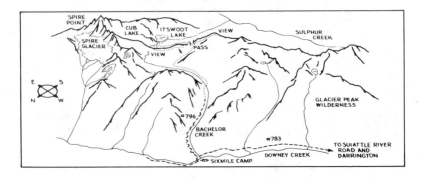

Glacier Peak from end of Bachelor Meadows trail

Rather than descend, walk ¼ mile westward from the pass along a narrow ridge to a superb view of Dome Peak and the glistening Dome Glacier. A stone's throw below are the two lakes. South is Glacier Peak. By camping either on the ridge or at Lake Itswoot, one can explore meadow slopes eastward to a 6200-foot ridge with an even more complete view of Dome. Take pity on Cub Lake and don't camp there—its shores have been too much mangled by fishermen and climbers.

Old road: 345
New road: 26

Glacier Peak and Milk Creek valley

SUIATTLE RIVER
Glacier Peak Wilderness

35 MILK CREEK– DOLLY CREEK– VISTA CREEK LOOP

Loop trip 33 miles
Allow 3–5 days
High point 6000 feet
Elevation gain 4400 feet

Hikable mid-July through
mid-October
USGS Glacier Peak

A section of the Pacific Crest Trail climbing high on the north flanks of Glacier Peak. Massive flower fields and close-up views of the mountain. Plan to spend an extra day, at least, roaming alpine ridges.

Drive the Suiattle River road (Hike 33) 23 miles to the end, elevation 1600 feet. Walk the abandoned road 1 mile to a Y at the former road-end; take the right fork. The Milk Creek trail drops a few steps, crosses the river on a bridge, and enters the Glacier Peak Wilderness. The way begins in glorious forest; at a mile or so is an awesome grove of ancient and huge cedars, hemlocks, and Douglas firs. Going somewhat level, sometimes uphill, passing cold streams, the path rounds a ridge and enters the valley of Milk Creek.

The trail enters a broad field of greenery at 3 miles, 2400 feet, with a stunning look up to the ice, a satisfying reward for a short trip. A pleasant campsite in the forest by the river ½ mile before the field.

From here the trial ascends gently, then steadily, passing campsites in the woods, and meets the Pacific Crest Trail at 7½ miles, 3900 feet. A short bit before the junction, under an overhanging rock, is Whistle Pig Camp—a nice spot on a rainy night, though with room for only several sleepers. Other small camps have been squirmed into the brush at and near the junction, purely from desperation.

Turn left at the junction and plod upward on a series of 36 switchbacks (growing views of Glacier Peak and toward Mica Lake and Fire Mountain) to the crest of Milk Creek Ridge at 11½ miles, 6000 feet. The climbers' route to the summit of Glacier leaves the trail here; hikers can follow way trails higher past flowers for hours before difficulties turn them back.

The trail traverses the flowery basin of the East Fork Milk Creek headwaters, crosses a ridge into the source of Dolly Creek, and at 14 miles comes to Vista Ridge and a camp, 5500 feet.

Flower gardens spread in every direction and views are grand north to Miners Ridge, Plummer Mountain, Dome Peak, and beyond. Glacier Peak is too close and foreshortened to be seen at its best. The trip schedule should include one or more walking-around days from the Vista Ridge camp. Wander up the crest to a 7000-foot knoll. Even better, hike north in meadows to 6500-foot Grassy Point, offering impressive views up and down the green valley of the Suiattle River, but especially a mind-blasting spectacle of the white-glaciered volcano.

From the ridge the trail descends a long series of switchbacks into forest. At 20 miles, 3000 feet, is a campsite by the crossing of Vista Creek. At 21¼ miles is a junction with the Suiattle River trail and at 22 miles, 2700 feet, is a camp beside the Suiattle River. Here the trail crosses Skyline Bridge and proceeds 11 miles down the valley, in 33 miles reaching the road-end and completing the loop.

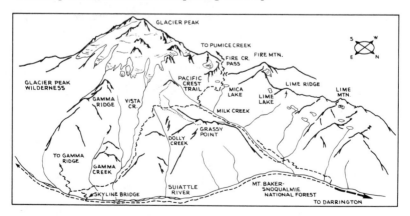

36   IMAGE LAKE

Round trip to Image Lake 32 miles
Allow 2–3 days
High point 6100 feet
Elevation gain 4400 feet

Hikable mid-July through
  October
USGS Glacier Peak and Holden

A 2-mile-high volcano, the image of its glaciers reflected in an alpine tarn. Meadow ridges for dreamwalking. The long sweep of Suiattle River forests. Casting ballots with their feet, hikers have voted this a supreme climax of the alpine world of the North Cascades and the nation. Incredibly, Kennecott Copper Corporation may take advantage of a serious flaw in the Wilderness Act and dig an open-pit mine here, in the very heart of the Glacier Peak Wilderness.

Drive Suiattle River road No. 26 (Hike 33) 23 miles to the end, elevation 1600 feet. Walk abandoned roadway 1 mile to the former road-end and a Y; go left on the Suiattle River trail, largely level, partly in ancient trees, partly in young trees, sometimes with looks to the river, crossing small tributaries, to Canyon Creek Shelter, 6½ miles, 2300 feet. At about 9½ miles, 2800 feet, is a creek with small campsites on both sides. Just beyond is a trail junction; go left on Miners Ridge trail No. 785. The forest switchbacks are relentless and dry but with occasional glimpses, then spectacular views, out to the valley and the volcano. At 12½ miles are two welcome streams at the edge of meadow country and at 13 miles, 4800 feet, is a junction; campsites here.

Miners Cabin trail No. 795, leading to Suiattle Pass, goes straight ahead from the junction; take the left fork to Image Lake. Switchback up and up, into blueberry and flower meadows with expanding views, to a junction atop Miners Ridge, about 15 miles, 6150 feet. A ¼-mile trail leads to Miners Ridge Lookout, 6210 feet. The main trail goes right ¾ mile, traversing, then dropping a bit, to 6050-foot Image Lake.

Solitude is not the name of the game here. If privacy is your pleasure,

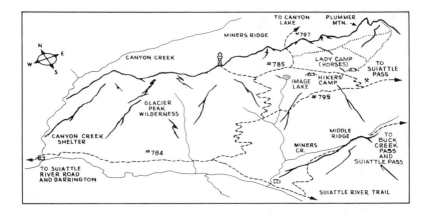

Image Lake and Glacier Peak

you'll have a busy time dodging from this nook to that corner. Indeed, so dense is the summer population that the Forest Service, to protect fragile meadows, has prohibited camping around and above the lake; it further has banned swimming when the water is low, to keep the water pure. Below the lake ¼ mile is a hikers' camp. A mile away at Lady Camp are accommodations for horses and mice. (On a bench above the trail look for the lovely lady carved in a tree by a sheepherder in about 1916.)

Exploring the basin, climbing the 6758-foot knoll above, visiting the fire lookout, walking the Canyon Lake trail into the headwaters of Canyon Creek—thus one may fill memorable days. By no means omit the finest wandering of all, along the wide crest of Miners Ridge, through flower gardens, looking north to Dome Peak and south across Suiattle forests to Glacier Peak. Experienced scramblers can ascend steep heather to the 7870-foot summit of Plummer Mountain and wide horizons of wild peaks.

Also, hike the grassy trail east 1 mile to lovely Lady Camp Basin. Here is the west edge of the ½-mile-wide open-pit mine Kennecott wants to dig; this blasphemy has been prevented so far by violent objections from citizen-hikers but can only be stopped for good and all by your letters to congressmen and senators urging them to exercise the right of eminent domain and purchase the patented mining claims. From Lady Camp-the trail drops some 500 feet in ½ mile to a junction with the Suiattle-Pass trail, which can be followed 1¾ miles back to the Image Lake trail junction.

37 SUIATTLE RIVER TO LAKE CHELAN

One-way trip 29½ miles
Allow 5–7 days
High point 6438 feet
Elevation gain about 5000 feet

Hikable mid-July through
   September
USGS Glacier Peak, Holden,
   Lucerne

A rich, extended sampler of the Glacier Peak Wilderness, beginning in green-mossy westside trees, rising to flowers of Miners Ridge and views of Glacier Peak, crossing Suiattle and Cloudy Passes, descending parklands of Lyman Lake to rainshadow forests of Railroad Creek and Lake Chelan. The traverse can be done in either direction; the west-to-east route is described here.

Drive to the Suiattle River road-end, 1600 feet, and hike 11 miles on the Suiattle River trail to the 4800-foot junction with the Image Lake trail (Hike 36).

Continue straight ahead on Miners Cabin trail, climbing 1¾ miles to a second junction with the Image Lake trail, 5500 feet. (The lake can—and should, if time allows—be included in the trip by taking the lake trail, which is 4½ miles long from end to end, thus adding some 3 extra miles and about 600 feet of extra elevation gained and lost.) In trees just past the junction are miners' shacks belonging to Kennecott Copper and a spring, a bad-weather campsite. The way now contours, crossing one

Lyman Lake

huge and many small avalanche paths, entering open slopes with grand views to Fortress, Chiwawa, and other peaks at the head of Miners Creek, passing more miners' junk in a small flat, and at 17 miles reaches Suiattle Pass, 5983 feet. A bit before the pass and below the trail is a pleasant camp on a meadow bench.

The trail drops some 300 feet into headwaters of South Fork Agnes Creek (when the snow is gone the drop can be partially avoided by taking a rough hiker-only alternate path) and climbs to the most spectacular views and gardens of the trip at 6438-foot Cloudy Pass, 19 miles. (From here, easy meadows demand a sidetrip to 7915-foot Cloudy Peak and along the ridge toward 8068-foot North Star Mountain.)

Descend magnificent flowers, then subalpine forest, to 5587-foot Lyman Lake, 21 miles. There are campsites in the woods north of the lake and at the outlet, but camps above, under Cloudy Peak, have better views and fewer bugs. If a campfire is built, use an existing fire ring. (From the lake outlet, a hiker-only trail climbs 500 feet to Upper Lyman Lake, alpine camps, and a mandatory sidetrip to the toe of Lyman Glacier.) At the lake begin bear problems which continue the full length of the Railroad Creek valley; look to the defense of your good things.

The trail drops past the outlet creek of Lyman Lake, where frothy water pours down long, clean granite slabs, and switchbacks into forests of Railroad Creek; views of Crown Point Falls and Hart Lake. After boggy walking and several bridges, at 24½ miles, 3989 feet, is Rebel Camp and at 25½ miles is Hart Lake. Good camping at both.

The last portion of the route is over blocks of rock under a tall cliff, past tumbling waterfalls, occasional views of high peaks, to beaver bottom and green jungle, and finally a jeep track and baseball field to the abandoned mining town of Holden, 29½ miles, 3200 feet.

Holden Village Inc. uses the old town as a religious retreat but may sell a hiker ice cream. A road goes 12 miles down to Lucerne, on Lake Chelan, a hot and dusty walk (a parallel trail is planned for future construction). From May 15 to October 15 (in 1981, anyhow) a bus from Lucerne Resort makes four daily round trips, permitting hikers to catch the *Lady of the Lake* downlake to Chelan (Hike 74) and a bus home.

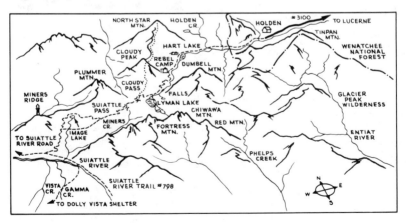

38 AROUND GLACIER PEAK

One-way trip (north and east
  section) 52 miles
Allow 5 days minimum
High point 6409 feet
  (Little Giant Pass)
Elevation gain 9800 feet
  To: Buck Creek Pass 4100 feet
    Little Giant Pass 3800 feet
    Boulder Pass 1550 feet
Hikable late July through
  September
USGS Glacier Peak and Holden

One-way trip (south and west
  section) 43 miles
Allow 5 days minimum
High point 6450 feet (Red Pass)
  Elevation gain 5700 feet
  To: White Pass 3700 feet
    Red Pass 700 feet
    Fire Creek Pass 2000 feet
Hikable late July through
  September
USGS Glacier Peak and Holden

Mt. Rainier National Park has the renowned Wonderland Trail; the Glacier Peak Wilderness offers an equally classic around-the-mountain hike. The 96-mile circuit with an estimated 15,500 feet of climbing includes virgin forests, glacial streams, alpine meadows, and ever-changing views of the "last wild volcano."

The complete trip requires a minimum 10 days, and this makes no allowance for explorations and bad-weather layovers. However, the loop breaks logically into two sections which can be taken separately. Perhaps the ideal schedule is to do the entire circuit on a single two-week

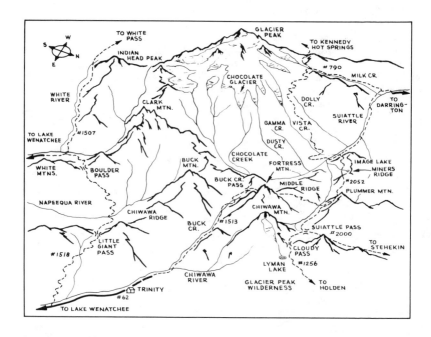

Ptarmigan in summer plumage

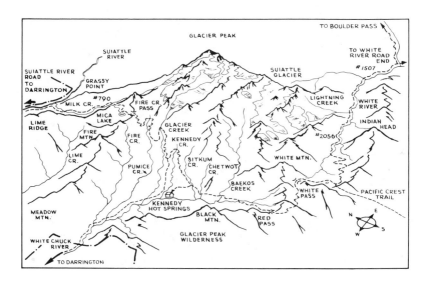

jaunt, keeping packs to a reasonable weight by arranging to be met midway with additional supplies.

NORTH AND EAST SECTION

Begin at Suiattle River road-end (Hike 33). Hike 11 miles along the Suiattle River on trail No. 784 to a junction with the Pacific Crest Trail. Go right 4½ miles to Middle Ridge trail and climb 5 miles to Buck Creek Pass.

(Two partial alternate routes can be taken; each adds a day and many extra rewards. One is the Milk Creek–Dolly–Vista trail (Hike 35), which starts at Suiattle River road-end and rejoins the main route near the 10-mile marker; this alternate adds 12 miles and 3200 feet of elevation gain to the total. The other is the Image Lake–Miners Ridge trail (Hike 36), which leaves the main route at 9½ miles and rejoins it 6 miles below Buck Creek Pass; this alternate adds 8 miles and 1700 feet of elevation gain. The two alternates can be combined on a single trip; first do the Milk Creek–Dolly–Vista trail, then backtrack 1 mile to begin the Image Lake–Miners Ridge trail.)

Descend 9½ miles from Buck Creek Pass to Trinity (Hike 69) and walk 5½ miles down the Chiwawa River road to Little Giant trail No. 1518. Climb 4¾ miles to Little Giant Pass (Hike 67) and descend 1¾ miles into the Napeequa River valley and a junction with Boulder Pass trail No. 1562. Climb 6½ miles over the pass and down to the White River trail (Hike 65). If the trip is to be broken at this point, hike 3½ miles downriver to the White River road.

A possible itinerary (excluding the alternates) would be: Day One, 11 miles and a 1150-foot climb to Miners Creek (the best camping is on the river ¼ mile beyond Miners Creek); Day Two, 9½ miles and a 3200-foot climb to Buck Creek Pass; Day Three, descend 3350 feet in 15 miles to Maple Creek; Day Four, climb 3900 feet, descend 2300 feet, in the 6½ miles to Napeequa River; Day Five, 10 miles to White River road-end, a climb of 1550 feet and a descent of 3350 feet. However, frequent campsites along the route allow shorter days or different days.

SOUTH AND WEST SECTION

Begin at White River road-end. Hike 14¼ miles on White River trail No. 1507 to an intersection with the Pacific Crest Trail. Continue north on the crest 2 miles to White Pass (Hike 65).

From White Pass contour and climb to Red Pass in 2 miles, then descend the White Chuck River (Hike 41) 7 miles to a junction. For the main route, climb right on the Pacific Crest Trail, crossing headwaters of Kennedy Creek, Glacier Creek, Pumice Creek, and Fire Creek and reaching Fire Creek Pass in 8 miles (Hike 40).

(For an inviting alternate, go 1½ miles from the junction downriver to Kennedy Hot Springs, enjoy a hot bath, then continue a short ½ mile to the Kennedy Ridge trail (Hike 40) and climb to rejoin the main route; this alternate adds 1¼ miles and 800 feet of elevation gain to the total.)

From Fire Creek Pass, the snowiest part of the entire circuit, descend a valley of moraines and ponds, past the magnificent cold cirque of Mica Lake, reaching the Dolly-Vista trail junction in 4 miles. Continue 7½

Indian Head Peak from White Pass

miles down Milk Creek trail to the Suiattle River road-end (Hike 35).

A possible itinerary would be: Day One, 9 miles and climb 800 feet to Lightning Creek; Day Two, 9¼ miles, a gain of 2100 feet and a loss of 1000 feet, to Glacier Peak Meadows; Day Three, drop 1700 feet and climb 2250 on the 9½ miles to Pumice Creek; Day Four, 500 feet up and 900 feet down on 4¼ miles to Mica Lake; Day Five, 11 miles and 3800 feet down to Suiattle River road. Again, frequent campsites allow shorter or different days.

39 MEADOW MOUNTAIN—FIRE MOUNTAIN

Round trip to 5800-foot viewpoint
16½ miles
Allow 2 days
High point 5800 feet
Elevation gain 3300 feet
Hikable July through October
USGS Pugh Mountain and Glacier
Peak

One-way trip from Meadow
Mountain road-end to White
Chuck River road-end 20 miles
Allow 2–4 days
High point 5800 feet
Elevation gain 4400 feet, including
ups and downs
Hikable July through October

Meadows laced with alpine trees, views to White Chuck forests and Glacier Peak ice, and a long parkland ridge for roaming, with sidetrips to cirque lakes.

Drive from Darrington on the Mountain Loop Highway 10.5 miles to the White Chuck River road. Turn left 5.5 miles to Straight Creek road No. 27, shortly beyond the crossing of the White Chuck River. Turn left 2 miles, climbing and switchbacking, following "Meadow Mountain" signs at all junctions, to a gate and parking area, 2500 feet.

Walk 5 miles on road No. 2710, now driven only by government employees, passing up a spur to Crystal Lake to the road-end, 3400 feet, and views of Glacier Peak, White Chuck Mountain, and Mt. Pugh.

The trail climbs a steep 1¼ miles (but in deep, cool forest) to the first meadow. Cross a bubbling brook in an open basin and then choose either of two destinations, both offering splendid views down to the green valley and out to the peaks. For the easiest, follow a faint way trail 1 mile westward to a high knoll, about 5600 feet. For the best, and with the most flowers, hike the main trail 2 miles eastward, climbing to a 5800-foot spur ridge from Meadow Mountain.

For one of the great backpacking ridge walks in the Glacier Peak Wilderness, take the up-and-down trail traversing the ridge east toward Fire Mountain. Earlier camps are possible, but the first site with guaranteed all-summer water is Hunter's Camp at 9 miles, ½ mile beyond the 5800-foot viewpoint, in a bouldery basin to which the trail drops to avoid cliffs of Meadow Mountain.

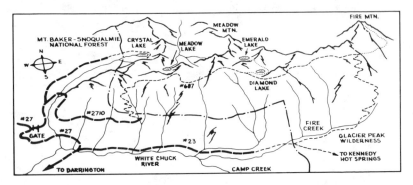

Glacier Peak from Meadow Mountain

Going up, then down, then up again, at 10¼ miles the trail touches the 5850-foot ridge crest. From here, descend 1 mile northwest on a much-used but not-obvious and easily lost path to 5300-foot Diamond Lake. From the east side of the lake climb a wide gully up the low ridge and descend extremely steep slopes (no trail) to Emerald Lake, 5200 feet. Good camps at both; stay 100 feet from the shores.

The main trail continues along the ridge to a low saddle at about 11 miles. The path proceeds east through patches of trees, grassy swales, sidehill flowers, and views.

At 12½ miles is a magnificent camp in a cliff-walled basin and at 14 miles, beneath Fire Mountain, are charming garden camps near the site of long-gone Fire Chief Shelter. From this area experienced off-trail travelers can find an easy but not obvious route to the summit of 6591-foot Fire Mountain; if the terrain gets steep and scary, you're on the wrong route—turn back.

The trail descends an old burn to Fire Creek forests, joining the White Chuck trail at 18½ miles, 1½ miles from the White Chuck River road. By use of two cars, one parked at each road-end, hikers can enjoy a 20-mile one-way trip along the full length of the ridge trail; a 3-day schedule allows for sidetrips, but more days could easily be spent exploring.

Old road: 314 327 3128
New road: 23 27 2710

40 KENNEDY RIDGE AND HOT SPRINGS

Round trip to Kennedy Hot Springs 11 miles
Hiking time 5 hours
High point 3300 feet
Elevation gain 1000 feet
Hikable May through November
One day or backpack
USGS Glacier Peak

Round trip to Kennedy Ridge moraine 18 miles
Hiking time 8–10 hours
High point 6200 feet
Elevation gain 4000 feet
Hikable July through October

Two hikes which can be done separately or combined. A short-and-low trip leads through tall, old trees, beside a roaring river, to a tingling bath in volcano-warmed waters—the most mob-jammed spot in the Glacier Peak Wilderness. A long-and-high trip climbs to alpine flowers with a close look at icefalls tumbling from Glacier Peak.

Drive from Darrington on the Mountain Loop Highway 10.5 miles to White Chuck River road No. 23. Turn left 11 miles to the road-end parking area and campground, elevation 2300 feet.

The wide, gentle White Chuck River trail has become—deservedly—the most popular valley walk in the Glacier Peak area. The way goes through virgin forest always near and sometimes beside the ice-fed river, beneath striking cliffs of volcanic tuff, crossing the frothing tributaries of Fire, Pumice, and Glacier Creeks. At 5 miles, 3300 feet, is a junction with the Kennedy Ridge trail.

Kennedy Hot Springs: In 1976 a monster flood ravaged the White Chuck River trail to Kennedy Creek. The evidence remains but the trail has been restored ½ mile to the guard station, hot springs, and camp, 3300 feet. Cross the river on a bridge, turn left past the trail to Lake Byrne (Hike 42), and in a few yards come to steaming, mineralized waters seeping from the earth. A tublike pool about 5 feet square and 5 feet deep has been dug, just big enough for three or four people. The water is

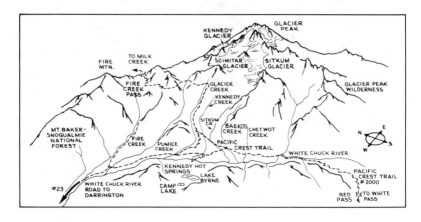

Glacier Peak and Scimitar Glacier on right, from Kennedy Ridge

not as hot as the Japanese like it, but the idea is the same—submerging to your chin and letting the bubbling heat relax your muscles. The water is usually a yellowish-reddish murk, but never mind; to clean away the iron oxide, one can always plunge into the icy river, several yards away. (This is the way the Finns like it—hot, then cold).

Perhaps not everyone will want a bath; some 2500 people sign the Kennedy register every year, which means the waiting line gets long in good weather. It likely would be a lot shorter if folks knew what the latest coliform bacteria count was.

Kennedy Ridge: From the junction at 5 miles, just before crossing Kennedy Creek, climb left on the Kennedy Ridge trail. (A full canteen is needed.) The steep forest way, with occasional glimpses of ice, joins the Pacific Crest Trail at 2 miles, 4150 feet. The Crest Trail switchbacks through cliffs of red and gray andesite, then along heather parklands on a moraine crest, swinging left to reach the welcome wet slash (and campsite) of Glacier Creek at 5650 feet, 4 miles from the White Chuck River trail.

Leave the trail and climb open subalpine forests on the old moraine, then in ½ mile step suddenly out onto raw boulders of a much newer moraine. See the Kennedy and Scimitar Glaciers tumbling from the summit of the volcano. See glacial debris and cataracts below the ice. See valley forests, peaks beyond.

It's a shame to turn back at the edge of so much good highland roaming. Just 1 mile from Glacier Creek, over Glacier Ridge, are the splendid meadows and camps of Pumice Creek, and in 3½ miles more is Fire Creek Pass. With a schedule of 3 or more days, these and other delights can be enjoyed.

41 WHITE CHUCK GLACIER

Round trip to White Chuck
  Glacier 28 miles
Allow 4 days minimum
High point about 6500 feet

Elevation gain 4200 feet
Hikable late July through
  September
USGS Glacier Peak

Begin beside a loud river in deep forest. Walk miles through big trees; climb to little trees and wide meadows. Roam flowers and waterfalls and moraines to a broad glacier. Wander gardens and ridges. In the opinion of some experts, this is the supreme low-to-high tour of the Glacier Peak Wilderness.

Drive to the White Chuck River road-end, 2300 feet, and hike 5½ miles to 3300-foot Kennedy Hot Springs (Hike 40).

Ascend steeply then gently to join the Pacific Crest Trail at Sitkum Creek, 3850 feet, 7 miles from the road; camping space is available here when Kennedy is full-up, as it often is. The Crest Trail continues along the valley, passing the avalanche track and meadow-marsh of Chetwot Creek, fording Baekos Creek, and at 9½ miles, 4000 feet, crossing a high bridge over the rocky chasm and thundering falls of the White Chuck River.

Now the trail climbs a valley step. Trees are smaller and so is the river, assembling itself from snow-fed tributaries. A little meadow gives promise of what lies above. More subalpine forest. Then the way enters the tremendous open basin of Glacier Peak Meadows. At 12 miles, 5400 feet, is the site of the long-gone Glacier Peak Shelter, and magnificent campsites everywhere around.

As a base for easy hiker-type explorations, this highland valley of flowers and creeks and snowfields is unsurpassed in the North Cascades.

First off, if your hike is mid-August or later, visit the ice; before that it is covered with snow. Climb meadows around the valley corner east, taking any of many appealing routes to a chilly flatland of moss and meanders, to moraines and meltwater, and finally the White Chuck Glacier. The white plateau is tempting, but only climbers with rope and ice ax should venture on its surface.

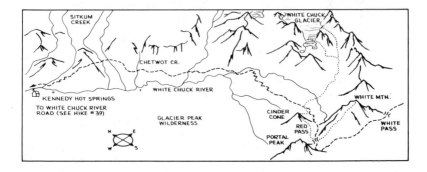

Glacier Peak from White Mountain

For another trip, investigate the intriguing White Chuck Cinder Cone, remnant of a volcano smaller and newer than Glacier Peak. Scramble meadows higher to the 6999-foot summit of Portal Peak.

If your visit is in late July or early August it is flower time on White Mountain. Therefore, hike the Crest Trail 2 miles up a wintry, rocky basin to 6450-foot Red Pass; from here, continue on the trail to White Pass (in early July be careful of the steep snow slopes) or leave the trail in about ½ mile and follow the flower crest to the summit of 7030-foot White Mountain.

Every direction calls. Invent your own wanderings. The minimum trip to the glacier can be done in 3 days but any itinerary of less than a week will leave the visitor frustrated, determined to return soon to finish the job at leisure.

Campsites other than those mentioned above are plentiful along the trail and throughout the high basin. However, as a conservation rule to be followed here and everywhere, camps should be placed in trees adjacent to meadows, not in the actual meadows, which are so fragile that only a few nights of camping can destroy nature's work of decades.

Old road: 314
New road: 23

42 LOST CREEK RIDGE

**Round trip to Round Lake
viewpoint 10 miles
Hiking time 6–8 hours
High point 5550 feet
Elevation gain 3550 feet
Hikable July through October
One day or backpack
USGS Sloan Peak**

**Round trip to Lake Byrne 24 miles
Allow 3 days minimum
High point 6000 feet
Elevation gain about 6500 feet,
including ups and downs in and
out
Hikable August through October
USGS Glacier Peak and Sloan
Peak**

A long ridge of green meadows, alpine lakes, and wide views of peaks near and far—one of the most memorable highland trails in the Glacier Peak region. The ridge can be ascended from either end for day trips or overnight camps, or walked the full length on an extended backpack. However, the middle section of the route is a boot-beaten path, often overgrown with vegetation. Particularly in the fog, hikers must be careful not to get lost on Lost Ridge.

Drive from Darrington on the Mountain Loop Highway 17 miles to North Fork Sauk River road No. 49. Turn left 3 miles to a small parking area and trail sign, elevation 2000 feet.

The trail goes gently along the valley ½ mile, then climbs steeply through open woods, with occasional views of impressive Sloan Peak, to 4425-foot Bingley Gap, 3 miles. The way continues some 2 miles up and along the ridge to meadows and a 5550-foot saddle overlooking Round Lake, 5100 feet. (A steep sidetrail descends to the lake and good camps.) Scramble up the grassy knoll east of the saddle for more views of Sloan

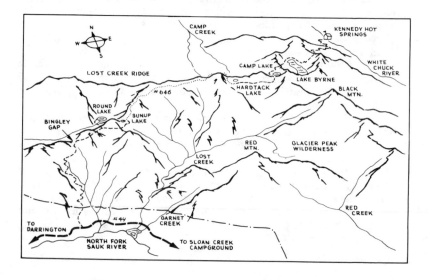

Sloan Peak from Lost Creek Ridge trail

and a look at Glacier Peak. Here is the place for day trippers to have lunch, soak up the scenery, and return home; generally the trail is reasonably snowfree by early July.

Beyond this point the up-and-down trail is sketchy, very snowy until late July, and requires careful route-finding. (The section from ¾ mile past Sunup Lake to Hardtack Lake is only partly a "constructed" trail with scattered sections of good tread and boot-built or hoof-built track.) However, the going is easy and glorious—always near or on the crest, mostly past vast meadows, through open basins, near small lakes, with constant and changing views, and a choice of delightful camps. At 11 miles, the trail now good, is 5650-foot Camp Lake, set in a cliff-walled cirque. From here the trail climbs to a 6000-foot knob, drops a few feet to the rocky basin of "Little Siberia," then descends to famous Lake Byrne, 12 miles, 5550 feet. Flowers and rocks and waterfalls of the basin and adjoining ridges demand leisurely exploration, ever dominated by the tall white volcano rising beyond White Chuck River forests. However, campsites at Lake Byrne are so small, poor, and overused that explorations should be basecamped at Camp Lake or Kennedy Hot springs.

From the lake the trail abruptly drops 2250 feet in 2 miles to Kennedy Hot Springs (Hike 40), 5½ miles from the White Chuck River road. If Lake Byrne is the primary goal, the quickest route is from this road, gaining 3200 feet in 7½ miles for a very long day or reasonable weekend. If transportation can be arranged, such as by use of two cars, a 19-mile one-way trip can be done from one road to the other; allow 3 days or more.

43   SLOAN PEAK MEADOWS

Round trip 8 miles
Hiking time 7 hours
High point 4800 feet
Elevation gain 2900 feet

Hikable mid-July through
  September
One day or backpack
USGS Sloan Peak

The big-time, big-corporation prospectors of today chatter about the sky in fleets of helicopters and never touch the ground except to drill holes in it and heap garbage on it. Their predecessors of 50 to 100 years ago, earthbound "dirty miners in search of shining gold," spent half their time building trails—often steep, but wide and solid enough for pack-trains. Hundreds of miles of trails still in use were engineered by these old-timers, who never found gold or anything else of value, earned nothing for their sweat but a shirt that needed a bath.

One bit of their handiwork, the Cougar Creek trail, climbs from the North Fork Sauk River to meadows on the side of Sloan Peak. This would be a glorious spot to spend a couple of days roaming, but lacking dirty miners to maintain it, the trail is so mean that hauling camping gear to the high country would try the cheerfulness of a Sherpa. Even as a day trip it's no simple stroll. The crossings of the North Fork Sauk and Cougar Creek are always difficult and frequently impossible. If in doubt, return to the car and go someplace else, such as Lost Creek Ridge (Hike 42).

Drive from Darrington 17 miles on the Mountain Loop Highway to North Fork Sauk River road No. 49 and turn left 4.6 miles to the trailhead, signed "Climbers' Trail," elevation 1900 feet.

Walk ½ mile to the river on abandoned road, in several places flooded by beaver ponds. The bridge is decades gone, and unless a logjam can be found upstream or down the trip is over—the river is much too deep and swift to ford safely.

On the far side of the river the trail follows an old logging railroad grade ¼ mile, then gains 500 feet up an old clearcut to the old miners' trail. Steep but wide, the relict ascends a long 2 miles to a rotten-log (ob-

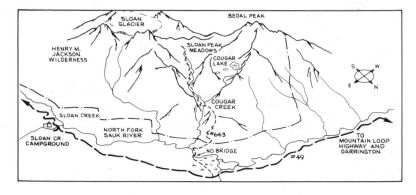

Cougar Creek

viously not permanent) crossing of Cougar Creek between two water-falls. In the next 2 miles the creek is crossed twice more—or perhaps not at all on a hot day when meltwater is roaring. The way continues relentlessly up, crossing four more creeks, each at the base of a waterfall. (Waterfalls are one of the best parts of this hike.)

At a very long 4 miles, elevation 4800 feet, a small meadow invites camping, in views up to Sloan Glacier and the summit cliffs of Sloan Peak and out east to Red Mountain and Glacier Peak. The slopes above the camp meadow invite wandering—which, however, should go only to the first steep snowfield unless the party has climbing gear and skills.

Old road: 308
New road: 49

44 BALD EAGLE LOOP

**One-way trip 24 miles plus 2-mile
  walk on road**
Hiking time 3 days
High point 6000 feet
Elevation gain 4500 feet

**Hikable late July through
  September**
**USGS Blanca Lake, Benchmark
  Mountain, Glacier Peak, Sloan
  Peak**

A ramble through miles of alpine trees and meadows on lonesome
trails used more by deer and marmots than people, which is surprising
considering the beauty. The trip must be planned with care to end each
day at a place with camping space—and water, which is scarce on the
high ridges. After a spot at 1 mile on the abandoned road, the next for-
sure water is at Spring Camp, 9 miles. However, in early summer there
normally are snowbanks that can be cooked in a pot.

Drive from Darrington 17 miles on the Mountain Loop Highway and
turn left on North Fork Sauk River road No. 49. In 7 miles, pass Sloan
Creek Campground, the end of the loop trip. Drive another 2 miles to a
junction with an unnumbered road and turn right on it a few hundred
feet to Sloan Creek and a washed-out bridge, the present (1984) Bald
Mountain trailhead, elevation 2400 feet, the start of the loop trip. A good
plan is to unload packs here and park the car back near the campground,
where you'll be coming out.

Walk 2½ miles on abandoned logging road to the end and find the start
of trail No. 1050, elevation 3200 feet. The way traverses a clearcut, enters forest, and climbs a sometimes muddy 1½ miles to Curry Gap, 4000
feet, and a junction. Go left on Bald Eagle trail No. 650, climbing nearly
to the top of 5668-foot Bald Eagle Mountain. With ups and downs, pass
Long John Camp (often dry) at 8 miles from the washed-out bridge and
Spring Camp at 9 miles. The trail then climbs within a few yards of the
crest of 5946-foot June Mountain. Be sure to take the short sidetrip to the
summit for views of Sloan Peak, Monte Cristo peaks, Glacier Peak, valleys, and forest. The tread on the north side of June Mountain may be

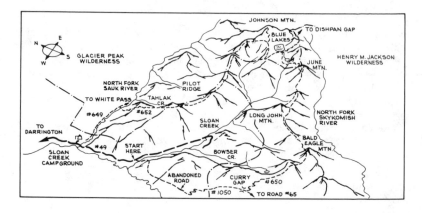

covered by steep, hard snow. If so, climb above—with care, since the heather also is steep and slippery.

At 12½ miles is a junction. The trail to the right continues 3 miles to Dishpan Gap and the Pacific Crest Trail. Go left on trail No. 652, dropping 500 feet, and at 14 miles reach campsites near 5500-foot Blue Lake, usually frozen until mid-August.

From Blue Lake the trail climbs 500 feet onto Pilot Ridge for 5 miles of some of the finest ridge walking in the North Cascades. Finally the trail leaves the ridge and drops 3000 feet in an endless series of short, steep switchbacks to North Fork Sauk River trail No. 649, at 11½ miles from Blue Lake reaching Sloan Creek Campground, 24 miles from the start. If you adopted the good plan your car awaits you here, rather than 2 miles away at the washed-out bridge.

Old road: 308   308B
New road: 49   no number

Monte Cristo Peaks from Bald Mountain trail

45   GOAT FLATS

Round trip to Goat Flats 9½ miles
Hiking time 6 hours
High point 4700 feet
Elevation gain 2000 feet

Hikable late July through
   October
One day or backpack
USGS Granite Falls and Silverton

The rock spires and icefields of Three Fingers Mountain stand near the west edge of the North Cascades, rising above lowlands and salt water, prominent on the skyline from as far away as Seattle. On a ridge of the mountain are the lovely alpine meadows of Goat Flats, the most beautiful in the Verlot area. Once upon a time a great network of trails linked the North and South Forks of the Stillaguamish River. Now most of the forest land is chopped up by logging roads, the trails ruined or abandoned or neglected. The hike to Goat Flats follows a small remnant of the old pedestrian network.

Drive the Mountain Loop Highway 6.5 miles east from Granite Falls to Forest Service road No. 41, and turn left 1.5 miles to a major junction. Go left on road 41, passing several sideroads and also the Meadow Mountain trail (an alternate but longer route). At 18 miles from the Mountain Loop Highway turn right on road No. (4100)025 and in .2 mile find the trailhead, elevation 2800 feet.

Trail No. 641 is a classic example of how tread can be completely worn out by the combined efforts of hiking feet and running water. The 2½ miles to Saddle Lake are all roots and rocks and gullies, such slow walking that to do them in less than 2 hours is to risk twisted ankles and broken legs. But take the better with the bitter: Improving the trail would increase hiker traffic at Goat Flats, already severely overused. So walk carefully, slowly, blessing the roots and rocks and gullies or at least stifling your curses.

Just across the outlet of 3800-foot Saddle Lake is a junction. The trail to the right leads to campsites and a shelter on the far side of the lake

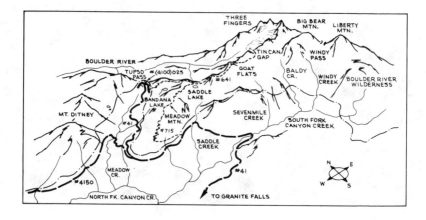

Fogbound Goat Flats

and continues to Meadow Mountain, a tree-covered hill. Go left to Three Fingers and Goat Flats.

From the lake the trail ascends steep slopes in forests to rolling meadows with acres and acres of blueberries and heather. The meadows are broken by groves of alpine trees and dotted with ponds—one in particular, several hundred feet below the trail, offers an excellent camp.

Some 2¼ miles from Saddle Lake the trail enters the meadow plateau of 4700-foot Goat Flats. Near the center is an historic artifact, an ancient log shelter once used as a patrol cabin, now serving as headquarters for local rodents. The meadows are paying the price of beauty, suffering badly from trampling. Visitors will want to leave the trail to pick blueberries and seek viewpoints but, as much as possible, should keep to beaten paths. Camping would better be done along the ridge before the Flats; if here, it should be at existing sites and without wood fire.

For most hikers the Flats are far enough, offering a close-up view of the cliffs and ice of Three Fingers, looks south to Pilchuck, north to Whitehorse and Mt. Baker, west to salt waterways and the Olympics. Campers get the best: sunsets on peaks and valleys, farm and city lights in the far-below lowland night, a perspective on megalopolis and wildness.

For hikers who want more, the trail goes on, traversing meadows and then climbing steeply up a rocky basin to 6400-foot Tin Can Gap, above the Three Fingers Glacier. From here a climbers' route weaves along an airy ridge to the foot of the pinnacle of the 6854-foot South Peak of Three Fingers, atop which is perched a lookout cabin built in the 1930s. The pinnacle is mounted by a series of ladders. In order to build the cabin the Forest Service dynamited a platform on the summit; tradition says the original summit never was climbed before it was destroyed. Tradition also says one lookout was so stricken by vertigo he had to telephone Forest Service supervisors to come help him down the ladder. Hikers will not want to go beyond Tin Can Gap.

46 MOUNT DICKERMAN

Round trip 8½ miles
Hiking time 8–9 hours
High point 5723 feet
Elevation gain 3800 feet

Hikable late July through
  October
One day
USGS Bedal

All too few trails remain, outside wilderness areas and national parks, that begin in valley bottoms and climb unmarred forests to meadows.

October snowfall on Mount Dickerman. Del Campo Peak in distance

The way to Dickerman is strenuous but the complete experience of life zones from low to high, plus the summit views, are worth every drop of sweat.

Drive from Verlot on the Mountain Loop Highway 16.5 miles to a small parking area and easily overlooked trail sign, elevation 1900 feet, about 2.5 miles beyond Big Four Picnic Area.

Trail No. 710 doesn't fool around. Switchbacks instantly commence, climbing up and up and up through lovely cool forest; except perhaps in late summer, several small creeks provide pauses that refresh. Tantalizing glimpses through timber give promise of scenery above. A bit past 2 miles lower-elevation trees yield to Alaska cedars and subalpine firs. Then the forest thins as the trail traverses under towering cliffs onto flatter terrain. Near here, in a sheltered hollow to the west, is a little lakelet produced by snowmelt and reached by a faint path; camping is possible.

The next ½ mile ranks among the most famous blueberry patches in the Cascades; in season, grazing hikers may find progress very slow indeed. In the fall, photographers find the blazing colors equally obstructive. Now, too, the horizons grow.

The final mile is somewhat steeper, switchbacking meadows to the broad summit, as friendly a sackout spot as one can find.

Abrupt cliffs drop toward Perry Creek forests, far below. Beyond are Stillaguamish Peak and Mt. Forgotten. To the east rise Glacier Peak, the horn of Sloan Peak, and all the Monte Cristo peaks. And across the South Fork Stillaguamish River are rugged Big Four Mountain and the striking rock slabs of Vesper Peak. This is only a small part of the panorama in every direction.

*Picking blueberries on
Mount Dickerman*

47 SUNRISE MINE TRAIL– HEADLEE PASS

Round trip 5 miles
Hiking time 5 hours
High point 4600 feet
Elevation gain 2500 feet

Hikable August and September
One day
USGS Silverton and Bedal

".....Theirs not to reason why, Theirs but to do and die: Into the valley of Death rode the six hundred....."

Judging by the avalanche debris, the narrow valley ascended by the Sunrise Mine trail must be bombarded by snow, rock, and broken trees from the first snowfall in October until all the snow has slid from surrounding peaks sometime after mid-July. Hikers may feel they *are* the Light Brigade as they trudge into the valley, but if they make sure not to do so until the heavy artillery has ceased for the summer, the risk of dying while doing is no greater than on any other steep, rough, and often snow-covered terrain. The happy demise of the Monte Cristo road has put that area's several popular trails much deeper in de facto wilderness, glory be, more and more hikers with limited time have been finding the Sunrise Mine Trail on their own. Best that they (you) be warned what to expect.

Drive the Mountain Loop Highway 17.6 miles from the Verlot Public Service Center (formerly the Verlot Ranger Station) toward (not to) Barlow Pass. Turn right 2.3 miles on Sunrise Mine road No. 4065 to the road-end and trailhead, elevation 2100 feet. (The final ½ mile often is blocked by a slide.)

In the first ½ mile through forest the root-and-rock rough trail crosses four creeks. The second ½ mile, still rough, switchbacks steeply up a fern-covered hillside, rounds a corner, and levels briefly as the trail enters the steep, narrow valley of death or whatever.

Avalanche fans may remain unmelted all summer, or even for years. Just because you're technically "on" a trail don't be silly about steep, hard snow. Unless the way is clear, be satisfied with the valley view of

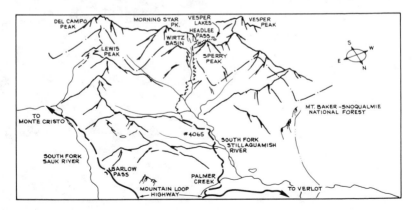

Headlee Pass trail

peaks piercing the sky.

The miners who built the trail begrudged time that could be spent more entertainingly, if not profitably, digging holes in the ground and sought to gain maximum elevation with minimum distance. No fancy-Dan 10-percent grade for *them*—the final mile, gaining 1200 feet to Headlee Pass, is 15–20 percent. The last 500 feet is in a slot gully where the grade has to be re-made every summer by unpaid volunteers.

Headlee Pass, 4600 feet, is a thin cut in the ridge with rather limited views, confined by cliffs on three sides and snowy Vesper Peak to the east. The trail continues a short distance beyond the pass to an end at the edge of a giant rockslide; at one time it went to Sunrise Mine. A faint way trail crosses the slide to tiny Headlee Lake, often snowbound even at Labor Day.

Old road: 3020
New road: 4065

48   GOAT LAKE

Round trip 10 miles
Hiking time 5 hours
High point 3162 feet
Elevation gain 1280 feet

Hikable mid-June through
  October
One day or backpack
USGS Sloan Peak and Bedal

   A subalpine lake beneath cliffs and glaciers, a popular destination with hikers of all ages. Wander beside clear, cold water, investigate artifacts of long-ago mining, and admire snow-fed waterfalls frothing down

Goat Lake and Foggy Peak

rock walls. The trail (foot travel only) partly traces the route of a wagon road dating from the late 19th century.

Drive from Verlot on the Mountain Loop Highway 19.5 miles to Barlow Pass, then north about 4 miles to Elliott Creek road No. 4080. Turn right 1 mile to a gate, parking area, and trailhead, elevation 1900 feet.

The recently abandoned road can be walked but is a mile longer and not as pretty as trail No. 647 (may be unsigned) which mainly follows an ancient wagon road, mostly in forest, in sight and loud sound of cascade-roaring Elliott Creek. At 3⅓ miles pass the end of the abandoned logging road and continue gently climbing. At 4¼ miles the trail leaves the wagon road, steepens, and switchbacks upward, rejoining the road just before the lake outlet at 4½ miles, 3162 feet.

For an interesting sidetrip, at about the 4-mile mark the wagon road diverges rightward from the trail and crosses Elliott Creek to decrepit remains of a mining settlement. The road then switchbacks and in roughly ½ mile recrosses the creek on risky remnants of a bridge to meet the trail.

Enjoy the views of Foggy Peak. Prowl relics of what was, some 75 years ago, a busy mining town. In summer sunshine, take a brisk swim.

Beyond the outlet is a nice spot to picnic. The trail continues left around the shore, eventually disappearing in alder and vine maple. On a rocky knoll before the brush begins is a particularly fine place to sit and stare and eat lunch before going home.

Because campers have overused the lakeshore areas, these are now restricted to picknicking. Camping is permitted only at the old hotel site on a knoll above the outlet.

For variety on the way back, hike the logging road, not as much fun as the trail but with better views from old clearcuts.

Old road: 309 322
New road: 4080 20

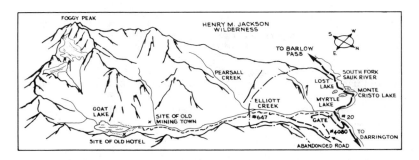

Sheep Gap Mountain from Gothic Basin

SOUTH FORK SAUK RIVER
Unprotected area

 # GOTHIC BASIN

Round trip from Barlow Pass 9 miles
Hiking time 9 hours
High point 5000 feet
Elevation gain 2600 feet

Hikable late July through early October
One day or backpack
USGS Monte Cristo

A glacier-gouged basin designed for wandering. Rounded buttresses polished and scratched by ice, sparkling ponds in scooped-out rock, an Arctic-barren cirque lake, loud waterfalls, meadow nooks, old mines, ore samples, and views of Monte Cristo peaks.

From 1909 to 1912 the Northwest Mining Company operated a 7,000-foot aerial tram from Weden House to a mine just below the basin lip. Little evidence is left except a few bits of rusty iron, some rotten wood, and the trail. For years after the railroad fell into disuse the headwaters of the South Fork Sauk reverted to wildness. Then, in the 1940s, the American dream of getting everywhere by car produced a road to Monte Cristo. As a day-after-Christmas present to pedestrians, in 1980 the Sauk River washed out long stretches. (In destruction of silly roads is the preservation of wilderness.)

Drive from the Verlot Public Service Center 19.5 miles to Barlow Pass and park near the gated Monte Cristo road, elevation 2360 feet.

Walk the Monte Cristo road 1 mile to the crossing of the Sauk River and just before crossing find a new trailhead on the right-hand side, behind an outhouse, elevation 2400 feet. The miners' trail started from Weden House, ¾ mile farther, but keeping a bridge over the braided channels was nigh impossible. In 1983, therefore, members of Volunteers of Washington (VOW), led by Will Thompson, roughed out a path ½ mile along the riverbank to intersect the old trail.

The sturdy miners didn't waste effort on switchbacks, and the trail is steep all the way. At 1½ miles is a series of three streams rushing down slot gorges possibly snow-filled and dangerous until early August; here too are flowers, a mine, and views across Weden Creek to Silvertip Peak. The trail enters brush, the tread gets skimpy and requires some careful walking, and the grade continues grueling. "King Kong's Showerbath" demands a halt amid unpleasantness. The Consolidated Mine invites a sidetrip. After an especially straight-up and rock-scrambling stretch, the way emerges into a final ½ mile of heather and flowers, traversing the valley wall on meadow shelves.

At 3 miles, 5000 feet, the trail cuts through the ridge into Gothic Basin and ends in a meadow among buttresses. A good campsite here and many others throughout the basin. Wood is scarce; bring a stove.

Now, explorations. In the lower basin are flower gardens, artifacts of old-time (and as recent as 1969) prospecting, waterfall gorges, and views down to Weden Creek and across to the Monte Cristo group. Especially fascinating are the rocks: limestone, sandstone, conglomerate, granite, and iron-red mineralized zones, all plucked and polished by the ice, the dominant brownish limestone weathered into oddly beautiful forms. Follow the stream bed or the buttress crest 300 feet higher to Foggy (Crater) Lake, in a solemn cirque under Gothic and Del Campo Peaks. Scramble slabs and talus and blossoms to 5500-foot Foggy Pass between Gothic and Del Campo, for higher views.

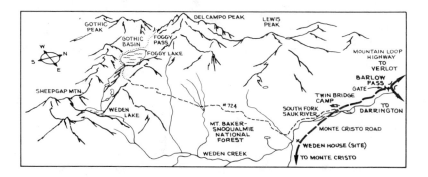

50 SILVER LAKE–TWIN LAKES

**Round trip from Barlow Pass to
Silver Lake 11 miles
Hiking time 8 hours
High point 4350 feet
Elevation gain 3000 feet
Hikable July through October
Backpack
USGS Monte Cristo**

**Round trip to Twin Lakes 17 miles
Hiking time 12 hours
High point 5400 feet
Elevation gain 3500 feet in, 1000
out**

Three beautiful lakes, especially lovely in fall colors. The nearest and easiest, Silver Lake, is tucked in a cirque of cliffs, waterfalls, and meadows. Twin Lakes, 3 grueling miles farther, are twin pools of deep blue beneath the great east face of Columbia Peak.

The authors don't want to hear any hikers whimpering about the December 26, 1980 flood that ripped up the road to Monte Cristo and forced them to walk 4 extra miles, each way. The Christmas flood was the best thing that's happened to this valley since the railroad shut down. The 4 miles now free of automobiles are the most scenic valley walk, forest walk, river walk in the area, with many excellent backpacker campsites, a terrific place to introduce little children to a life away from automobiles. Further, those 4 miles multiplied by 2 convert certain former day walks amid crowds to lonesome wildland backpacks. If you phone the

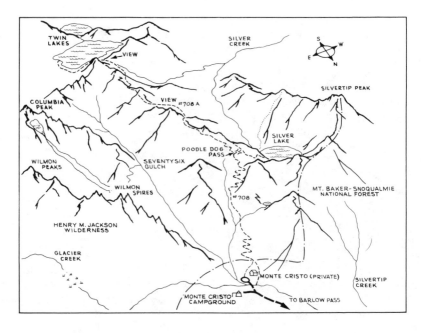

Silver Lake and Silvertip Peak

Silvertip Peak from Twin Lakes trail

Verlot Service Center (206-691-7791) for the latest road information, and they say it's still closed, break into a cheer and tell Snohomish County to keep it that way.

Drive the Mountain Loop Highway 19.5 miles from the Verlot Public Service Center to Barlow Pass and park near the gated Monte Cristo road, elevation 2360 feet.

Hike the Monte Cristo road 4 delightful miles to a junction. The left is to Glacier Basin. Take the right toward Monte Cristo townsite, cross the Sauk River, and in a few feet reach the trailhead, elevation 2753 feet, signed "Silver Lake."

The trail is steep, eroded by water and boots, and cluttered by boulders, giant roots, and stumps from clearcut on private property, so though it's only 1½ miles to Silver Lake, expect to spend 2 hours getting there. At 4350 feet the way crosses Poodle Dog Pass. Here the Silver Lake and the Twin Lakes trails separate.

For Silver Lake, go right from the pass ¼ mile to the shore, 4260 feet. Camping is possible by the outlet but the space is cramped and muddy and the last easy firewood was burned up along about 1947; bring a stove. For the best views and picnics cross the outlet and climb open slopes 700 feet to a shoulder of Silvertip Peak. Look down Silver Creek toward Mineral City, and beyond Silver Lake to the Monte Cristo peaks. In season, graze blue fruit.

For Twin Lakes, go left on a boot-beaten track that follows an old miners' trail. The way is strenuous and rugged, gaining (and partly losing) 1500 feet in the 2½ miles to a viewpoint 650 feet above the lakes. Though the route is well defined it would be easy to lose in snow, so don't go before August. In the first mile the upsy-downsy trail rounds a ridge with views out Silver Creek to logging roads. After dropping to pass under a cliff, at about 2 miles it climbs to a viewpoint over the deep hole of Seventysix Gulch to Wilmon Spires.

Walk on—and scramble along, above cliffs—the ridge crest. Some 150 feet before the highest point of the ridge the trail contours right toward an obvious pass, and at 2½ miles reaches the lakes view, far enough for most hikers. Make a wrong turn here and you're in cliffs. To reach the lakes go right, descending to the obvious pass and then following the trail down a wide terrace. Campsites are plentiful but not wood; carry a stove.

Clark's nutcracker

51 GLACIER BASIN

Round trip from Barlow Pass 13½ miles
Allow 2 days
High point 4500 feet
Elevation gain 2100 feet
Hikable July through October
USGS Monte Cristo and Blanca Lake

Round trip from Monte Cristo 5 miles
Hiking time 5 hours
Elevation gain 1700 feet
One day

Meadows and boulders, flowers and snowfields, cold streams for wading and soft grass for napping, all in a dream basin tucked amid fierce peaks.

Until the flood of December 26, 1980, this was so short and popular a hike any observer could plainly see the eventual total devastation of the scene. The only salvation in sight was that popularity was generating unpopularity. Now the hike is long—too long for a day or even a relaxed weekend—and more glorious than it's been since the 1940s, when the automobile poked its nose into this valley. It would be a mad, mad world that reopened the road to Monte Cristo and thus rejected Mother Nature's gift.

Drive the Mountain Loop Highway 19.5 miles from the Verlot Public Service Center to Barlow Pass and park near the gated Monte Cristo road, elevation 2360 feet. (You may wish to call the Service Center to inquire about the road—see Hike 50.)

Walk the road 4⅓ miles, noting the many excellent spots to camp by the river and introduce children to wilderness, or to basecamp for day hikes to high country. From the road split, 2800 feet, the right goes to Monte Cristo townsite and the Silver Lake trail. Climb left a short bit to Monte Cristo Campground and Glacier Basin trail No. 719. The start is on overgrown mining-logging road. At ½ mile is a wide swath of gravel and white water where Glacier Creek regularly goes crazy in winter, as on Christmas of 1980; cross on temporary log bridges, marked by temporary plastic ribbons. The road-trail continues 1 more mile to the end, now a scenic campsite.

The "true" trail commences at a moderate grade in open greenery but

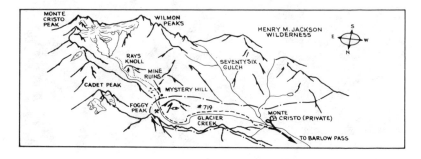

Glacier Basin

quickly plunges into Sitka alder and Alaska cedar and tilts straight up. Stop for a rest on a rock outcrop above a magnificent waterfall before tackling the next stretch, the worst, blistering hot and fly-bedeviled in sunny summertime. The "trail" is so eroded by years of snowmelt and boots that were it not for the alder handholds the rock slabs and mud walls would require mountaineering equipment. Going up, think how bad it's going to be coming *down*. But there's only ½ mile of the worst (an hour up, an hour down). The track then eases out in a gulch filled with talus, snow, and whistling marmots.

The difficulties are not quite over. When the water is high the trail is flooded and hikers must scramble over boulders. At 4500 feet, 2½ miles from Monte Cristo Campground, with startling abruptness the way opens into the basin—the meandering creeks, the flat fields of grass and blossoms, and the cliffs and glaciers of Cadet and Monte Cristo and Wilman Peaks, the sharp thrust of Wilmon Spires.

What to do now? Sit and look, have lunch, watch the dippers. Or roam among boulders and wade sandy creeks and maybe organize a snowball fight. Or climb scree slopes to explore old mines. Or take a loitering walk to Ray's Knoll (named for climber Ray Rigg) and views over the basin and down the valley. Scramblers can continue up an easy gully to a higher cirque with glaciers, moraines, waterfalls, and broader views.

But please be kind to the basin meadows. Walk softly. And camp not in the flower flats but on a flat area partway up tree-covered Mystery Hill, to the right as you enter the basin. No fires!

52 BALD MOUNTAIN

One-way trip about 9½ miles
Hiking time 6 hours
High point 4500 feet
Elevation gain from Stillaguamish
2100 feet, from Sultan 1900 feet

Hikable July through October
One day or backpack
USGS Silverton and Index
South Fork Stillaguamish River

A fine high route traverses the 7-mile ridge separating Sultan Basin and the South Fork Stillaguamish River. Walk the complete way, partly in views of valleys, lakes, and peaks, and partly in deep forest. Or just visit the scenic climax—a dozen small lakes in huckleberry-heather meadows near the summit of 4851-foot Bald Mountain. This climax can be attained from either end: The distance is less from the Sultan start.

Stillaguamish start: Drive the Mountain Loop Highway from Granite Falls to 5 miles past the Verlot Public Service Center and turn right on road No. 4020, signed "Bear Lake Trail" and "Bald Mountain Trail." At 2.7 miles from the highway turn right on road No. 4021, signed "Bald Mountain." At 4.3 miles go uphill left. Stay right at the next Y and at a bit more than 5 miles reach a large Department of Natural Resources sign and parking lot, elevation 2100 feet.

Walk a steep cat road up a few hundred feet to the trail, which proceeds from old clearcut into old virgin forest, much of the way on puncheon. At ¾ mile pass a sidetrail to Beaver Plant Lake and in a scant mile reach a Y. The right fork goes a short bit to Upper Ashland Lake and camps. Keep left.

The trail climbs around the end of Bald Ridge in grand forest, at 3 miles topping a 3950-foot saddle with views of Three Fingers, the Stillaguamish, and Clear Lake, directly below. At about 4 miles the trail, to pass under cliffs, switchbacks down and down 500 feet into the head of Pilchuck River, here is the first water since the lakes area. The lost elevation is regained and at about 6½ miles is a 4400-foot saddle under the highest peak of Bald Mountain. Here begin those promised meadows.

Sultan start: This end of the trail can be reached from either the town of Sultan or from Granite Falls as described here.

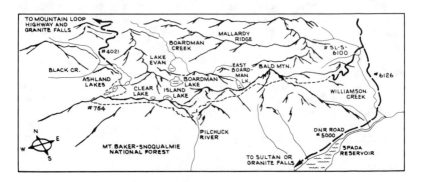

One of the Cutthroat Lakes

At the second stop sign in Granite Falls, turn right on South Alder Street. At 0.2 miles turn left on East Pioneer Street signed "Lake Roesiger." At 4.5 miles turn left on DNR road No. 5000 (a large graveled road with a very small road sign). This road has numerous spurs so when in doubt look carefully for the small signs. The road follows the Pilchuck River for miles and then switches from the Pilchuck to the Sultan River watershed. At 17 miles from Granite Falls pass the junction with the road to Sulton which crosses Culmback Dam.

Stay on road 5000 (which may also be marked with the Forest Service No. 6126). The views become spectacular and the road steep. At 21 miles from Granite Falls cross Williamson Creek, and at 22.5 miles turn left on DNR road 6100, cross Williamson Creek again, and start climbing. At 1.7 miles from Williamson Creek keep left. At 2 miles leave SL-S-6100 and go right. At 2.6 miles reach a junction and the Bald Mountain parking area, elevation about 2600 feet.

Hike the road, switchbacking left, keeping to the right at the first spur and left at the second. At 1 mile the road ends and foot trail enters forest. At 2 miles the forest becomes more alpine and at 2¾ miles from the parking lot the trail reaches a junction. The left fork contours around the south side of Bald Mountain 7 miles to Ashland Lakes as described above; the right fork drops a short mile to Cutthroat Lakes, a dozen or more delightful tarns and small lakes. Plenty of campsites but in late summer running water may be hard to find.

Old road:	3015	3015B	2901	292A	SL-S-6100
New road:	4020	4021	6120	6126	SL-S-6100

53 BLANCA LAKE

Round trip to lake 8 miles
Hiking time 6–8 hours
High point 4600 feet
Elevation gain 2700 feet in, 600 feet out

Hikable July through October
One day or backpack
USGS Blanca Lake

The rugged cliffs of Kyes, Monte Cristo, and Columbia Peaks above, the white mass of the Columbia Glacier in the upper trough, and the deep waters of ice-fed Blanca Lake filling the lower cirque. A steep forest climb ending in a grand views, with further explorations available to the experienced off-trail traveler.

Drive US 2 to Index junction and turn left on the North Fork Skykomish River road 14 miles to Garland Mineral Springs. At a junction .5 mile beyond the springs turn left on road No. 63 the 2 miles to Blanca Lake trail sign and parking area, elevation 1900 feet.

The trail immediately gets down to the business of grinding out elevation and never neglects that assignment, relentlessly switchbacking up and up in forest, eventually with partial views out to Glacier Peak. At 3 miles the way reaches the ridge top at 4600 feet, the highest point of the trip. In a few hundred yards is shallow little Virgin Lake, amid meadows and trees of a saddle on the very crest. Acceptable camping here for those who don't wish to carry packs farther, but no water in late summer.

Now the trail goes down, deteriorating into a mere route as it sidehills through trees with glimpses of blue-green water, dropping 600 feet in 1 mile and reaching the 3972-foot lake at the outlet. Relax and enjoy the wind-rippled, sun-sparkling lake, ¾ mile long, the Columbia Glacier, the spectacular peaks. Where the trail hits the lake, and across the outlet stream on the west shore, are a number of overused but fairly decent campsites. Don't expect to find any easy wood; carry a stove.

Experienced hikers can explore along the rough west shore to the braided stream channels and waterfalls and flowers at the head of the lake. Those with proper mountaineering background and equipment can climb the Columbia Glacier to the col between Columbia and Monte Cristo Peaks and look down to Glacier Basin. The descent into the basin

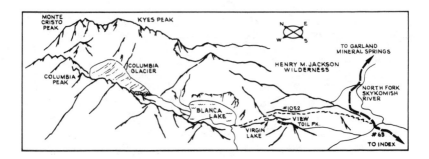

Air view of Lake Blanca and Kyes Peak

is not technically difficult, but strictly for parties skilled in use of the ice ax.

For a spectacular view of lake and mountains, hike to the top of 5128-foot Toil Peak, the first of two wooded bumps between Virgin Lake and Troublesome Mountain. On the highest point of the trail above Virgin Lake find a faint path traversing heather meadows southward, climbing at times steeply to the top.

Old road: 290
New road: 63

Mount Rainier from Benchmark Mountain

SKYKOMISH RIVER
Henry M. Jackson Wilderness

54 WEST CADY RIDGE LOOP

Short loop trip 17 miles
Allow 2 days
High point 5816 feet
Elevation gain 3300 feet
Hikable mid-July through late
September
USGS Blanca Lake and
Benchmark Mountain

Long loop trip 23½ miles
Allow 2–3 days
Elevation gain 4700 feet

An easy loop through miles of forest and flower-covered alpine meadows, or a longer loop with more miles of forest and meadows. Both start on the North Fork Skykomish River trail and travel part of the way on the Pacific Crest National Scenic Trail. Both have a 1½-mile road walk to connect the beginning and end; if transportation can be arranged between the two trailheads, subtract 1½ miles and 500 feet of elevation gain from the trip log.

Except for West Cady Ridge good campsites are scattered along the way. For the short loop plan to camp high on Pass Creek. For the long loop camp the first night 4 or 5 miles up the trail and the second night on the Crest Trail near Pass Creek.

From US 2 at Index junction turn left on North Fork Skykomish River road 20 miles to the end and the North Fork Skykomish trailhead, elevation 3000 feet. Unload packs here and drive back 1.4 miles to where the loop will end at West Cady Ridge trailhead, elevation 2500 feet. Leave the car here and walk back up the road.

Hike 1½ miles on North Fork trail No. 1051 to the junction with Pass Creek trail No. 1053, signed "Cady Pass 3½ miles"; elevation, 3200 feet.

For the short loop go right, crossing the North Fork on a footlog, then climbing a sometimes muddy and brushy trail to the Pacific Crest Trail, 5 miles from the road, elevation 4200 feet. Campsites on the Crest Trail just after crossing Pass Creek.

For the long loop, back at the Pass Creek junction continue up the North Fork trail on sometimes excellent and sometimes poor tread. At about 4 miles from the road cross the North Fork Skykomish River on a footlog to a nice campsite. At 5 miles the path traverses a large huckleberry parkland with water and camping space. From here the way climbs to Dishpan Gap and the Pacific Crest Trail, 7½ miles from the road, elevation 5600 feet.

Head south on the Crest Trail (Hike 63) 4 miles through beautiful alpine meadows, passing Wards Pass and Lake Sally Ann to Cady Pass; ½ mile beyond the pass join the short loop at Pass Creek, elevation 4200 feet.

From Pass Creek continue south on the Crest Trail 2¼ miles and go right on West Cady Ridge trail No. 1054, elevation 4900 feet. Here begin the 4 glorious miles of meadows. Be sure to take in the highest point of the ridge, 5816-foot Benchmark Mountain, surrounded by fields of heather and flowers and horizons of views, including Sloan Peak, the Monte Cristo peaks, Baker, and Rainier.

A delightful walk in alpine meadows follows the ups and downs of 4-mile-long West Cady Ridge. At its abrupt end the trail descends a series of short switchbacks, at 8 miles from the Crest Trail reaching the North Fork a short distance from the road-end.

Old road: 290
New road: 63

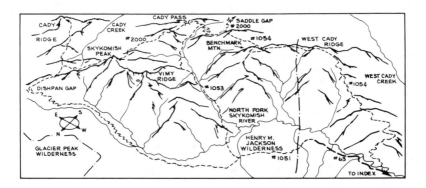

55 BARCLAY AND EAGLE LAKES

Round trip to Eagle Lake 8½ miles
Hiking time 6 hours
High point 3888 feet
Elevation gain 1700 feet

Hikable late June through
 October
One day or backpack
USGS Baring

For many years Barclay Lake ranked among the most popular low-elevation hikes in the Cascades, passing through pleasant old forest to the base of the tremendous north wall of Mt. Baring, a trip good in early spring and late fall when higher country was deep in snow. The wall remains, and the lake, but not much forest. Tragically, the walk to Barclay Lake no long deserves, by itself, inclusion in this book. However, there is still Eagle Lake, amid trees, meadows, and peaks, and offering a staggering cross-valley look at the north wall of Baring, a legend among climbers and to date ascended only once.

Drive US 2 some 6 miles east from Index junction. Turn left at Baring on 635 Place NE, cross railroad tracks, and go 4.3 miles on road No. 6024 to the trailhead, elevation 2200 feet.

The trail, with minor ups and downs and numerous mudholes, meanders through what remains of the forest of Barclay Creek, in 1½ miles reaching Barclay Lake, 2422 feet, and at 2¼ miles ending near the inlet stream. Camping at several spots along the shore and also a neck-stretching look up and up the precipice at 6123-foot Baring Mountain.

At the lakehead, just where the trail leaves the water by a small campsite, find a meager path climbing 1000 feet straight up steep forest. For a bit the way is on rockslide, then briefly levels and resumes climbing beside another rockslide. The grade abruptly flattens at a viewpoint above Stone Lake and contours to 3888-foot Eagle Lake.

By the shore is a private cabin, kept locked; the owner maintains a campsite for public use near the outlet.

For more views, and for meadows, wander up the easy slopes of 5936-

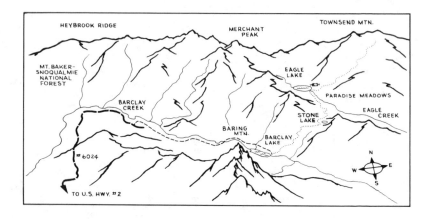

North wall of Baring Mountain from Eagle Lake trail

foot Townsend Mountain, or from the outlet roam downstream through the lovely forest, heather, and marsh of Paradise Meadow.

Now then. As you are sitting in Paradise Meadow nursing bruises and sprains and wiping sweat from your eyes, you may be hailed by a fisherman who is astounded at your suffering and stupidity, inasmuch as he is just a half-hour away from his car, parked on a logging road up Eagle Creek. And you go home and write a letter demanding to know why this guidebook has put you through this ordeal. Well, what makes it an ordeal is not the steep climb, which enriches the wilderness experience, but learning a road is so near (though not by trail—it's a brush route). Why isn't the road gated, banning public vehicles, and thus placing Eagle Lake back in deep wilderness where it belongs?

Old road: 278
New road: 6024

56 SCORPION MOUNTAIN

Round trip 8 miles
Hiking time 6 hours
High point 5540 feet
**Elevation gain 2300 feet in, 300
feet out**

Hikable July through October
One day
**USGS Evergreen Mountain and
Captain Point**

Looking for view from an easy trail? Try Evergreen Mountain. Looking for a pleasant family walk? Choose any other destination but Scorpion! Even the access road, carved into a steep hillside stripped bare of trees, is difficult. And there is no water on the path, making at least one

Monte Cristo Peaks from Scorpion Mountain

loaded canteen essential. However, hikers seeking solitude and a nice view at the end of a tough trail will find Scorpion worth a day's effort.

Drive US 2 to Skykomish. Just beyond town turn left on Beckler River road No. 65. At 7 miles turn right on road No. 6520, signed "Johnson Creek" and "Johnson Ridge Trail." At 1.7 miles from Beckler River road keep straight ahead at a junction and at 5.6 miles turn right on an un-numbered road and continue to its end at 7 miles, about 3500 feet. If the going is too hairy, park and walk the last mile. From the road-end climb ¾ mile up a shadeless clearcut, picking from the maze of cat roads one that can be followed to the ridge top, where the trail starts.

The seldom-used trail was cleared in 1967 in the process of fighting a series of little fires, all fortunately extinguished before reaching propor-tions of the devastating Evergreen Mountain fire which occurred at the same time. The trail is obscured here and there by windfalls but there is no problem detouring around them. If the tread is lost, just follow the ridge top.

The heavily wooded ridge crest occasionally offers glimpses of rocky 6190-foot Mt. Fernow to the south. At 2¼ miles the trail passes over the top of 5056-foot Sunrise Mountain, with a view of Glacier Peak, and then drops about 300 feet before climbing nearly to the top of 5540-foot Scor-pion Mountain at 4 miles. Leave the path at its highest point and follow the ridge a few hundred feet to the summit, flanked by a lush carpet of grass and flowers and surrounded by a panorama of the Cascades.

The trail continues around the southern shoulder of the mountain and drops 500 feet to tiny Joan Lake at 4½ miles.

Volunteers are reopening 5½ miles of an old trail from Scorpion Moun-tain to Captain Point and Scenic.

Old road:	280	273	273A
New road:	65	6520	no number

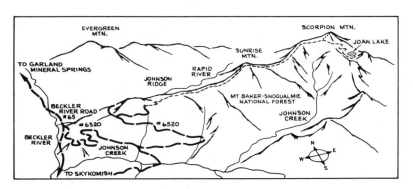

Upper Fortune Pond

SKYKOMISH RIVER
Henry M. Jackson Wilderness

57 A PEACH, A PEAR, AND A TOPPING

Round trip to Pear Lake 15 miles
Allow 2 days
High point 5300 feet
Elevation gain 3200 feet in, 500 feet out

Hikable July through October
USGS Captain Point and Benchmark Mountain

Savor flower and heather gardens ringing three alpine lakes and a spatter of ponds along the Pacific Crest Trail. And if all these sweet things seem to call for whipped cream, stroll to a peak for a panorama of a horizonful of valleys and mountains.

To approach from the east, drive road No. 6701 from the Little Wenatchee River (see Hike 61) and at 4 miles past the junction with road No. (6701)400 find Top Lake trail No. 1506. From the more popular west, drive US 2 to Skykomish and just east of town turn north on Beckler River road No. 65. At 7 miles turn right on Rapid River road No. 6530. At 11.4 miles is the start of Meadow Creek trail No. 1057, elevation 2100 feet.

Beginning amid the ravages of the 1967 Evergreen Mountain fire and subsequent salvage logging, the trail (a goshawful goo from churning by

Bear tracks on shore of upper Fortune Pond

horses, which also have ruined hillside tread) gains almost 1000 feet switchbacking out of Rapid River valley. At about 1 mile the burn is left, forest entered, and the grade moderates and contours into Meadow Creek drainage, crossing Meadow Creek at 3 miles by hopping boulders (there aren't really enough). At 3¾ miles recross the creek to a junction with an abandoned trail to Cady Ridge. The way climbs steeply from Meadow Creek into Cady Creek drainage. At 6½ miles the Crest Trail is reached at the lower of the two Fortune Ponds, 4700 feet.

Walk the Crest Trail south. At 7¾ miles cross 5200-foot Frozen Finger Pass between Cady Creek and Rapid River and drop to Pear Lake, 8 miles, 4809 feet. No camping within 100 feet of the shores here or at Fortune Ponds. Peach Lake, at the same elevation over the ridge south, is best reached by contouring off trail around the ridge end and below cliffs, passing narrow Grass Lake. Top Lake is attained via ½ mile more on the Crest Trail and another ½ mile on trail No. 1506. For the promised land of views, leave the trail at Fortune Ponds and ascend Fortune Mountain, 5903 feet.

Old road:	270	280	2801	2713
New road:	6530	65	(6701)400	6701

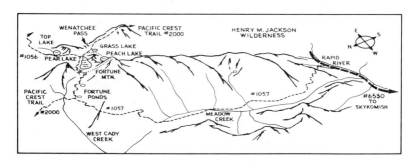

Lake Valhalla from Pacific Crest Trail

NASON CREEK
Unprotected area

LAKE VALHALLA

Round trip 11 miles
Hiking time 6 hours
High point 5100 feet
Elevation gain 1100 feet

Hikable mid-July through
   October
One day or backpack
USGS Labyrinth Mountain

North from Stevens Pass the Pacific Crest Trail roams by a splendid succession of meadowy alpine lakes. First in line is Lake Valhalla, set in a cirque under the cliffs of Lichtenberg Mountain.

Drive US 2 to Stevens Pass, elevation 4061 feet, and park in the lot at the east end of the summit area. Find the trail beside the PUD substation.

The way begins along the original grade of the Great Northern Railroad, used when trains went over the top of the pass; the right of way was abandoned upon completion of the first Cascade Tunnel (predecessor of the present tunnel) early in the century.

From the open hillside views extend beyond the pass to ski slopes and down Stevens Creek to Nason Creek and far east out the valley. Below is the roar of highway traffic. In 1½ miles the gentle path rounds the end of the ridge and enters the drainage of Nason Creek. Here a sidetrail drops east ½ mile to the old Cascade Tunnel, now employed as a research station by University of Washington geophysicists.

The main trail descends a bit to cross a little stream, climbs a ridge, and at 3½ miles enters a basin of meadows and marsh, with a fair campsite at 3¾ miles. Staying east and below the Cascade Crest, the way ascends easily to a 5100-foot spur, then drops to the rocky shore of the 4830-foot lake.

Heavily used and frequently crowded camps lie among trees near the outlet; wood is hard to come by, so carry a stove. For explorations climb heather meadows to the summit of 5920-foot Lichtenberg and broad views or continue north on the Pacific Crest Trail (Hike 100) as far as time and energy allow.

A much shorter (5½ miles round trip) but less scenic approach is via the Smith Brook trail (Hike 59) which joins the Pacific Crest Trail at Union Gap 1 mile from the road. The Crest Trail leads south from the Gap 1¾ miles to Lake Valhalla.

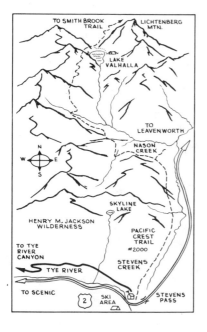

Pipsissewa or prince's pine

59 LAKE JANUS AND GRIZZLY PEAK

**Round trip to Grizzly Peak 17
miles**
Hiking time 6–8 hours
High point 5597 feet
**Elevation gain 2200 feet in, 800
feet out**

**Hikable mid-July through
October**
One day or backpack
**USGS Labyrinth Mountain and
Captain Point**

A beautiful alpine lake and a long ridge trail, sometimes in Western Washington and sometimes in Eastern Washington and sometimes straddling the fence. An easy but spectacular stretch of the Pacific Crest Trail. The trip can be done in a day but at least a weekend should be planned—the lake is inviting and "looking around the next corner" is bound to be irresistible.

Drive US 2 east 4.5 miles from Stevens Pass and turn left on Smith Brook road No. 6702. Cross Nason Creek bridge, turn left, and follow the road 3.5 miles toward Rainy Pass to the Smith Brook trailhead, elevation 3800 feet.

Climb 1 mile on trail No. 1590 to 4680-foot Union Gap and the junction with the Pacific Crest Trail. Turn right, dropping 700 feet down the west side of the crest to round cliffs of Union Peak, then regaining part of the elevation before reaching 4146-foot Lake Janus, 2½ miles from the Gap. The trail goes through pleasant forest with the far-off sound of Rapid River. Though the grade is gentle the tread is badly water-eroded in places from years of heavy use.

The lake is everything an alpine lake should be—sparkling water surrounded by meadows and tall trees and topped by the bright green slopes of 6007-foot Jove Peak. Numerous camps are available, including a mountain memorial cabin that has not been treated kindly. Wood is scarce near the camps so carry a stove.

From the lake the trail enters forest on smooth and easy tread, climbs 1100 feet in 1½ miles to the Cascade Crest, contours around the Eastern Washington side of a small hill, and then ducks around a corner back into Western Washington, a process repeated frequently on the way to

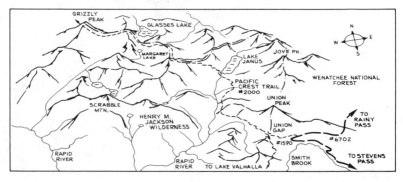

Lake Janus

Grizzly Peak. Carry water; there's little along the way.

Every turn of the crest-wandering trail offers new views. Look east down into Lake Creek and Little Wenatchee River drainage and across to nearby Labyrinth Mountain. Look north to Glacier Peak. Look west down to the Rapid River and out to peaks above the Skykomish. At 2½ miles from Lake Janus is a glimpse of Margaret Lake, some 400 feet below the trail. A short ½ mile beyond is a view down to Glasses Lake and larger Heather Lake; this is a good turnaround point for day hikers.

At about 5¼ miles from Lake Janus the trail climbs within a few feet of the top of 5597-foot Grizzly Peak and more panoramas—but unfortunately not of Glacier Peak, cut off by a nameless peak ½ mile north. The trail also goes close to the summit of the nameless peak, with a view of Glacier Peak; succumbing to this temptation will lead to further temptations, on and on along the Pacific Crest Trail.

Old road:　　2728
New road:　　6702

Alpine Lookout

NASON CREEK
Unprotected area

60 NASON RIDGE

**Round trip to Rock Mountain 8
 miles**
Hiking time 7 hours
High point 6852 feet
Elevation gain 3400 feet
Hikable August through October
One day or backpack
**USGS Wenatchee Lake and
 Labyrinth Mountain**

**Round trip to Alpine Lookout 10½
 miles**
Hiking time 6 hours
High point 6200 feet
Elevation gain 1700 feet
One day

A prime tour for experienced navigators is the magnificent journey the full length of Nason Ridge, 26-miles through wide-sky highlands from near the Cascade Crest to near Lake Wenatchee. Most hikers, though, sample the high delights on day or weekend hikes via four access trails, the two most popular of which are described here.

Snowy Creek to Rock Mountain: This pleasant way to Nason Ridge starts in cool forest, by small creeks, and climbs to alpine meadows and cliffs.

Drive US 2 east 4.5 miles from Stevens Pass and turn left on Smith Brook road No. 6702 (Hike 59). Cross Rainy Pass and in approximately 5 miles, at a major switchback, go straight ahead on road No. 6705 another 3.5 miles to the crossing of Snowy Creek and the trailhead, elevation 3500 feet.

Snowy Creek trail No. 1531 starts in clearcut, then enters forest. At 2 miles, 3800 feet, pass a campsite in a large, level meadow below cliffs of Rock Mountain. Tread vanishes in the meadow but reappears halfway

Mountain goats in protected area around Alpine Lookout

across, on the left. The next 2 miles are grueling, entering trees and leaving them, climbing 1800 feet to the ridge of Rock Mountain. From the junction on the ridge it's ⅓ mile to the 6852-foot summit, formerly site of a lookout cabin. (From the junction the way drops ¾ mile to the 6200-foot intersection with the Rock Mountain trail, which climbs in 4 miles and 3500 feet from US 2 at a point 9 miles east of Stevens Pass.)

Alpine Lookout: Drive US 2 east from Stevens Pass about 17 miles to a highway department rest area. A few hundred feet beyond, turn left on Butcher Creek road No. 6910. Cross Nason Creek, avoid a spur road, turn right at 2.5 miles, and drive almost to the road-end. Find the trailhead (Round Mountain trail No. 1529) at 4100 feet. Climb 1000 feet in 1½ miles to the junction with the Nason Ridge trail No. 1583 and continue climbing west 3¾ miles to the lookout, 6200 feet.

Old road:　　2728　2744　2717
New road:　　6702　6705　6910

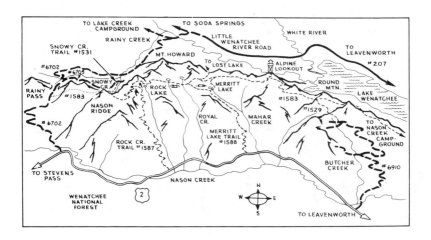

MINOTAUR LAKE

Round trip to Minotaur Lake 6 miles
Hiking time 5 hours
High point 5500 feet
Elevation gain 2000 feet

Hikable mid-July through October
One day or backpack
USGS Labyrinth Mountain

Minotaur Lake lies in a Grecian setting. Above and beyond are the rock walls of 6376-foot Labyrinth Mountain. Below is Theseus Lake. Heather meadows and alpine firs complete the mythological scene. No longer are seven girls and seven boys annually given in sacrifice to Minotaur, but each year visitors pay (in season) a tribute to the gods as the bugs take a libation of blood.

Drive US 2 east from Stevens Pass 19 miles and turn left to Lake Wenatchee. Pass the state park road, the roads to Plain and Fish Lake, and continue to Lake Wenatchee Ranger Station and 1.5 miles beyond to a junction. Go left on Little Wenatchee River road No. 65 for 6 miles, then turn left again, cross the river first on road No. 6702 then No. 67 for 8 miles, then go right on road No. 6704 (this junction also can be reached from the Smith Brook–Rainy Pass road No. 6702, Hike 60) and 1 more mile to the trailhead, elevation 3800 feet.

The way begins on North Fork Rainy Creek trail No. 1516, maintained but muddy. The trail switchbacks up a hill, drops to cross an unnamed

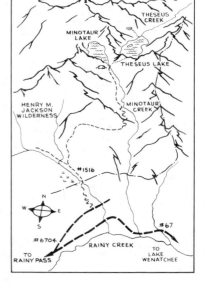

Cow parsnip

Theseus Lake

creek, and follows this stream ¾ mile. The North Fork trail goes on, but at about 1 mile find an unmaintained fishermen's path shooting straight up. There is no formal tread, only the groove pounded by many boots, gaining 1500 feet in the next mile. Views are limited to a few glimpses out through trees. At the end of the long, steep, dry ascent the trail turns downvalley ½ mile, losing 100 feet, then turns again and heads up Minotaur Creek. Forest gives way to highland meadows and at 3 miles is 5550-foot Minotaur Lake.

In trees around the shore are several good campsites. Cross the outlet and walk a few yards northeast to see 5060-foot Theseus Lake; a very steep path leads down to more good camps and the shores of the lake.

For broader views of mountains west to Stevens Pass, north to Glacier Peak, and east beyond Lake Wenatchee, scramble easily to open ridges above the lakes and wander the crests.

Old road: 283 2714 2728B 2728
New road: 65 6702 6704   67

62 HEATHER LAKE

**Round trip to Heather Lake 6½
  miles**
Hiking time 4 hours
High point 3953 feet
Elevation gain 1300 feet

Hikable July through October
One day or backpack
**USGS Labyrinth Mountain and
  Captain Point**

Waters of the ½-mile-long lake-in-the-woods reflect rocks and gardens
of Grizzly Peak. A family could be happy here for days, prowling about

Heather Lake from Pacific Crest Trail near Grizzly Peak

from a comfortable basecamp. So could doughty adventurers seeking more strenuous explorations.

From the upper end of Lake Wenatchee (Hike 61), drive 6 miles on Little Wenatchee River road No. 65, turn left on road No. 6702, cross the river, and in .5 mile go right on road No. 6701, following the river upstream. In 4.7 miles turn left onto road No. (6701)510. In 300 feet keep right and in another 2.3 miles reach the trailhead at the road-end, elevation 2700 feet. This trail also can be reached from the east side of Stevens Pass on Forest Road No. 6702, signed "Smith Brook Road" (Hike 60), a 12-mile dirt road climbing over 4600-foot Rainy Pass to road No. 6701 near the Little Wenatchee River.

The trail is a constant (nearly) joy, the minor ups and downs of the first 1½ miles, netting only 100 feet, easing muscles into their task. Having done so, it turns stern, crossing Lake Creek on a bridge and heading up seriously, leaving no doubt why machines and horses are forbidden. At 2½ miles, after gaining 900 feet, the grade relents and joy resumes in the last ¾ mile to Heather Lake, 3953 feet, with fine camps and a cozy privy.

The bare schist near the lake outlet, studded with tiny garnets, displays the grinding done by the glacier that scooped out the lake basin. Once these slabs were smooth, but eons of erosion have eaten away the polish, leaving only the grooves.

Attractive to the ambitious navigator with USGS map and compass, a way trail rounds the left side of the lake. At the far end follow a small stream south, climbing 700 feet in ½ mile to Glasses Lake, 4626 feet, so named because from neighboring peaks it looks like a pair of eyeglasses.

Old road: 283   2728   2713   2713E
New road: 65   6702   6701   (6701)510

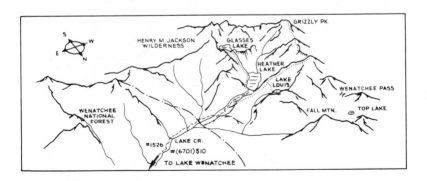

63 CADY PASS— MEANDER MEADOWS LOOP

Loop trip 17½ miles; sidetrip 14 miles more	Elevation gain 2000 feet, for sidetrip add 2100 feet
Allow 3–5 days	Hikable July through September
High point 5600 feet; sidetrip 6450 feet	USGS Bench Mark Mountain, Poe Mountain, Glacier Peak

A loop hike splendid in its own right, with an opportunity for a sidetrip to White Pass along what some argue is the most beautiful segment of the entire Pacific Crest National Scenic Trail, certainly offering one of the longest meadow walks anywhere in the Cascade Range.

Drive 14.5 miles on Little Wenatchee River road No. 65 (Hike 61) to its end near Little Wenatchee Ford Campground. Park here and walk back down the road a short bit to the trailhead, elevation 3000 feet.

Trail No. 1501 drops to a bridge over the Little Wenatchee River. In ¼ mile pass the Cady Ridge trail and follow Cady Creek 5 miles, gaining 1700 feet (including ups and downs), to wooded and waterless 4300-foot Cady Pass. Turn right (north) on the Pacific Crest Trail, climbing 1300 feet in 2 miles to break out above timberline on the divide between Cady Creek and Pass Creek. Now the way goes around this side or that of one small knoll after another, alternating between Eastern Washington and Western Washington. Then comes a traverse along the east slope of 6368-foot Skykomish Peak. At 2½ miles from Cady Pass (8 miles from the road) is 5479-foot Lake Sally Ann, a charming little tarn amid cliff-bordered meadows; this is the first dependable campsite on the trip, and badly overused. Less than ½ mile farther is an intersection with the Cady Ridge trail and another camp in a broad meadow. Climb a waterfall-sparkling basin to 5680-foot Wards Pass and roam parkland atop and near the crest past Dishpan Gap to 5450-foot Sauk Pass, 5½ miles from Cady Pass (10½ miles from the road) and a junction with trail No. 1525, the return route by way of Meander Meadows. For a basecamp descend meadows to the best possible campsite or a mile farther to some super spots.

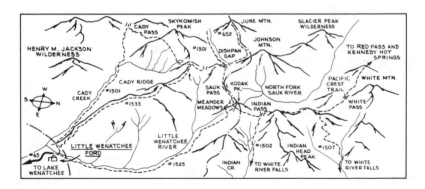

Meander Meadows

For the sidetrip continue on the Crest Trail 7 miles to 6450-foot Red Pass, with more flower-covered meadows and a spectacular view of Glacier Peak. The way goes up (1900 feet) and down (900 feet) the ridge top, totalling for the round trip 14 miles of hiking and 2400 feet of climbing—worth it.

The sidetrip begins by traversing green slopes of Kodak Peak to a saddle. (Take a few minutes to carry your camera, Kodak or other, to the 6121-foot summit.) Descend across a gorgeous alpine basin and down forest to mostly wooded Indian Pass, 5000 feet, 1½ miles from Sauk Pass. Pleasant campsites in the pass—but usually no water except in early summer.

Climb forest, climb gardens around the side of Indian Head Peak to tiny Kid Pond and beyond to 5378-foot Lower White Pass, 3 miles from Sauk Pass, and a junction with the White River trail. The next 1½ miles have the climax meadows, past Reflection Pond into flower fields culminating at 5904-foot White Pass, 4½ miles from Sauk Pass. For dramatic views of Glacier Peak and the White Chuck Glacier walk the Crest Trail west another 1½ miles to Red Pass.

Having done (or not) the sidetrip, finish the loop from Meander Meadows by following trail No. 1525 down 2 miles of flowers (if not eaten by domestic sheep) and another 5 miles of forest and meadow.

Old road: 283
New road: 65

Mountain daisy

LITTLE WENATCHEE RIVER
Unprotected area

POE MOUNTAIN

Round trip 6 miles
Hiking time 4 hours
High point 6015 feet
Elevation gain 2900 feet

Hikable late June through
October
USGS Poe Mountain

What the map calls "Wenatchee Ridge" is unofficially known as "Poet Ridge," due to a government mapmaker of yore having named its various high points Bryant Peak, Longfellow Mountain, Poe Mountain, Irving Peak, Whittier Peak, and Mt. Jonathan (whoever he was). Discriminating students of literature call it "Poetaster Ridge" and lament the taste of government mapmakers of yore. Poe is not the highest of the lot but has so commanding a view it was once the site of a lookout cabin. The panorama includes the Little Wenatchee River valley from Meander Meadows to Soda Springs, forests of Nason Ridge, and mountains of the Cascade Crest. Views in other directions are blocked by various poets. Glacier Peak, Sloan, Monte Cristo, Hinman, and Rainier can be seen above distant ridges.

The two trails to Poe Mountain are the same length and, when ups and downs are taken into account, have nearly the same elevation gain. The better choice on a hot day would be the ridge route, reached from road No. 6504, starting at an elevation of 4000 feet. The direct route from the west described here should be done early in the morning before the sun blisters the trail. Carry water; there's none along the way save dewdrops.

Drive Little Wenatchee River road No. 65 to the end, elevation 3900 feet (Hike 63).

Glacier Peak and Poet Ridge from Poe Mountain

Walk ¼ mile on Little Wenatchee River trail No. 1525 and turn right on Poe Mountain trail No. 1520. The rate of gain is about 1000 feet per mile, ideal for getting there firstest with the mostest rubber left on the lugs. Shade trees are scarce but views are plentiful, enlarging at each upward rest-step. Just below the top the way joins the ridge trail, No. 1543, for the final ¼ mile to the meadowy summit.

Old road: 283 2817
New road: 65 6504

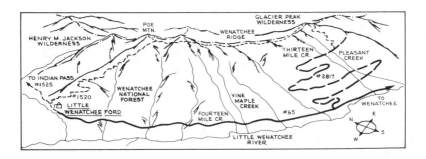

65 NAPEEQUA VALLEY VIA BOULDER PASS

Round trip to Napeequa ford 26 miles

Allow 3–7 days

High point (Boulder Pass) 6250 feet

Elevation gain 4250 feet in, 2000 feet out

Hikable early August through October

USGS Holden and Glacier Peak

The Napeequa River has designed its fabled Napeequa valley neatly to keep people out, exiting via a cliff-walled gorge that never has had any sort of trail and entering from glaciers and precipices inaccessible except to climbers. Each of the only two reasonable entries is over an exceedingly high pass and a wide, deep, swift river. Hikers may well climb to the top of Boulder Pass, drop to the floor of Napeequa valley—and find themselves cut off from the fabled green meadows by the Napeequa River. Then, if they get across the flood alive, they can expect to be eaten

Napeequa River

alive by flies as big as the flowers and as numerous. Pretty pictures simply don't tell the whole story.

Drive to Lake Wenatchee Ranger Station (Hike 61) and continue 1.5 miles to a junction. Keep right on the White River road No. 64 to the end and trailhead, elevation 2200 feet. Hike the White River trail 4 pleasant, virtually level miles through lovely virgin forest to the Boulder Pass trail No. 1562, 2470 feet. Subsequent mileages are calculated from this junction.

The well-graded trail climbs steadily to Boulder Pass. In about 2½ miles is a crossing of Boulder Creek, hazardous in high water. At 4 miles is 5000-foot Basin Camp, under the walls of 8676-foot Clark Mountain. This is a logical and splendid spot to end the first day—and also a grand base for an extra day exploring a very faint path west to a 6150-foot saddle overlooking the White River. To find the path, cross the creek from camp to a point just under a slab of red rock on the opposite side of the valley. Even without tread the going would be fairly easy up open meadows.

From Basin Camp the trail climbs 2½ miles to 6250-Boulder Pass, the meadowy saddle to the immediate east of Clark Mountain. Look down into the Napeequa valley and over to Little Giant Pass (Hike 67). The hike to here, 10¾ miles from the road, makes a strenuous but richly rewarding 2–3 day trip.

Descend switchbacks 2¼ miles to the valley floor—and trouble—at 4340 feet. The Forest Service is unable to keep a bridge across the swift-flowing Napeequa River, which perhaps can be safely forded at this point in late August but many summers never is less than very risky.

If you can manage to cross, explorations are limited only by the time available. Follow the trail up the wide, green valley floor, probably the floor of an ancient lake, 5 or 6 miles; good camps are numerous. In ½ mile look to glaciers on Clark Mountain. In 2 miles pass under the falls of Louis Creek. Wander on and on, higher and higher, better and better, to trail's end in the moraines and creeks of Napeequa Basin, a deep hole half-ringed by dazzling glaciers, one of which tumbles nearly to the basin floor. Experienced off-trail travelers can find meager sidetrails into the hanging valleys of Louis Creek and North Fork Napeequa and climb to Louis Basin or 6876-foot High Pass.

Old road: 298
New road: 64

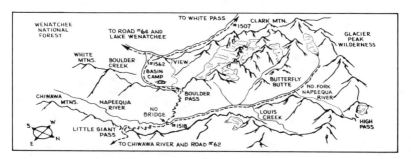

66 MAD RIVER

Round trip to Blue Creek Guard Station 11 miles
Hiking time 6 hours
High point 5400 feet
Elevation gain 1250 feet

Hikable late June through October
One day or backpack
USGS Sugarloaf, Chikamin, Silver Falls

Miles and miles of easy, pleasant roaming in the Entiat Mountains. Trails follow noisy creeks through picturesque glades, trails cross vast meadows of brilliant flowers, trails round shores of little lakes, and trails climb a mountain—all in all, a grand area for a weekend or for a week-long family vacation. Unfortunately, however, though there are 150 square miles here of wilderness (unprotected), the Forest Service permits motorcycles on the trails after they dry out in mid-July.

Some hikers may prefer to climb to the highlands via trail from the Entiat River road to avoid the poor access road from the Chiwawa; nevertheless, the latter approach is described—it's a horror for great big family sedans but not too bad for small and agile cars.

From Highway 2 between Stevens Pass and Leavenworth turn east on Highway 207 toward Lake Wenatchee State Park. Pass the park and at 4 miles, just past the Wenatchee River bridge, go straight ahead on a paved country road. Stick with this road, dodging sideroads to Fish Lake and the Chiwawa River road, and at 10.5 miles cross the Chiwawa River in the middle of a vacation-home development. Turn north on the old Chiwawa River road No. 61 for 1.6 miles and turn right on road No. 6101. At 7.3 miles from the bridge, after a final steep and narrow 2 miles that only a jeep or beetle could love, is Maverick Saddle. An even rougher road, probably best walked, leads .3 mile to the trailhead, signed "Mad River trail 1409." Elevation, 4250 feet.

The trail goes downriver 15 miles to Pine Flat on the Entiat River. It also goes upriver, your way to go. In 1 mile cross a bridge over the Mad

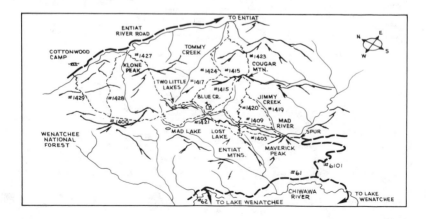

Mad River near Blue Creek Patrol Cabin

River—at this point really just a pretty creek. At 1½ miles is Jimmy Creek trail, first of three routes to the summit of 6719-foot Cougar Mountain. At 3 miles is an intersection with a trail that goes right to the top of Cougar, left to Lost Lake. At 4 miles cross Mad River on a driftwood log and at 4½ miles recross near a junction with Tyee Ridge trail No. 1415, the third way up Cougar. At 5 miles is a broad meadow and at 5½ miles Blue Creek Guard Station, a splendid spot for a basecamp.

Many loops attract the explorer. One is to two little lakes named Two Little Lakes, with a short sidetrip up 6834-foot Klone Peak and a return past Mad Lake, set in an enormous meadow which in early summer dries out and becomes solid blue-red with lupine and paintbrush. Other loops are to Lost Lake and around Cougar Mountain. Pleasant alternative returns from the guard station are via Lost Lake.

Old road: 2746   2722
New road: 61   6101

67 NAPEEQUA VALLEY VIA LITTLE GIANT PASS

Round trip to the pass 9½ miles
Hiking time 9 hours
High point 6409 feet
Elevation gain 4200 feet in, 300
  feet out

Hikable early August through
  September
One day or backpack
USGS Holden

Climb to the famous view of the fabled Napeequa valley. Look down on the silvery river meandering through green meadows of the old lakebed. See the gleaming ice on Clark Mountain and Tenpeak, glimpse a piece of Glacier Peak. But you gotta really want it. Strong mountaineers turn pale at memories of Little Giant in sunshine and flytime. However, though more grueling than the Boulder Pass entry (Hike 65), the trail is 5 miles shorter and has no fearsome ford of the Napeequa to face. Ah, but it does have a fearsome ford of the Chiwawa River. But that's at the very beginning, so you get the bad news in time to choose another destination should the flood be boiling halfway up your Kelty.

Drive US 2 east from Stevens Pass 19 miles and turn left toward Lake Wenatchee. A short distance past the Wenatchee River bridge keep right at a Y and go 1.5 miles. Turn left on paved road No. 62. Follow this road, crossing the Chiwawa River on a concrete bridge. Proceed upvalley on the Chiwawa River road about 19 miles. Spot a barricaded sideroad left, signed "Bridge Out." Park here, elevation 2600 feet.

Longingly inspect remains of the bridge taken out by a flood in 1972. Look around for a possible logjam. Finding none, try the wade, if you are fairly sure you can survive it, and if you do, follow roads through abandoned Maple Creek Campground toward the mountainside. Just short of a little tin cabin, cross a footbridge over a wash to the right and pretty soon pick up the trail. The old straight-up sheep driveway of evil reputation has been partly replaced (and the sheep are long gone from here, too)

Glacier lily

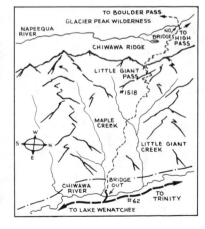

Napeequa River from Little Giant Pass. Clark Mountain on left

by a trail that was nicely engineered, if steep, but is deteriorating rapidly from lack of maintenance. The way climbs the valley of Maple Creek in pretty pine forest, crosses a saddle, and drops to South Fork Little Giant Creek at about 2½ miles from the river, elevation 4000 feet. Campsites on both sides.

Now the way steepens and at 3 miles half scrambles up a broad rib of bare schist that splits the valley in two and on a sunny day will fry your boots. But in ⅓ mile creeks begin, and camps that get progressively better, the last on a scenic meadow knoll at 4 miles. A lovely ascent in greenery and marmots leads to the 6409-foot pass and the boundary of Glacier Peak Wilderness, 4⅔ miles from the river.

Better views can be obtained by scrambling up the knobs on either side of the pass, which in addition to being a sensational grandstand is a glory of flowers.

The trail down to the Napeequa is poorly maintained if at all, yet suffices for hikers—but not for horses or sheep, and bleached bones prove it. Watch your step—at spots a misstep could add you to the casualty list. The distance to the 4200-foot valley floor is 2 miles, and if the views don't have you raving the blossoms will. Or, in season, the flies. The trail proceeds upvalley 1⅓ miles to the site of the bridge that is gone and the ford that remains to cross the river to the Boulder Pass trail (Hike 65). The best camps hereabouts are on gravel bars.

68 SPIDER MEADOW

**Round trip to upper Spider
  Meadow 12½ miles**
Hiking time 8 hours
High point 5100 feet
Elevation gain 1700 feet

**Hikable mid-July through
  October**
One day or backpack
USGS Holden

A glorious valley-bottom meadow in a seeming cul-de-sac amid rugged peaks. Yet the trail ingeniously breaks through the cliffs and climbs to a little "glacier" and a grand overlook of Lyman Basin and summits of the Cascade Crest. For hikers trained in use of the ice ax this can be merely the beginning of a long and classic loop trip.

Drive about 22 miles on the Chiwawa River road No. 62 (Hike 67) and turn right on No. 6211, the Phelps Creek road, 2 miles to a gate and the trailhead, elevation 3500 feet.

Spider Meadow

The walk begins past the gate on the road, which is still used by miners almost to the wilderness boundary.

The gentle grade goes up and down in forest, passing the Carne Mountain trail in ¼ mile, Box Creek in 1 mile, Chipmunk Creek in 1¾ miles, and the Glacier Peak Wilderness boundary in 2⅔ miles. At 3½ miles, 4175 feet, are the crossing of Leroy Creek, the junction with Leroy Creek trail, a campsite, and the end of the old road.

The way continues through forest interspersed with flower gardens. At 5¼ miles, 4700 feet, is the spectacular opening-out into Spider Meadow. Red Mountain shows its cliffs and snows; the views include other walls enclosing Phelps headwaters—no way can be seen to escape the valley, an apparent dead end. A mile of flower walking leads to the crossing of Phelps Creek, 6¼ miles, 5000 feet. A bit beyond are ruins of Ed Linston's cabin. Good camps here and throughout Spider Meadow. Hikers with only a day or a weekend may turn back here, well content.

But there is much more. Follow the trail upward through the meadow, boulder-hop Phelps Creek, and follow the trail upward. At 6½ miles, 5300 feet, is a junction. The right fork follows Phelps Creek to more meadows and the end of the valley under Dumbbell Mountain.

The left fork is a steep, hot, and very dry miners' trail climbing 1100 feet to the lower end of Spider Glacier at 6400 feet. Here are several tiny but spectacular campsites. No wood but lots of water and lots of views downvalley to Spider Meadow, Mt. Maude, and Seven-Fingered Jack.

Immediately above is the narrow snowfield of Spider "Glacier." In a short mile, either up the snow-filled gully or along the easy and scenic rock spur to the east, is 7100-foot Spider Pass. Look down to the Lyman Glacier, the ice-devastated upper Lyman Basin, and the greenery of the lower basin.

An old trail ascends ¼ mile from the pass to a mine tunnel. One must marvel at the dogged energy of Ed Linston, who hauled machinery and supplies to so airy a spot. After being badly injured by a dynamite explosion in the mine he was helped down the mountain by his brother. He recovered to spend many more years roaming the Cascades, passing away in 1969 at the age of 82.

Old road: 311   3000
New road: 62   6211

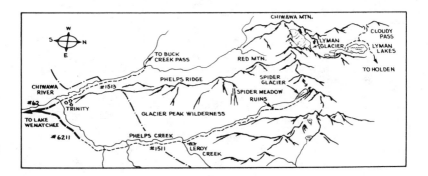

Triad Lake from High Pass trail

CHIWAWA RIVER
Glacier Peak Wilderness

69 BUCK CREEK PASS–
HIGH PASS

Round trip 19 miles   **Elevation gain 3200 feet**
Allow 2–3 days   **Hikable July through October**
High point 6000 feet   **USGS Holden**

In a mountain range full to overflowing with "unique places," two things have given Buck Creek Pass fame: an unusual richness of flower gardens rising from creek bottoms to high summits, and the exceptional view of the grandest ice streams of Glacier Peak, seen across the broad, forested valley of the Suiattle River.

The trail lends itself to a variety of trips short and long: a day's walk as far as time allows, a weekend at the pass, or a week of explorations.

Drive about 24 miles on the Chiwawa River road No. 62 (Hike 67) to the end at Phelps Creek, elevation 2772 feet, next to the old mining town of Trinity.

Walk across the Phelps Creek bridge into Trinity and follow trail signs past the buildings and over the valley floor until the old roads become trail. At 1¼ miles a sign announces entry into the Glacier Peak Wilderness. A nice creek here in forest shade. The abandoned road climbs moderately to a junction at 1½ miles. The road leads straight ahead toward mining claims on Red Mountain; the trail turns left.

Tread goes up and down within sound of the Chiwawa River, at 2¾ miles crosses the "river" (now just a fast-moving creek) and enters the valley of Buck Creek. Just beyond the bridge is a large campsite.

The trail climbs a valley step, levels out and passes a forest camp in a patch of grass, switchbacks up another glacier-gouged step, and emerges from trees to traverse a wide avalanche meadow at 5 miles, 4300 feet. This is a good turnaround for a day hike, offering a view of the cliffs and hanging glaciers on the north wall of 8573-foot Buck Mountain.

There are many small campsites along the way. Most notable are those at 7 miles, 4500 feet, across Buck Creek on a green meadow, and another a quarter of a mile farther up the trail in the woods. From this point the trail starts a series of long switchbacks, climbing on a 10-percent grade to a 6000-foot point overlooking Buck Creek Pass, 9½ miles. For camping, drop about 200 feet into the pass.

Explorations? Enough for a magnificent week.

Start with an evening wander to Flower Dome to watch Suiattle forests darken into night while the snows of Glacier Peak glow pink.

For a spectacular sunrise, after dinner carry your sleeping bag to the top of Liberty Cap.

Try an interesting sheepmen's track. Walk the main trail back toward Trinity about ½ mile from the pass to a large basin with several streams. A few feet before emerging from forest into basin meadows, go left on an unmarked way trail that traverses flower gardens below Helmet Butte and Fortress Mountain, past delightful campsites, disappearing in some 2 miles at 6100 feet.

Don't miss the dead-end trail toward (not to) High Pass. Find it on the south side of Buck Creek Pass and ascend around Liberty Cap and as far as the way is not covered with dangerously steep snow. The end, 3 miles from Buck Creek Pass, is in a 7200-foot saddle overlooking the wintry basin of Triad Lake. Getting from trail's end to High Pass is a task for climbers.

Old road: 311
New road: 62

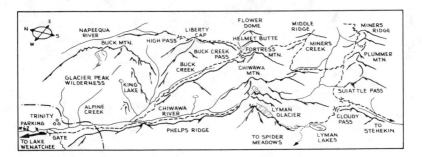

70 LARCH LAKES LOOP

Round trip (shorter loop) 18 miles
Allow 2–3 days
High point 6500 feet
Elevation gain 3400 feet

Hikable mid-July through
** September**
USGS Lucerne

Two clear lakes surrounded by alpine trees and meadows nestled under cliffs of Fifth of July Mountain. An entryway to miles and miles of up-and-down high trails along the Entiat Mountains.

Drive US 97 north from Wenatchee up the Columbia River to Entiat. Turn left 38 miles on Entiat River road No. 51 to the end at Cottonwood Campground, elevation 3144 feet.

Hike the Entiat River trail 5 miles to Larch Lakes trail, 3800 feet. The way crosses the Entiat River, goes ¼ mile through stately forest, and then begins a grueling climb of 1900 feet in 2½ miles, switchbacking up a treeless, shadeless, waterless south slope. On a hot day the best plan is to loiter by the river until late afternoon, when sun has left the hillside—or

Upper Larch Lake

better yet, cook dinner by the river and make the ascent in the cool of the evening. Waiting until morning does no good; the hillside gets the first rays of sun.

Before starting up, note the waterfall high on the hillside to the west. Elevation of this falls (which comes from the lake outlet) provides a measure of how much climbing remains to be done.

The tortuous switchbacks abruptly flatten into a traverse along the shores of 5700-foot Lower Larch Lake, leading to a large meadow and acres of flat ground for camping. The trail continues a short ½ mile to Upper Larch Lake, more meadows, and the junction with the Pomas Creek trail. Here is a choice of loop trips.

For the longer of the two, climb north some 700 feet to Larch Lakes Pass, then amble on to 6350-foot Pomas Pass and down Pomas Creek to a junction with the Ice Creek trail, 6 miles from Upper Larch Lake. Go left to Ice Lakes (Hike 72) or right to the Entiat River trail.

For the shorter and more popular loop, follow the trail south around Upper Larch Lake. Tread disappears in meadows and several starts can be seen on the wooded hillside left of Fifth of July Mountain. The correct path goes into the woods at the base of the slope a couple of hundred feet from a granite "island" in the meadow.

The trail climbs steadily more than a mile, with airy views down to Larch Lakes, then contours the mountain to a 6500-foot junction with the Cow Creek trail, the return route via Myrtle Lake.

The ascent of Fifth of July Mountain is a must. Though the north face of the peak is a tall, rugged cliff, there's an easy side. Leave packs at the junction and climb the Garland Peak trail a mile south to 7000-foot Cow Creek Pass (some signs say Fifth of July Pass) and ascend the gentle south slope to the 7696-foot summit and a 360-degree panorama of Glacier, Clark, Maude, Rainier, and other peaks beyond counting.

The Cow Creek trail descends a steep 2 miles to the edge of Cow Creek Meadows, just out of sight of the trail and offering a splendid camp, 5100 feet. Another 2 miles drop to sparkling, motorcycle-loud Myrtle Lake, 3700 feet, ½ mile from the Entiat River trail, reached at a point 3½ miles from the road-end.

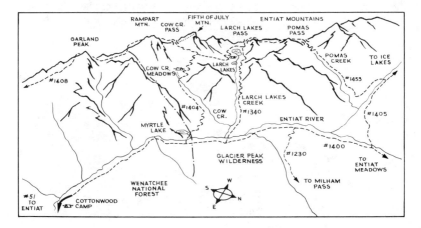

71 MILHAM PASS— EMERALD PARK

Round trip from road to Milham Pass 25 miles
One-way trip to Lake Chelan 22½ miles
Allow 2–4 days
High point 6663 feet

Elevation gain 2700 feet
Elevation loss to Lake Chelan 5500 feet
Hikable mid-July through September
USGS Lucerne

A high pass surrounded by the snowy summits of Pinnacle Mountain and Saska, Emerald, and Cardinal Peaks, all standing well above 8000 feet. If transportation can be arranged, a one-way trip can be made down into the lovely meadows of Emerald Park and out to Lake Chelan. Alternatively, of course, the approach to Milham Pass can begin from the lake.

Drive the Entiat River road (Hike 70) to the end, elevation 3144 feet.

Hike the Entiat River trail 6½ miles to the Snowbrushy Creek trail, 3900 feet. A few hundred feet below the junction is an excellent campsite in Snowbrushy Meadow.

The first mile climbs steeply from the Entiat valley into the Snowbrushy valley. Then the way parallels the creek, continuing a steady but reasonable ascent through open forest and large meadows. At about 2½ miles from the Entiat trail is the first decent camp, in trees; beyond are numerous sites in flowers and grass. At 3 miles the trail crosses a 5700-foot meadow under Gopher Mountain, with views of Saska Peak spires at the valley head and back out to Fifth of July Mountain, across the Entiat.

The was passes junctions with the Pyramid Mountain trail, climbing east to high viewpoints, and indistinct 45-Mile Sheep Driveway, climbing northwest over Borealis Ridge and descending to the Entiat River trail—offering a longer but more scenic return route.

From about 4½ miles the grade steepens for the final ascent to 6663-foot Milham Pass, 6 miles from the Entiat trail and 12½ miles from the road. To get the best views, scramble a few hundred feet up the ridge to the south, taking due caution among large and loose boulders on steep sections of the slope. The scramble is rewarded by a look down to the

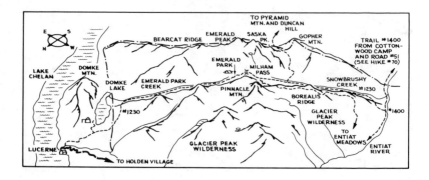

bright green meadow of Emerald Park and out east to peaks beyond Lake Chelan.

To continue to Lake Chelan, follow the Emerald Park Creek trail, which goes along the crest of the pass a few hundred feet north, then drops abruptly. A large snowfield generally covers the tread here until mid-July; descend with care.

About 2 miles below the pass the trail enters the big meadow of Emerald Park, 5400 feet; a fine camp here. The next 6 miles to the Domke Lake trail, in sunbaked brush and scrub, then forest, are steep and rough.

From the Domke Lake junction, 2200 feet, a sidetrail leads a short mile to the 2192-foot lake and a campground. The main trail descends 2 miles from the junction to Lucerne, 10 miles from Milham Pass, on the shores of 1096-foot Lake Chelan. For boat service on the lake, see Hike 74.

Old road: 317
New road: 51

Emerald Park from Milham Pass

72 ENTIAT MEADOWS AND ICE LAKES

Round trip to Lower Ice Lake 28 miles
Allow 3–5 days
High point (knoll above lower lake) 6900 feet
Elevation gain 4200 feet
Hikable August through September
USGS Holden and Lucerne

Round trip to Entiat Meadows 30 miles
Allow 3–4 days or more
High point 5500 feet
Elevation gain 2400 feet
Hikable July through October

A long trail with many byways to glory and at the two ends a pair of climaxes: a vast meadow under small glaciers hanging on the walls of a row of 9000-foot peaks, and two high, remote lakes set in cirque basins close under cliffs of 9082-foot Mt. Maude, with alpine trees standing out starkly in a barren, glaciated landscape reminiscent of Khyber Pass.

Drive to the end of the Entiat River road (Hike 70), elevation 3144 feet.

Hike the Entiat River trail No. 1400, engineered by the Forest Service the first 4½ miles into a motorcycle expressway; stay alert to avoid being knocked down or run over, especially by unsupervised children. At 3½ miles is the turnoff to the Cow Creek trail and Myrtle Lake, destination of most razzers. At 5 miles is the Larch Lakes trail (Hike 70) and at 5½ miles a campsite by Snowbrushy Creek. At 6½ miles, 3900 feet, is a beautiful camp below the trail in a Snowbrushy meadow; here too is the Snowbrushy Creek trail to Milham Pass (Hike 71), and at 8¼ miles, 4300 feet, reach the split.

Ice Lakes: The Ice Creek trail goes left a short bit to a camp and a two-log bridge over the river. The way climbs gradually in forest the first mile, then drops 400 feet to Ice Creek. At 1½ miles, 4300 feet, is a junction with the Pomas Creek trail, an excellent alternate return route via Larch Lakes (Hike 70).

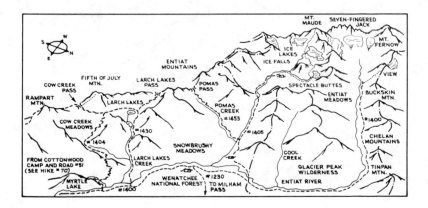

Ice Falls

The route goes along the river bottom, alternating between small alpine trees and meadows. At about 3 miles is a crossing of Ice Creek; since a footlog seldom is available and the channel is too wide to jump, be prepared to wade—and find out how well the creek lives up to its name. In another mile is another crossing, but this time the creek can be stepped over on rocks. At some 4½ miles from the Entiat trail, formal tread ends in a rocky meadow and delightful campsite, 5500 feet. The noisy creek drowns the sound of a pretty waterfall tumbling from Upper Ice Lake.

From the trail-end a boot-built path follows the rocky meadow north to the valley head, passing the waterfall. Generally keep right of the creek, but cross to the left when the going looks easier there. The valley ends in a steep, green hillside; above, in hanging cirques, lie the lakes. From a starting point to the right of the creek, scramble up game traces, crossing the creek and climbing between cliffs to its left. The way emerges onto a rocky knoll 100 feet above 6800-foot Lower Ice Lake, 6 miles from the

Ice Lake

Entiat trail. Camp on pumice barrens, not the fragile heather; no fires permitted.

Upper Ice Lake is a mile farther. Head southwest in a shallow alpine valley, below cliffs, to the outlet stream and follow the waters up to the 7200-foot lake, beautifully cold and desolate.

Mt. Maude cliffs are impressive from the lakes. However, the long and gentle south ridge of the peak offers an easy stroll. The scramble to the ridge, though, is not a complete cinch; patches of steep snow remain in summer and require an ice ax for safe passage. Maude is the only 9000-

footer in the Cascades accessible to hikers, but they must be experienced hikers thoroughly familiar with the ice ax and the rules of safe travel on steep terrain. The summit views extend from Glacier Peak to the Columbia Plateau, from Mt. Rainier to an infinite alpine wilderness north.

Entiat Meadows: The way to the split is principally through forest; the final 7 miles up the Entiat River alternate between trees and meadows. Though sheep have not been allowed in the valley for years, some meadows still show deep rutting from thousands of hooves, and some of the native flowers have never grown back.

At 13 miles, having gained only some 2000 feet thus far, the grade steepens a little for a final 1¼ miles and then, at about 5500 feet, the tread fades out in fields of heather and flowers. The camps are fine throughout the miles-long Entiat Meadows and the views are grand—up the cliffs of the huge cirque to the summits of Fernow, Seven-Fingered Jack, and Maude, all above 9000 feet, and to remnants of the Entiat Glacier, which in days of glory excavated the cirque and gave the valley its contours.

If ambition persists, scramble up grassy slopes of the ridge to the north and look down into Railroad Creek and the town of Holden.

Old road: 317
New road: 51

Lunch stop in Entiat Meadows

73 PYRAMID MOUNTAIN

Round trip 19 miles
Allow 2 days
High point 8247 feet
Elevation gain 4500 feet

Hikable mid-July through
September
USGS Lucerne

The views from this old lookout site extend over range upon range of snow mountains in the Glacier Peak Wilderness, over heat-hazy plateaus of the Columbia Basin, and straight down 7000 feet to Lake Chelan, so far below that binoculars are needed to spot the *Lady of the Lake*. One has to wonder why the spot was chosen for a fire lookout—the scenery is all rock, ice, and water, hardly anything in sight that might burn.

The two ways to Pyramid Mountain are the same length and have about the same elevation gain. The spectacular route from Big Hill Road starts at an elevation of 6500 feet and goes 9½ up-and-down miles to the summit, with campsites at 4 and 7 miles. However, the drive to the trailhead is so long and difficult that the recommended route, described here, is the south Pyramid Creek trail, featuring an interesting transition from valley forest to mountain barren.

Thanks to the Forest Service the area is overrun with machines. The hiking trail was rebuilt with wide tread, little creeks were provided with sturdy little bridges, and fords of big creeks were graded to a smoothness permitting wheels to splash through without slowing. Even so, hikers continue to be the majority here; to receive justice, they're going to have to do some yelling about the tyranny of the minority.

Drive the Entiat River road (which becomes road No. 51) 32.5 miles and turn left 4.1 miles on North Entiat River road No. 5606 to the trailhead, elevation 4000 feet.

Begin in forest on trail No. 1437, going over Crow Creek. In 1 mile cross Pyramid Creek and at 1¼ miles turn right on South Pyramid Creek trail No. 1439. At 5½ miles, 5800 feet, are the last creekside campsites.

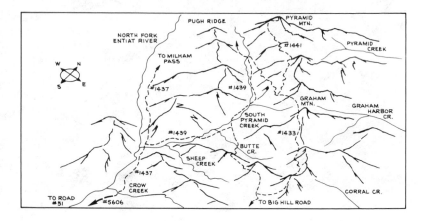

At the junction here go right on Pyramid Mountain trail No. 1433, climbing 1¼ miles to another junction; go left here on Pyramid Viewpoint trail No. 1441. An up-and down traverse emerges from trees, reaches a small campsite in ½ mile, and yields to steep and steeper tread climbing to the 8246-foot summit, 9½ miles from the road.

Artifacts of the vanished lookout abound: the leveled summit, scraps of metal, and an open-air john that may have the most spectacular view of any such facility in the Northwest.

Old road: 317   317B
New road: 51   5606

View from summit of Pyramid Mountain

74 CHELAN LAKESHORE TRAIL

One-way trip from Prince Creek
17½ miles
Allow 3–4 days
High point 1700 feet
Elevation gain perhaps 3000 feet,
including ups and downs
Hikable late March through early
June

USGS Lucerne, Prince Creek, Sun
Mountain, Stehekin

One-way trip from Moore 6½ miles
Allow 2 days
High point 1600 feet
Elevation gain about 900 feet,
including ups and downs

The way to know Lake Chelan is to walk beside it, sometimes by waves slapping the shore, sometimes on high bluffs with sweeping views. There are green lawns atop rock buttresses, groves of old Ponderosa pine and Douglas fir, glades of mystic aspen, slot gorges with frothing waterfalls. The views and trees and many of the creeks are grand in any season, but spring is the prime time, when the sun is dependable but not too weighty, cool breezes blow, and the flowers are in rich bloom. Early on, the trail is lined by trillium, chocolate lily, glacier lily, spring beauty, yellowbells, Johnny-jump-up, red currant, and more. Later on, the show features spring gold, prairie star, blue-eyed Mary, naked broomrape, primrose monkeyflower, death camas, balsamroot, miners lettuce, calypso, and more.

Drive to the town of Chelan or up the lake to Field Point and board the passenger boat. Contact the National Park Service Information Center in Seattle before the trip to learn the current schedule. The past pattern has been a single trip daily from mid-May to mid-September, uplake in early morning, downlake in early afternoon, and Sunday-Monday-Wednesday-Friday trips the rest of the year (no Sunday boat in mid-winter).

For a 2-day trip, hikers can start at Moore with day packs and have their overnight gear dumped on the dock at Stehekin to await them; this gives an afternoon on the trail and a morning poking around Stehekin.

To do the full 17½ miles from Prince Creek to Stehekin the nice allowance is 4 days (including the going-home day), though 3 are tolerable. The map fails to convey that though the trail never climbs higher than

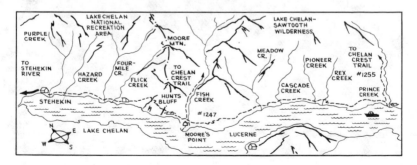

Lake Chelan and McGregor Mountain from Hunts Point

1700 feet and generally is some several hundred feet above the shore (1098 feet above sea level), it irrationally manages to go uphill virtually the whole way.

At Prince Creek hikers have the choice of being put off downlake from the creek, perhaps to stay the first night at the campground there, or uplake (a campsite here, too) to save ½ mile of trail. Tell the boatman which you prefer.

Since the hour of debarkation at Prince Creek is about 11 a.m., most hikers camp the first night in the vicinity of Meadow Creek, 7 miles, after crossing Rattlesnake, Rex, Pioneer, and Cascade Creeks. The shelter cabin in the dark woods at Meadow Creek is unattractive except in a storm.

By the nice plan, a relaxed second day attains the trail's high point at 1700 feet on a long, wide shelf, descends to Fish Creek, 10½ miles from Prince Creek, then takes the sidetrail ½ mile down the creek to Moore's Point, once a famous resort and now a spacious Forest Service campground. Spend the afternoon exploring the old homestead, including an ancient orchard and the New Englandlike stone walls fencing a deer pasture.

The 6½ miles from Fish Creek to Stehekin are an easy morning for a 3-day trip. (Since the boat doesn't go downlake until afternoon, a party can finish the trip the morning of "boat day.") The way starts by climbing to 1600 feet on Hunts Bluff. The views of lake and mountains are so climactic that many a party carries a bucket of water up in order to spend the night. The trail then drops to the lake, crossing more creeks, and comes to Lakeshore (Flick Creek) Shelter, a choice camp on a jut of forest and rock out into the waves. It never again climbs high, wandering the base of cliffs and through woods to Flick Creek, Fourmile Creek, Hazard Creek, and finally Stehekin, 17½ miles. (To be technical, the sign here says "Fish Creek 6.6, Prince Creek 17.2.")

Overnight camping is permitted where the trail enters the Stehekin complex (this campground is designated "overflow") and ¼ mile up the road at Purple Point Campground.

Horsethief Basin

LAKE CHELAN—STEHEKIN RIVER
Partially in Lake Chelan—Sawtooth Wilderness

75 CHELAN SUMMIT TRAIL

One-way trip from Summer
 Blossom 38 miles
Allow 5–9 days
High point 7840 feet
Elevation gain about 10,000 feet

Hikable early July through
 September
USGS South Navarre, Martin
 Peak, Prince Creek, Oval Peak,
 Sun Mountain, Stehekin

A miles-and-miles and days-and-days paradise of easy-roaming ridges and flower gardens and spectacular views westward over the deep trench of (mostly unseen) Lake Chelan to the main range of the Cascades. Snow-free hiking starts earlier, and the weather is better, than in the main range, which traps many winter snows and summer drizzles. Only twice before the final plunge does the trail dip as low as 5500 feet, in forest;

eight times it climbs over passes or shoulders, the highest 7840 feet; mainly it goes up and down (a lot) through meadows and parkland on the slopes of peaks that run as high as 8795-foot Oval Peak, in the Sawtooth Group. Good-to-magnificent camps are spaced at intervals of 2 to 3 miles or less. Sidetrips (on and off trails) to lakes, passes, and peaks are so many that one is constantly tempted; for that reason a party should allow extra days for wandering.

The trail can be sampled by short trips from either end or via feeder trails from Lake Chelan on one side or the Methow and Twisp Rivers on the other. (For examples of the latter, see Hikes 81 and 82.) The perfect dream trip is hiking the whole length from Summer Blossom to Stehekin, but this requires either a two-car switcharound or a very helpful friend to do drop-off and pickup duty. Further, the road routes to Summer Blossom range from dismaying to impossible. Some cars simply can't get there. Some years no cars can. Most parties thus settle for a nearly perfect dream trip that starts on a feeder trail from the lake and uses the *Lady of the Lake* (Hike 74) to handle the drop-off and pickup.

Summer Blossom is achieved on a road that is very sporty for jeeps but a misery for passenger cars. The least bad approach is from the Methow Valley. From Pateros on the Columbia River drive the Methow Valley Highway 17 miles toward Twisp. Just before crossing the Methow River the seventh time turn left on Gold Creek Road. In 1 mile turn left on road No. 4340 and in 1 mile more left again on road No. 4330, which begins as well-graded gravel, the better to inveigle you, my dears. At about 5.5 miles from this junction is another; go right, following the sign, "Cooper Mountain Road 7." These 7 miles grow steeper, narrower, slipperier, spookier. The junction with Cooper Mountain Road is in a scenic parkland saddle on the divide between the Methow River and Lake Chelan. Turn right 9 miles on road No. 82 sliced just far enough into the flowery sidehill for two hikers to walk side by side comfortably. At 23.5 miles from the Methow Valley Highway is Summer Blossom trailhead, eleva-

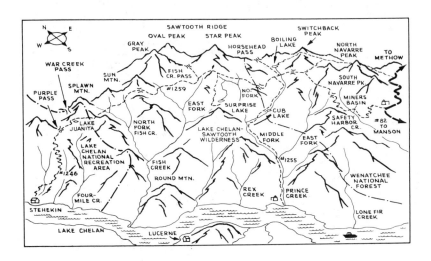

Chickadee in a mid-September snowstorm

tion 6440 feet. Start here, on hiker-only trail, rather than the motorcycle razzerway that begins 2 miles farther along at South Navarre Campground.

Ascend "Narvie Basin," as old-timers pronounce "Navarre," spotting fine and lonesome camps at a distance from the trail, and then the ridge of North Navarre Peak, topping out at 7840 feet, a quick stroll from the summit. The way stays high more than 2 wildly scenic miles before dropping to join the main trail (from South Navarre) at the 7400-foot pass between Horsethief Basin (in Safety Harbor Creek) and East Fork Prince Creek headwaters, at 6 miles from the start.

The disgusting news is that for miles north from here the trail must be shared with razzers—which, however, don't run in the snowy early summer and, if hikers keep those complaining letters pouring in, folks, eventually will not run at all. The good news is the broad meadow basin of the East Fork through which the way swings, rounding the foot of 8321-foot Switchback Peak (an old trail switchbacks nearly to the summit) to the 7120-foot pass (8 miles) to Middle Fork Prince Creek. Down and around another wide parkland, at 10 miles are the junction with the Middle Fork Prince Creek trail and a basecamp for sidetrips to Boiling Lake and Hoodoo Pass and all.

(The Middle Fork Prince Creek trail is the best feeder for a tidy loop. Have the *Lady* drop you at Prince Creek, on the uplake side (Hike 74) and gain 5500 feet in 12 miles. Camps at 4, 6, and 8 miles from the lake.)

The trail climbs to Chipmunk Pass, the 7050-foot saddle (11½ miles) to North Fork Prince Creek, and here enters the Lake Chelan–Sawtooth Wilderness, the end of motorcycles. It descends to a 5560-foot low point in forest (14 miles) and climbs to flowers again and the 7400-foot pass (18½ miles) to East Fork Fish Creek. In odd-numbered years, sheep that have been driven up Buttermilk Creek here graze northward, devouring the flowers and fouling the water. (That's *another* letter for you to write the Forest Service.)

View from side of Navarre Peak

A short, steep drop leads to a 6800-foot junction with the trail to Fish Creek Pass (the sheep route). From a camp here, sidetrips include a stroll to larch-ringed Star Lake beneath the great wall of Star Peak and scrambles to the summits of 8690-foot Star Peak and 8392-foot Courtney Peak. On the other hand, if camp is made after a meadow traverse to Twin Springs Camp in Horseshoe Basin, there are sidetrips to Tuckaway Lake, Gray Peak, and Oval Lakes.

The way ascends to the 7400-foot pass (22 miles) to North Fork Fish Creek, descends to 5520-foot woods (24½ miles), and climbs through gardens (camps off the trail, near Deephole Spring) to a 7250-foot pass (27½ miles) to Fourmile Creek. A descent and an upsy-downsy traverse lead to Lake Juanita, 6665 feet, 30 miles. The quick and terrific sidetrip here is to Boulder Butte, 7350 feet, one-time lookout site.

At 30½ miles is 6880-foot Purple Pass, famous for the gasps drawn by the sudden sight—5800 feet below—of wind-rippled, sun-sparkled waters of Lake Chelan, seeming close enough for a swan dive. Hundreds of switchbacks take your poor old knees down Hazard and Purple Creeks to Stehekin, 38 miles, and the ice cream.

| Old road: | 3109 | 3107 | 3001 |
| New road: | 4340 | 4330 | 82 |

Lyman Glacier and Chiwawa Mountain

LAKE CHELAN–STEHEKIN RIVER
Glacier Peak Wilderness

76 AGNES CREEK– LYMAN LAKE LOOP

Loop trip 43 miles
Hiking time 3–7 days
High point 6438 feet
Elevation gain 4900 feet

Hikable mid-July through
  September
USGS McGregor Mountain, Mt.
  Lyall, Agnes Mountain,
  Stehekin, Holden

Here's a favorite of loopers: ascending one of the supreme long-and-wild, low-to-high valleys of the North Cascades to Suiattle Pass, then climbing over Cloudy Pass and descending past Lyman Lake and Holden Village to Lake Chelan.

Hikes from Lake Chelan involve nonusual transportation to and from trailheads. In this case there are the *Lady of the Lake* (Hike 74), which drops the party off at Stehekin and picks it up at Lucerne, the shuttle bus up the Stehekin road, and the Lucerne bus down from Holden Village (Hike 37). The trip plan must take into account that hikers probably won't get started on the trail until mid-afternoon of the first day and must be off the trail by mid-morning of the last day to catch the boat.

From Stehekin Landing ride the bus 11 miles to High Bridge Ranger Station. About 500 feet beyond the bridge, on the left side of the road, is Agnes Creek trailhead (Pacific Crest Trail No. 2000), elevation 1600 feet.

The trail drops a few feet, crosses Agnes Creek, and commences a long, easy grade in lovely forest with notable groves of cedar. Glimpses ahead of Agnes Mountain and glaciers on Dome Peak; to the rear, McGregor Mountain. A good stop the first night is Fivemile Camp, 2300 feet.

Take an extra day here for a fine sidetrip (or, in early summer when the loop is too snowy, a destination). Cross the Agnes on a bridge and hike West Fork Agnes trail 3 miles to the dead end at the edge of grassy Agnes Meadow, 2500 feet, beneath the high rock walls of Agnes Mountain and the glaciers of a half-dozen peaks. This sidetrip can be done in mid-June, when the meadow newly melted from the snow is all one yellow-and-white glow of glacier lily and spring beauty.

From Fivemile Camp the valley forest on the main trail continues superb, featuring a fine stand of large hemlock and fir near Swamp Creek; another good camp here at 8 miles.

At Hemlock Camp, 12 miles, the trail splits. The new Pacific Crest Trail crosses the river, climbs to high views on the side of the valley, and at 19 miles reaches timberline campsites at a junction, 5600 feet. You can also get here via the old valley trail, which may be the better choice in early summer, when the new trail is likely to be largely in snow.

For a mandatory sidetrip, go right at the junction 6 miles to Image Lake (Hike 36), for the day or overnight.

For the loop, go left over 6438-foot Cloudy Pass to Lyman Lake and another must-do sidetrip. Near the outlet of Lyman Lake find the trail climbing 400 feet in about 2 miles through flower fields and heather slopes, passing Upper Lyman Lake to Upper-Upper Lyman Lake, ringed by barren moraines left by the source of icebergs, the glacier flowing from 8459-foot Mt. Chiwawa.

Finish the loop down Railroad Creek to Holden Village; take the bus to Lucerne and the boat down Lake Chelan (Hike 37).

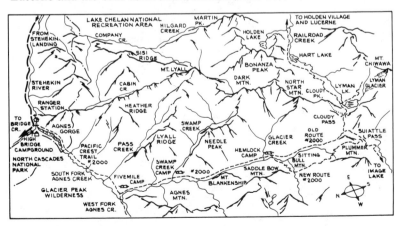

77 NORTH FORK BRIDGE CREEK

Round trip to cirque 21 miles
Allow 2–3 days
High point 4200 feet
Elevation gain 2000 feet

Hikable early July through
October
USGS McGregor Mountain and
Mt. Logan
Park Service backcountry use
permit required

The North Cascades are distinguished by tall peaks—and also by deep holes. Among the most magnificent holes in the range is the huge cirque at the head of North Fork Bridge Creek, where breezes ripple meadow grasses beneath the ice-hung precipices of 9160-foot Goode Mountain, 8515-foot Storm King Peak, and 9087-foot Mt. Logan.

Travel to Bridge Creek, 16 miles from Stehekin (Hikes 74 and 76). Just before the creek is the trailhead, elevation 2200 feet. The trail starts with a short, stiff climb of 400 feet, then goes up and down in woods, emerging to a view of Memaloose Ridge and reaching the bridge over Bridge Creek at 2½ miles, 2600 feet. Across the bridge and ¼ mile beyond is a junction; go left on the North Fork trail.

The way ascends steeply a bit and gentles out. From brushy openings in the forest are views of rugged cliffs—a promise of what is to come. To achieve fulfilment of the promise it is necessary to camp somewhere in the North Fork. There are three choices: Walker Park Camp, 5½ miles, 3120 feet, a miserable, fly-ridden pit; Grizzly Creek Camp, about 6 miles, 3200 feet, in open woods near the stream; and Grizzly Creek Horse Camp, 6⅓ miles, 3180 feet.

The ford of Grizzly Creek is not life-threatening except in snowmelt season, yet neither are its wide, cold, rushing waters a novice's joy. Beyond the creek the way leaves woods and wanders along the valley bottom in cottonwood groves, avalanche brush, and patches of grass. Immense views continue—up and up the 6000-foot north wall of Goode to icefalls of the Goode Glacier and towers of the summit.

At 7¼ miles, about 1⅔ miles past Grizzly Creek, maintained trail ends in North Fork Meadows. The old path continues, a bit less gentle. At

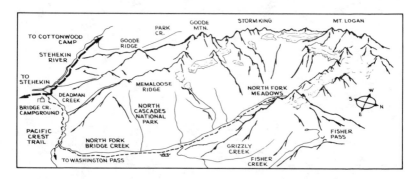

Mount Goode and upper North Fork Bridge Creek (Dick Brooks photo)

about 9½ miles, 3800 feet, is the site of famous Many Waterfalls Camp, where camping is now banned. The scene is glorious with wide fields of hip-high grass, the roar of many waterfalls from hanging glaciers, and neck-stretching gazes to Goode and Storm King.

Paths here are confusing; climb the brushy knoll above to a resumption of tread amid small and sparse trees. In a stand of old alpine timber that has escaped avalanches is the heather-surrounded wreckage of a miner's cabin. The trail emerges into grass and flowers of the cirque, 10½ miles, 4200 feet, and fades away. The views of Goode are better than ever and Logan's walls are close above the amphitheater.

Air view of Park Creek Pass. Mount Buckner, left, Mount Logan, right

LAKE CHELAN–STEHEKIN RIVER
North Cascades National Park

78   PARK CREEK PASS

Round trip to pass 16 miles
Allow 3–4 days
High point 6100 feet
Elevation gain 3900 feet

Hikable mid-July through
    September
USGS Goode Mountain and Mt.
    Logan
Park Service backcountry use
    permit required

A wild and alpine pass on the Cascade Crest between the 9000-foot summits of Mt. Buckner and Mt. Logan, dividing snow waters flowing east to the Stehekin River and Lake Chelan and snow waters flowing west to the Skagit River and the inland sea. The pass and its surroundings rank among the scenic climaxes of the North Cascades National Park. A base can be established at Buckner Camp for roaming, or a one-way trip made over the mountains from lowlands east to lowlands west. Keep in mind that there is no camping in the alpine areas around the pass. From the last permitted camp in Park Creek it is 5 miles, with a 2000-foot climb, over and down to Thunder Basin Camp.

Travel 18½ miles from Stehekin (Hikes 74 and 77) to Park Creek Campground and trailhead, elevation 2300 feet.

The trail switchbacks steeply from the Stehekin into the hanging valley of Park Creek, then goes along near the stream through forest and occasional open patches with views up to Goode Ridge. At 2 miles, 3200 feet, is a two-site designated camp and a footlog crossing of the creek. Beyond here the grade gentles, continuing mostly in trees but with openings that give looks to Park Creek Ridge. At 3 miles is an obscure junction with a rough-and-sketchy climbers' route to 7680-foot Goode Ridge and broad views; the scramble is for experienced hikers only, but well worth the effort.

Crossing numerous creeks in green avalanche tracks, views growing of high peaks, the trail ascends gradually to 4000 feet, 4½ miles. Now the way leaves the main valley of Park Creek, which falls from the glaciers of Mt. Buckner, and traverses and switchbacks steeply into a hanging side-valley, gradually emerging into parkland. At 7 miles, 5700 feet, the trail flattens out in a magnificent meadow laced by streams and dotted by clumps of alpine trees, the view dominated by the north wall of 8200-foot Booker Mountain.

A final wander in heather and blossoms leads to the rocky, snowy defile of 6100-foot Park Creek Pass, 8 miles from the Stehekin road.

In order to preserve the fragile meadows, camping is not permitted in the area near the pass; however, fair basecamps for exploration are located in the forest at 5 miles (Buckner Camp) and 2 miles west of the pass in Thunder Basin.

For one wandering, with grand views of Buckner, Booker, Storm King, and Goode (tallest of all at 9160 feet, third-highest non-volcanic peak in the Cascades), find an easy, flowery route to the ridge southeast of the pass, overlooking the head of Park Creek. For another, descend west from the pass about ½ mile, leave the trail, and contour meadows and moraines to a mind-expanding vista of the giant Boston Glacier and great peaks standing far above the deep valley of Thunder Creek.

If transportation can be arranged, a one-way trip can be made on down Thunder Creek to Diablo Lake (Hike 18).

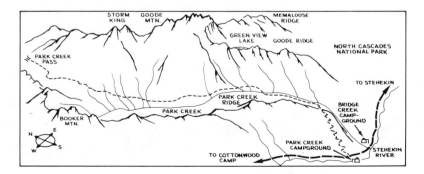

79 HORSESHOE BASIN (STEHEKIN)

**Round trip from Cascade River
  road 18 miles**
Allow 3–4 days
**Elevation gain 3000 feet in, 1800
  feet out**
Hikable July through October
**USGS Cascade Pass and Goode
  Mountain**
**Park Service backcountry use
  permit required**

**Round trip from Cottonwood
  Camp 8 miles**
Hiking time 5 hours
Elevation gain 2000 feet

Nine or more waterfalls tumble to the meadow floor of this cliff-ringed cirque. Above are glaciers on Sahale and Boston Peaks, both nearly 9000 feet, and the spires of Ripsaw Ridge. Wander the flowers and rocks and bubbling streams. The basin is well worth a visit in its own right, and

Glory Mountain, left, Trapper Mountain, right, from mine in Horseshoe Basin

makes a splendid sidetrip on the cross-mountain journey described in Hike 80.

The basin trail can be reached either from the west side of the Cascades or the east. For the west approach to the junction, ascend to Cascade Pass (Hike 29) and descend 3 miles into the Stehekin valley. For the east approach to the junction, travel to the end of auto road at Cottonwood Camp, 2800 feet, and walk the abandoned mining road 2 miles (Hikes 74 and 76).

At an elevation of 3600 feet on the Stehekin River trail, the old mining road (dating from the 1950s) switchbacks sharply in a rockslide, climbing around and up the mountainside to enter the hanging valley of Basin Creek. At 1½ miles the way emerges from brush and flattens out amid boulder-strewn meadows, 4200 feet. Impressive looks upward from flowery knolls to ice and crags, and a magical view and sound of white water on the glacier-excavated walls.

The old road continues ½ mile upward across the sloping floor of the basin to a mine tunnel at 4800 feet, close under the froth and splash of the falls. The Park Service has worked in the mine to make explorations safe; bring a flashlight. Hours can be spent roaming the basin, enjoying.

Experienced off-trail hikers can go higher. Cross the creek a short way below the mine and scramble brushy slopes, amid small cliffs to the right of the vertical walls, into the upper cirque of Horseshoe Basin. The ascent is not easy but doesn't require the ropes and other gear of mountain climbers; traces of an old miners' trail may be found, simplifying progress. Once on the high shelf under Mt. Buckner and Ripsaw Ridge the way is open for extended explorations, always looking down waterfalls to the lower basin and out to peaks beyond the Stehekin.

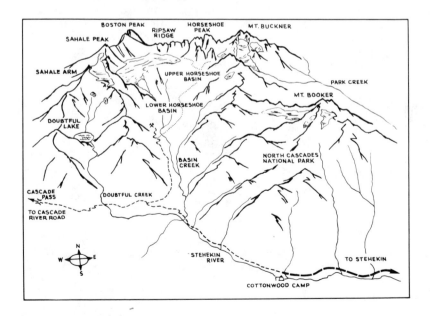

80 LAKE CHELAN TO CASCADE RIVER

One-way trip from Cottonwood
  Camp to Cascade River road 9
  miles
Hiking time 6 hours
High point (Cascade pass) 5400
  feet
Elevation gain 2600 feet
Hikable mid-July through
  mid-October
One day
USGS Goode Mountain and
  Cascade Pass

One-way Boy Scout hike from
  Prince Creek to Cascade River
  50 miles
Allow at least 6 days
Elevation gain 5900 feet, loss 2600
  feet
Park Service backcountry use
  permit required

A classic and historic cross-Cascades route from the Columbia River to
Puget Sound. The trip can begin from either side of the range, but for a
well-ordered progression of soup, salad, main course, and finally dessert
(rather than the reverse) the approach from the east is recommended.
The journey can be a quick-and-easy 9 miles or, by starting at Prince
Creek, a Boy Scout "50-mile hike."

Voyage Lake Chelan, elevation 1098 feet (Hike 74).

Begin the 50-mile hike at Prince Creek, then walk the quiet road from
the Stehekin boat landing to Cottonwood Camp, 2800 feet, 23 miles from
Stehekin and the end of automobile traffic. Hikers who don't need a merit
badge may ride the shuttle bus this far (Hike 76).

At Cottonwood Camp the way emerges from woods into avalanche
greenery and goes along the valley bottom, with views of ridges above, to
the grassy-and-bouldery avalanche fan at the crossing of Basin Creek,
3100 feet, 1½ miles from Cottonwood; campsite here. In another ¾ mile,

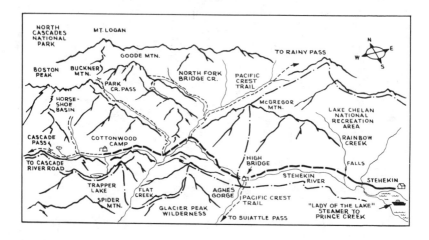

Stehekin valley and McGregor Mountain from Cascade Pass trail

at 3600 feet, is the junction with the route of Horseshoe Basin (Hike 79).

Excellent trail climbs an enormous talus to Doubtful Creek, 4100 feet, ¾ mile from the Horseshoe Basin junction. The ford can be difficult and extremely dangerous in high water, and falls above and below forbid any easy detour. Now the trail rises into a hot slope of slide alder, ascending in 12 gentle switchbacks to the crest of the wooded ridge above Pelton Basin and views. In the basin at 4820 feet, 5 miles, the Park Service has installed wooden tent platforms to allow camping in meadows without destroying them. This is a superb base for easy explorations.

A short mile more leads to 5400-foot Cascade Pass and broader views. A supertrail descends 3¾ miles to the end of the Cascade River road, 3600 feet (Hike 29).

FOGGY DEW CREEK

Round trip to Sunrise Lake 13 miles
Allow 2 days
High point 7200 feet
Elevation gain 3700 feet

Hikable mid-July through September
One day or backpack
USGS Hungry Mountain and Martin Peak

The name has magic for those who love the folk song, and the scene has more. Maybe the stiff climb of 3700 feet doesn't usually stir the poetry in a hiker's soul, but the loud waters of Foggy Dew Creek do, and the lake in a horseshoe cirque amid meadows, cliffs, and parklike larch and alpine firs. Try it in late September when the larch has turned to gold. However, since hunters are here then, maybe you'd prefer the midsummer solitude, caused in no small measure by the fishless condition of the shallow lake. A party could spend many days happily here, exploring the sidetrails on both sides of the divide, and, as well, the Chelan Summit Trail (Hike 75), to which this trail leads.

From Pateros on the Columbia River drive the Methow Valley Highway 17 miles toward Twisp. Just before crossing the Methow River, for the seventh time, turn left on a narrow country road 1 mile to a Forest Service sign. Turn left on road No. 4340. (From Twisp drive 15 miles toward Pateros. Just before crossing the Methow River, for the third time, turn right on a narrow country road. In 1.5 miles turn right at the above-mentioned Forest Service sign.) Whichever way you reach it, from this sign drive North Fork Gold Creek road No. 4340 for 5 miles and turn left on road No. (4340)200. At 9.1 miles are the road-end and trailhead, elevation 3490 feet.

Foggy Dew trail No. 417 starts in selectively logged (all the big pines) forest, climbs steadily, and at 2½ miles passes Foggy Dew Waterfall, something to sing about. At 3½ miles the valley and trail turn sharply right. At 4 miles cross a small tributary and at 5 miles come to a junction

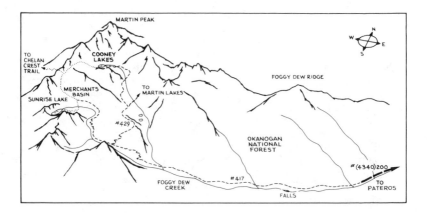

Sunrise Lake

with Martin Peak trail No. 429 and the end of the motorcyclists.

At 5½ miles, 6700 feet, steepness lessens and the path ascends moderately in ever-expanding meadows. At 6 miles reach Merchants Basin and a junction with a way trail to Sunrise Lake. From here the Foggy Dew trail to the Chelan Summit is seldom traveled and virtually vanishes in the meadow; a USGS map is essential to further navigation.

The well-used Sunrise Lake trail climbs ½ mile to the shores at 7200 feet, 6½ miles from the road. Campsites are lovely, explorations abound, and every prospect pleases. The lovely water may be contaminated by horses.

For a different way back, adding an extra 2 miles, 1200 feet, more meadows, and another lake to the round trip, at the trail junction in Merchants Basin find the seldom-used trail climbing toward an unnamed pass to the north. The tread is hidden in vegetation. Near the pass veer off to the right and in 1½ miles reach Cooney Lakes and return to the Foggy Dew trail by trail No. 429.

EAGLE LAKES

**Round trip to Lower Eagle Lake
10 miles**
Hiking time 5 hours
High point 6900 feet
**Elevation gain 2200 feet in, 200
feet out**
**Hikable mid-June through
September**
One day or backpack
USGS Martin Peak

**Round trip to Horsehead Pass 13
miles**
Hiking time 8 hours
High point 7590 feet
Elevation gain 2900 feet

Pretty Eagle Lakes under beetling crags. A 7590-foot pass overlooking Boiling Lake. A bushel of byways to other lakes and meadows. Easy-roaming routes to summits over 8000 feet, often-nameless points that are higher than many great and famous peaks elsewhere in the North Cascades. Views over forests and sagebrush to ranches in the Methow Valley, over vast deeps of the Lake Chelan trench to ice giants of the main range.

The first 4½ miles of the "National Recreation Trail" (whatever that is) have been rebuilt smooth and wide. If you feel like running, the corners are nicely banked. But don't suppose the fancy design is for the benefit of racing hikers or galloping horses. The motorcyclists spoke up and the hikers didn't, and the hikers' former trail has turned into a motorcycle path. To avoid dust and noise and the danger of being run over, it is recommended you do this trip in late June or early July when snow patches still stop wheels but not feet.

Drive road No. 4340 (Hike 81) to the junction with road No. (4340)200 and stay on 4340 for 1.6 more miles to a Y. Take the left road, No. (4340)300, 6 miles to the road-end and the start of Eagle Lakes trail No. 431, elevation 4700 feet.

After a nearly level first mile traversing under cliffs, ascent begins and continues steadily. At ½ mile pass the Crater Lakes trail, climbing 1700 feet in 3½ miles to two small lakes. At 2¼ miles pass the Martin Lakes trail, going by several lakes and in 9 miles joining the Foggy Dew trail.

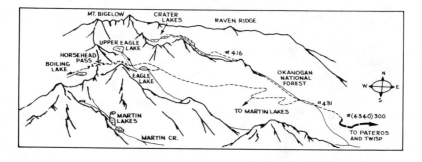

At 2¾ miles is a tiny spring and a possible camp. At 4½ miles, 6900 feet, is a Y. The left, a hikers-only trail, drops 200 feet, at 5 miles from the road reaching Lower Eagle Lake, 6490 feet, with plentiful campsites. The right, the main trail continues up, passing a short trail to 7110-foot Upper Eagle Lake and at 7½ miles reaching 7590-foot Horsehead Pass.

The trail descends 1 mile to Boiling Lake, a name that has led unknowing hikers to imagine it must be a hot puddle in a sunbaked desert. Not at all—it's a cool pool in green meadows, with pleasant camps in the trees. The "boiling" is a common phenomenon in mountain lakes, bubbles of air rising from bottom mud. The trail continues down a bit more to join the Chelan Summit Trail (Hike 75).

| Old road: | 3201 | 3110 | 3109 | 1 |
| New road: | 4340 | (4340)200 | (4340)300 | (1000)000 (or just 1) |

Eagle Lakes trail

Dagger Lake from Twisp Pass

TWISP RIVER
Lake Chelan–Sawtooth Wilderness

83 TWISP PASS– STILETTO VISTA

Round trip to Twisp Pass 9 miles
Hiking time 6–8 hours
High point 6064 feet
Elevation gain 2300 feet
Hikable late June through October

One day or backpack
USGS Gilbert and McAlester Mountain
Park Service backcountry use permit required for camping at Dagger Lake

Climb from Eastern Washington forest to Cascade Crest gardens, glacier-smoothed boulders, dramatic rock peaks, and views down into Bridge Creek and across to Goode and Logan. Then wander onward amid a glory of larch-dotted grass and flowers to an old lookout site with horizons so rich one wonders how the fire-spotter could ever have noticed smoke. For a special treat do the walk in autumn when the air is cool and the alpine country is blazing with color.

Drive the Methow Valley Highway (Hike 81) to Twisp and follow the

Twisp River road No. 44, signed "Gilbert" 25 miles to the end. A short bit before the road-end is a large trailhead parking area, elevation 3700 feet.

The trail begins by ascending moderately through woods, with occasional upvalley glimpses of pyramid-shaped Twisp Mountain. At 2 miles are a junction with Copper Pass trail No. 426, a camp and the last dependable water for a long, hot way. Ascend fairly steeply on soft-cushioned tread to 3 miles; stop for a rest on ice-polished buttresses with views down to valley-bottom forest and up to the ragged ridge of Hock Mountain, above the glaciated basin of the South Fork headwaters. The trail emerges from trees to traverse a rocky sidehill, the rough tread sometimes blasted from cliffs. At about 4 miles the route enters heather and flowers, coming in a short ½ mile to a small stream and pleasant campsites. A final ¼ mile climbs to Twisp Pass, 6064 feet, 4½ miles, on the border of the North Cascades National Park.

For wider views ascend meadows north and look down to Dagger Lake and Bridge Creek and across to Logan, Goode, Black, Frisco, and much more.

The trail drops steeply a mile to Dagger Lake and 4 more miles to Bridge Creek and a junction with the Pacific Crest Trail.

Don't go away without rambling the crest south from the pass about ¼ mile to the foot of Twisp Mountain and a magical surprise—a hidden little lake surrounded by grass and blossoms and alpine forest, a mountain home.

The open slopes north of the pass demand extended exploration. And here is another surprise. Hikers heading in the logical direction toward Stiletto Peak will stumble onto sketchy tread of an ancient trail. Follow the route up and down highlands, by sparkling creeks, to a green shelf under cliffs of 7660-foot Stiletto Peak, a fairy place of meandering streams and groves of wispy larch. Then comes a field of photogenic boulders, a rocky ridge, and the 7223-foot site of the old cabin. Look north over Copper Creek to Liberty Bell and Early Winter Spires, northwest to Tower, Cutthroat, Whistler, Arriva, and Black, southwest to McGregor, Glacier, and Bonanza, and south to Hock and Twisp—and these are merely a few of the peaks seen, not to mention the splendid valley. Stiletto Vista, former lookout site, is only 2 miles from Twisp Pass, an easy afternoon's round trip.

Old road: 349
New road: 44

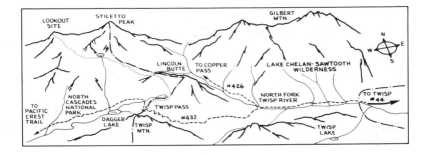

84 COPPER PASS

Round trip to pass 10 miles	One day
Hiking time 6 hours	Hikable July through
High point 6700 feet	mid-October
Elevation gain 3000 feet	USGS Gilbert and McAlester

The climb to the heathery pass is steep, but the color is worth it. Try the trip in July when glacier lilies and yellowbells are blooming, or in August for asters and cow parsnip and paintbrush and a few tucked-away gentians, or in late September when larch trees turn to gold.

The prospectors' trail of olden days connected the Twisp River to the Stehekin via Bridge Creek. Unused for decades, in 1981 and 1982 it was reopened to the pass by volunteers from the Sierra Club and Outward Bound. The trail down to Bridge Creek has not been brushed but can be found and used for a 3-day loop trip, returning via Twisp Pass (Hike 83). This alternative requires a backcountry permit for the North Cascades National Park, obtainable at the Twisp Ranger Station.

Drive the Twisp River road to the end, elevation 3700 feet (Hike 83).

Hike Twisp River trail No. 432 for 2 miles to a junction just before crossing North Fork Twisp River (dwindled to a creek); go straight on trail No. 426, signed "Copper Pass." With more ups than downs the way follows the North Fork, mostly in woods. At 3½ miles cross the stream to a nice campsite, 5200 feet.

There's nothing now but up. In ¼ mile is a view of a double waterfall, and a bit farther, ruins of an old cabin. Scarcely deigning to switchback, the trail aims at the sky, partly in trees and partly in meadows.

At 6700 feet, 5 miles, is the sky—which is to say, Copper Pass, where herbaceous meadows yield to heather meadows. Day hikers may gaze down Copper Creek, across to the rocky ridge of Early Winters Spire, out to faraway ice-clad Goode Mountain, eat lunch, and go home satisfied.

Loopers can readily see the trail dropping steeply to green meadows at the head of Copper Creek. A bit of searching at the far edge of the boggy meadow may be needed to find the resumption of tread in forest. In about 4 miles from the pass the path intersects the Pacific Crest Trail. Follow it

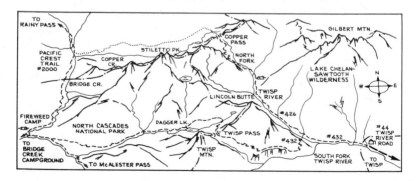

Copper Pass

down Bridge Creek 1 mile to enter North Cascades National Park, then 1 more mile to Fireweed Camp, 3600 feet. From Fireweed, 4 long, steep miles climb to Twisp Pass, 6064 feet, and 4 shorter miles drop to the trailhead, completing a loop of 21 miles with an elevation gain and loss of 5500 feet.

Old road: 349
New road: 44

85   ABERNATHY PASS

Round trip 18 miles
Allow 2 days
High point 6400 feet
Elevation gain 3300 feet

Hikable July through October
USGS Mazama and Silver Star
  Mountain

Finding the trails a bit too peopled for your solitudinous tastes? Try Cedar Creek. Climb splendid forests, first in a narrow V valley and then in a broad U trough between Silver Star and Gardner Mountains, which do not present themselves in sweeping panoramas but through many peeking-type windows. Proceed to Abernathy Pass for the big picture. Or strike off through the open woods and get really lonesome and very high on slopes of the Big Kangaroo.

Drive the North Cascades Highway 20 west 3.5 miles from Early Winters Campground or east 13 miles from Washington Pass and turn onto road No. 200, signed "Sandy Butte–Cedar Creek." At the road-end .9 mile, turn right into a large gravel pit. Cedar Creek trailhead No. 476 is atop the bank to the left, elevation 3100 feet.

Though the trail starts 400 vertical feet higher than the creek, to stay above the wild torrent it gains 500 feet in a short 2 miles to Cedar Falls, a spectacular twin waterfall, the destination of most hikers, many of whom stay at the camp here overnight despite the danger to their hearing.

The way continues to climb steeply to keep dry. At about 3 miles is a window view of the craggy summit of North Gardner Mountain. At 4 miles the post-glacial notch is left behind and the U-shaped glacial trough entered, with an accompanying flattening of the grade. The path crosses occasional aspen-dotted meadows that gives looks at the impressive shoulders of Silver Star right and Gardner left, and far up the valley to a wall of mountains, part of the Abernathy Peak massif.

The pleasant forest walk is enlivened by creeks that may or may not be log-bridged and in snowmelt time may or may not be easy to get over. Campsites are scattered along the way, including one at West Fork Cedar Creek and another, the best and the last, a scant mile farther at Middle Fork, 7 miles, 5000 feet. (The old mile markers predate the Sandy Butte road, so subtract a mile.)

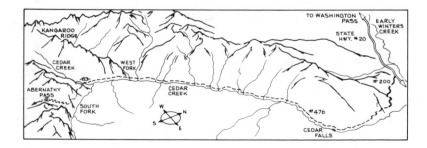

Cedar Creek Falls

The valley head appears to be a cul de sac, no possible route through the solid wall of granite peaks. Consequently the 2 miles and countless switchbacks that climb 1400 feet to Abernathy Pass, 6400 feet, seem a magic trick. The summit of the pass is a narrow cleft and the trail immediately drops to North Creek and the Twisp River. For views, therefore, scramble the granite knobs west from the pass, on striking ledges and slabs and buttresses, in picturesque pines and larches. The climax knob is ¾ mile, 7002 feet. Look north to Snagtooth Ridge and Silver Star Mountain, and south across North Creek to Gilbert Mountain and pyramid-shaped Reynolds Peak, and back down the long valley whence you came.

The greatest hiking hereabouts is on paths made by climbers. In open forests aromatic with Labrador tea and white rhododendron, and boggy glades dotted with insect-eating butterwort, then on steep heather meadows and rockslides, follow Middle Fork Cedar Creek to the south end of Kangaroo Ridge, or West Fork to the north end. Since this country has some of the most famous granite in the Cascades, watch out for mountain climbers snapping their carabiners.

86 CUTTHROAT PASS

**Round trip from Cutthroat Creek
road-end to Cutthroat Pass 12
miles
Hiking time 6–8 hours
High point 6800 feet
Elevation gain 2300 feet
Hikable July through
mid-October
One day or backpack
USGS Washington Pass**

**One-way trip from Rainy Pass to
Cutthroat road-end 10½ miles
Hiking time 6–7 hours
High point 6800 feet
Elevation gain 1900 feet**

A high ridge with impressive views, one of the most scenic sections of the Pacific Crest Trail. If transportation can be arranged, one can start at Rainy Pass and end at Cutthroat Creek, saving 400 feet of elevation gain. However, because a short sidetrip to sparkling Cutthroat Lake makes a refreshing rest stop, the trail is described starting from Cutthroat Creek.

Drive the North Cascades Highway 20 east from the Skagit Valley over Rainy and Washington Passes, or west from the Methow Valley 14 miles from Winthrop to Early Winters and 11 miles more to Cutthroat Creek. Beyond the bridge turn right on the Cutthroat Creek road 1 mile to the road-end and trailhead, elevation 4500 feet. The upper regions are dry so have a full canteen.

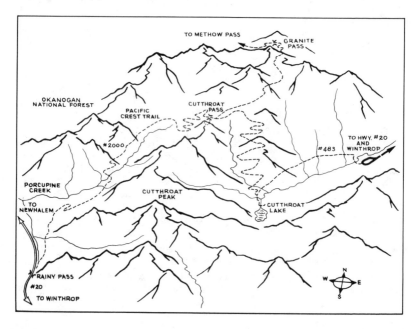

Cutthroat Peak

The trail quickly crosses Cutthroat Creek and begins a gentle 1¾-mile ascent amid sparse rainshadow forest to a junction with the Cutthroat Lake trail. The 4935-foot lake (no camping) is ¼ mile away, well worth it. Fill canteens here—the upper regions are dry.

The next 2½ miles climb through big trees and little trees to meadows and a campsite (no water in late summer). A final short 2 miles lead upward to 6800-foot Cutthroat Pass, about 6 miles from the road-end.

It is absolutely essential to stroll to the knoll south of the pass for a better look at the country. Cutthroat Peak, 7865 feet, stands high and close. Eastward are the barren west slopes of Silver Star. Mighty Liberty Bell sticks its head above a nearby ridge. Far southwest over Porcupine Creek is glacier-clad Dome Peak.

If time and energy permit, make a sidetrip 1 mile north on the Pacific Crest Trail to a knoll above Granite Pass and striking views down to Swamp Creek headwaters and across to 8444-foot Tower Mountain, 8366-foot Golden Horn, and Azurite, Black, and countless more peaks in the distance. This portion of the Crest Trail may be blocked by snow until mid-August; if so, drop below the tread and cross the snow where it isn't dangerously steep.

From Cutthroat Pass the Crest Trail descends Porcupine Creek a pleasant 5 miles to Rainy Pass, the first 2 miles in meadows and the rest of the way in cool forest with numerous creeks. The trail ends a few hundred feet west of the summit of 4840-foot Rainy Pass.

The best camping is on flat spots near the head of Porcupine Creek, but none are close to water. At 3½ miles from Rainy Pass, ½ mile off the trail to the west, is a well-watered meadow camp.

87 MAPLE PASS

Round trip to pass 8 miles
Hiking time 4½ hours
High point 6600 feet
Elevation gain 1800 feet

Hikable mid-July through
mid-October
One day
USGS Mt. Arriva, McGregor
Mountain, Rainy Pass

Lakes, little flower fields, small meadows, and big views sum up this delightful hike. The Forest Service built the trail to the pass, intending it to be a segment of the Pacific Crest Trail, only to discover what should have been obvious before, that the potential impact on fragile meadows by horse traffic would be disastrous. One certainly hopes it never will be

Corteo Peak from Maple Pass

completed down the far side of the pass (and therefore open to horses).

Drive the North Cascades Highway 20 east from the Skagit Valley or west from the Methow Valley to Rainy Pass and park at the south-side rest area. Find trail No. 740 signed "Lake Ann–Maple Pass." Elevation, 4855 feet.

As is typical of the Pacific Crest Freeway, the trail was blasted wide enough for a cavalry charge. However, unless this does become part of the Crest Trail, horses will continue to be banned, as they now are, and that's a mercy for the meadows. Elevation is gained at the easy grade typical of the freeway. At 1½ miles, 5400 feet, is a spur to Lake Ann, destination of most hikers. The ½-mile path goes along the outlet valley, nearly level, by two shallow lakelets, around marshes, to the shore. Camping is prohibited within ¼ mile of the lake due to the dense population.

The main trail ascends across a large rockslide, by 2 miles getting well above Lake Ann. At 3 miles is 6200-foot Heather Pass; from a switchback, look west to Black Peak, Lewis Peak and the cirque of Wing Lake, out of sight under the peak. A way trail traverses steep hillsides of heather, snow, and boulders to Lewis Lake and Wing Lake; camping at the latter.

The main trail continues from Heather Pass, contouring over the top of cliffs 1000 feet above Lake Ann to Maple Pass at 4 miles, 6600 feet, and there abruptly ends.

Boot-beaten tracks go left and right. The path west leads to a 6870-foot high point with close views of Corteo and Black Peaks. The path east leads to a shoulder of Frisco Mountain and views down Maple Creek and out toward icy-white Dome Peak, Spire Point, Mt. Resplendent, and Glacier Peak.

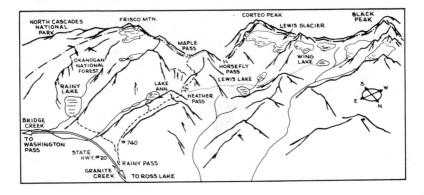

ROBINSON PASS

Round trip 18 miles	**Hikable late May through October**
Allow 2 days	**USGS Slate Peak, Robinson**
High point 6200 feet	**Mountain, Pasayten Peak, Mt.**
Elevation gain 2700 feet	**Lago, and Mazama**

The geography here is not of the big glacier-monster crag sort characteristic of the North Cascades National Park, but spectacular it is—high, massive, shaggy ridges, naked and cliffy, reminding of Montana, and enormous U-shaped glacial-trough valleys, and awesome swaths of climax avalanches sweeping down from crests thousands of feet to bottoms and up the other sides. Also, lovely streams rush through parkland forests. And among the greatest appeals, trips in what the local folk call the *"wilderness* Wilderness" are like taking a ride in a time machine back to the 1930s. Solitude! Though Robinson Creek is a main thoroughfare into the heart of the Pasayten Wilderness, and a favorite with horse people, most come in the fall hunting season. Summer is lonesome even on the main trail, and on byways one can roam a hundred miles and maybe never see another soul.

Drive the North Cascades Highway 20 from the Methow Valley 1.5 miles east of Early Winters Campground and turn left, cross the Methow River and go .4 mile to the hamlet of Mazama and turn left again, upvalley. At 7 miles pavement ends. At 9 miles cross Robinson Creek and turn right into a small campground, parking area, and trailhead, elevation 2500 feet.

The trail follows the creek ¼ mile, then switchbacks a couple hundred feet above the water. At 1½ miles enter the Pasayten Wilderness and shortly cross a bridge over Robinson Creek. Partly in rocky-brushy opens, partly in forest of big Ponderosa pines, then smaller firs, the way climbs steadily, moderately, just short of 3 miles crossing a steel bridge over Beauty Creek, which waterfalls down from Beauty Mountain, at 4 miles recrossing Robinson Creek on a bridge. The avalanche country has been entered, wide aisles cut in the forest, huge jackstraws piled up; from

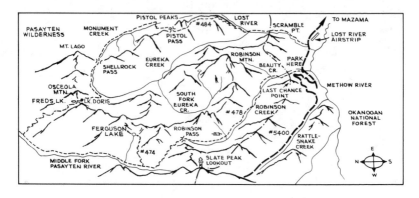

Robinson Pass and Slate Peak in clouds

here on the way is a constant garden.

At 6 miles are a log crossing of Robinson Creek, now much smaller, and Porcupine Camp, in the woods and unappealing except in a storm. To here, avalanche meadows have broken the forest. From now on strips of forest break the ridge-to-creek meadows. A nice camp is located in the first broad meadow above Porcupine; an even better in the second, at 6½ miles, 4900 feet, by the creek in a grove of large spruce trees; and a third just before Robinson Pass, in the trees 300 feet below the trail.

The trail sidehills through flower fields, rock gardens alternating with avalanche gardens, up to Robinson Pass at 9 miles, 6200 feet, a great broad gap through which the continental glacier flowed. Long-ago forest fires cleared the big timber and now the wildflowers blaze.

The pass is a trip in itself, but also is the takeoff for longer journeys. To begin, the open slopes above the pass invite easy roaming—to the left, up to big views from Peak 6935 and onward to Slate Pass, just 2 miles from Robinson Pass, and another mile to Slate Peak, or the other way on the long, lonesome heights of Gold Ridge; to the right, up to Peak 7720, and maybe along the ridge a mile to Devils Peak, or—climbers only—2 miles more to 8726-foot Robinson Mountain, the neighborhood giant.

If trail walking is preferred, descend Middle Fork Pasayten River, through gaspers of avalanches from Gold Ridge, the most impressive series of swaths in the Cascades; 15 miles from the pass is Soda Creek, and in another 8 miles, Canada. The classic long loop of the region is: down the Middle Fork 6½ miles; up by Freds Lake to a 7100-foot pass, down by Lake Doris and around the headwaters of Eureka Creek, under Osceola, Carru, and Lago, three peaks between 8585 and 8745 feet, and up to Shellrock Pass, 7500 feet, 8 miles from the Middle Fork trail; 8½ miles down forests of Monument Creek and up by Lake of the Woods to Pistol Pass, 7100 feet; and 10¾ infamous miles down, down, and down, hot and thirsty, to the Lost River and out to the Methow road, reached at a point 2 miles from Robinson Creek; total loop, 43 miles, much elevation gain and loss, allow a week.

89 GRASSHOPPER PASS

Round trip 11 miles
Hiking 6 hours
High point 7000 feet
Elevation gain 1000 feet in, 1000 feet out

Hikable July through October
One day or backpack
USGS Slate Peak

Wide-open, big-sky meadow ridges with grand views of giant peaks and forested valleys. The entire hike is above timberline, contouring hillsides, traversing gardens, and sometimes following the exact Cascade Crest.

Drive the North Cascades Highway 20 and turn off to Mazama (Hike 88). Continue 20 miles upvalley to 6198-foot Harts Pass. From the pass turn left on the Meadow Campground road 2 miles, keeping right at a fork, to the road-end and trailhead, elevation 6400 feet.

The Pacific Crest Trail immediately leaves the trees, going along an open slope below diggings of the Brown Bear Mine and above a pretty meadow. The first mile is a gentle ascent to the 6600-foot east shoulder of a 7400-foot peak. The way swings around the south slopes of this peak to a saddle, 7000 feet, overlooking Ninetynine Basin at the head of Slate Creek, then contours 7386-foot Tatie Peak to another saddle, 6900 feet, and a magnificent picture of Mt. Ballard.

A moderate descent, with a stretch of switchbacks, leads around a

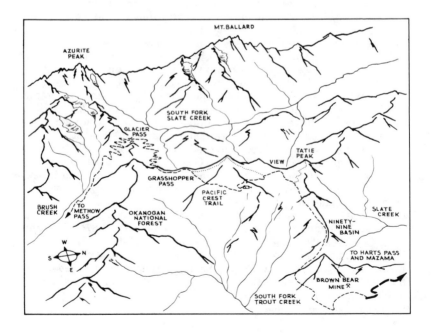

Azurite Peak and Grasshopper Pass

7500-foot peak. In a bouldery basin at 4 miles, 6600 feet, is the only dependable water on the trip, a cold little creek flowing from mossy rocks through a flower-and-heather meadow ringed by groves of larch. Splendid camps.

The trail climbs gradually a final mile to the broad swale of 6700-foot Grasshopper Pass. (Fine camps in early summer when snowmelt water is available.) But don't stop here—go ¼ mile more and a few feet higher on the ridge to a knob just before the trail starts down and down to Glacier Pass. The views are dramatic across Slate Creek forests to 8440-foot Azurite Peak and 8301-foot Mt. Ballard. Eastward are meadows and trees of Trout Creek, flowing to the Methow.

Each of the peaks contoured by the trail invites a sidetrip of easy but steep scrambling to the summit, and the wanderings are endless amid larches and pines and spruces, flowers blossoming from scree and buttress, and the rocks—colorful shales, slates, conglomerates, and sandstones, and an occasional igneous intrusion.

Experienced cross-country hikers don't really need the trail, but can scramble up and down the crest from road-end to Grasshopper Pass, climbing all three peaks. This route is not recommended with a heavy pack, but actually is the easiest way in early summer, when steep snow blocks the trail in several cold corners.

90   WINDY PASS

Round trip 7 miles
Hiking time 5 hours
High point 6900 feet
Elevation gain 500 feet in, 1000
   feet out

Hikable early July through
   October
One day or backpack
USGS Slate Peak and Pasayten
   Peak

In all the hundreds of miles of the Pacific Crest Trail in Washington, this ranks among the easiest and most scenic segments. The hike starts in meadows and stays high the entire way, contouring gardens thousands of feet above the trees of Slate Creek, magnificent views at every step.

Drive to Harts Pass (Hike 89) and turn right on the Slate Peak road about 1.5 miles to the first switchback and a small parking area at the trailhead, elevation 6800 feet.

If the trip is being done in early July, don't be discouraged if the road beyond Harts Pass is blocked by snow and the trail beginning is blinding-white; snow lingers here later than on any other portion of the hike, and mostly clear trail can be expected after a frosty start.

The Pacific Crest Trail gently climbs a meadow shelf the first ½ mile, contours steep slopes of Slate Peak, and drops into lovely little Benson Basin, with a creek and nice camps a few hundred feet below the tread. The way swings up and out to a spur ridge, contours to Buffalo Pass and another spur, and then descends above the gorgeous greenery of Barron Basin to 6257-foot Windy Pass and delightful camps in flowers and larch trees.

Sad to say, the wreckers have been here. Barron Basin is one of the most magnificent easy-to-reach glorylands in the Cascades, but much of it is private property and the miners have raised havoc, gouging delicate meadows with bulldozers, dumping garbage at will. This hike is bound to convert any casual walker into a fierce enemy of the ultra-permissive federal mining laws, which make it difficult if not impossible for the

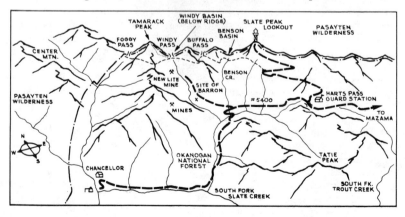

Forest Service to protect the land. Some of the desecration is very new but much is nearly a century old—note how long nature needs to restore ravaged meadows.

Sidetrips from the pass will make a person want the basin to be reclaimed for the public domain and placed within the Pasayten Wilderness, the boundary of which follows the divide, excluding the miner-mangled slopes to the west. Wander meadows north to the panoramas from 7290-foot Tamarack Peak, or walk the Crest Trail a short mile into Windy Basin, offering the best—and most heavily used—camps.

Views on the way? They start with Gardner Mountain, the Needles, Silver Star, Golden Horn, Tower Mountain, and especially the near bulks of Ballard and Azurite. Westerly, Jack and Crater dominate, but part of Baker can also be seen, and many more peaks. Easterly is the Pasayten country, high and remote.

Before or after the hike, take a sidetrip to the fire lookout on the 7440-foot summit of Slate Peak, formerly the highest point in Washington State accessible to automobiles; the road is now gated ¼ mile from the summit, and that's a help.

Old road: 374
New road: 5400

Pacific Crest Trail in Benson Basin. Mount Ballard in distance

91 THREE FOOLS TRAIL

One-way trip from Castle Pass to Ross Lake 27 miles
Allow 3–5 days
High point 7000 feet
Elevation gain about 10,000 feet
Hikable mid-July through September
USGS Slate Peak, Pasayten Peak, Shull Mountain, Castle Peak, Skagit Peak, Hozomeen Mountain

One-way trip from Harts Pass to Ross Lake 54 miles
Allow 7–9 days

One-way trip from near Allison Pass (Canada) to Ross Lake 38 miles
Allow 5–7 days

A classic highland wander from the Cascades Crest to Ross Lake, going up and down a lonesome trail through some of the wildest valleys, ridges, and meadows in the range. A one-way trip is recommended, starting at Harts Pass (or near Manning Park headquarters in Canada) and ending at the lake. (See note on border crossings, hike 100.) Special transportation arrangements are required: a drop-off at Harts Pass (or near Manning Park headquarters—see Hike 92); a pickup by boat from Ross Lake Resort (Hike 21)—though a party can, if desired, exit via the East Bank Trail.

Hike the Pacific Crest Trail (Hike 100) 27 miles from Harts Pass (or 11 miles from near Manning Park headquarters) to Castle Pass, elevation 5451 feet. Turn west on the Three Fools Trail (officially, Castle Pass trail No. 734), climbing steeply in forest, then meadows. At 3 miles, 6000 feet, enter a little basin with a welcome creeklet—the first dependable water since before Castle Pass, and the last for several more miles. Tread ascends from the basin, swings around a spur, descends meadows to a saddle, and climbs the crest to a 6534-foot knob that ranks among the most magnificent viewpoints of the region. Look north across the headwaters of Castle Creek to Castle Peak, Frosty Mountain in Canada, and Mt. Winthrop; look south across forests of Three Fools Creek to peaks along and west of the Cascade Crest; look in every direction and look for hours and never see all there is to see. The way drops from the knob and climbs

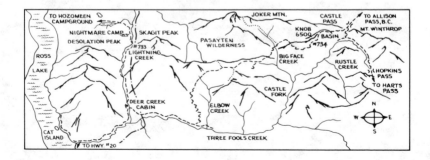

Woody Pass Peak from side of Three Fools Peak

ridge-top heather and parklands to 6 miles, 6400 feet, and a grandly scenic camp—but the only water, if any, is from snowmelt.

The trail angles down across a broad, steep flower garden, then switchbacks in what used to be forest until an avalanche roared down, wiping out a stretch of tread, to Big Face Creek, beneath the impressive wall of Joker Mountain. (At 6½ miles is a tumbling creek; below the trail here is a campsite on a tiny, wooded shelf.) At 8 miles, 5200 feet, the path reaches the valley bottom. For a mandatory sidetrip, fight through a bit of brush and climb the open basin to a high saddle with views out to Hozomeen and the Chilliwacks and below to a snowy cirque lake draining to Freezeout Creek.

The trail goes gently downstream in trees to a crossing of Big Face Creek at 8¾ miles, 4840 feet, then turns right in a gravel wash to the ford. A possible camp here.

A long climb begins up forest to avalanche greenery; when tread vanishes in the grass go directly uphill, watching for cut logs. The ascent continues in trees, opens to meadows, and at 11½ miles, 6350 feet, tops out in the wide green pass, with broad views, between Big Face and Elbow Creeks. A sidetrail drops ¼ mile to a campsite and meandering stream in the glorious park of Elbow Basin. The main trail—tread missing for long stretches—contours and climbs north around the basin to a grassy swale (and a scenic camp, if snowmelt is available) near the ridge crest at 13 miles. Be sure to walk to the 6687-foot plateau summit of the ridge and views: east to the Cascade Crest; south to Jack Mountain; west to the Pickets, Chilliwacks, Desolation, and especially the nearby towers of Hozomeen; north into Canada.

The trail descends near and along the crest, with a look down to the tempting cirque of Freezeout Lake (accessible via a steep scramble), passing through a spectacular silver forest. A stern drop commences—down and down hot and dry burn meadows and young trees. The mouth grows parched, the knees loose and floppy. At 18 miles, 2350 feet, the trail at last touches Three Fools Creek and a possible camp; stop for an

Grouse

Three Fools Peak from Lakeview Ridge (Harvey Manning photo)

orgy of drinking and foot-soaking, and an understanding of why this trip is not recommended to begin at Ross Lake.

Hopes of an easy downhill water-grade hike are quickly dashed by a 1000-foot climb. The trail then goes down, goes up, and down and up, and finally on a forest bench to Lightning Creek at 23 miles, 1920 feet. Just before the crossing is a junction with the trail north to Nightmare Camp and Hozomeen (Hike 19). Just beyond the ford is Deer Lick Cabin (locked) and a campsite.

Again the trail climbs 1000 feet and goes down and up, high on the side of the Lightning Creek gorge, coming at last to a superb overlook of Ross Lake, a thousand feet below. The conclusion is a switchbacking descent to the lakeshore and Lightning Creek Camp, 1600 feet, 27 miles from Castle Pass.

Old and new lookout buildings at Monument 83

UPPER METHOW RIVER– SIMILKAMEEN RIVER
Manning Provincial Park and Pasayten Wilderness

92 CASCADE LOOP TRAIL– MONUMENT 83

Loop trip 34 miles
Allow 2–3 days
High point 6550 feet
Elevation gain 4900 feet

Hikable late June through
October
USGS Frosty Creek and Castle
Peak

When built in the 1920s the fire lookout at Monument 83 probably was the most remote in the Cascades. It still is if approached from the United States, via Slate Peak, West Fork Pasayten River, the pass near Deadwood Lake, and the Boundary Trail—a wilderness walk of nearly 30 miles that is well worth the doing, especially if part of a loop that returns down the Pacific Crest Trail. However, since construction of Highway 3 across Manning Provincial Park, in Canada, Monument 83 is only 10 miles from a road and lies on the very popular Cascade Loop Trail, featuring miles of splendid forest, climaxes of alpine meadows, and the thrill of international travel.

Drive Highway 3 from Hope, British Columbia, across Allison Pass to Manning Provincial Park administration office, lodge, and visitors center ("Nature House"), where U.S. Forest Service wilderness permits (no longer needed) were available for camping in the Pasayten Wilderness. Park here, at the end of the loop hike, in order to have your car waiting, or drive 1.8 miles farther to the Monument 83 parking lot on the right side of the road, elevation 3700 feet.

The "trail" to Monument 83 is a rough, seldom-used service road, closed to public vehicles. In ¼ mile the way crosses the Similkameen River, then ascends gradually in forest along Chuwanten Creek and Monument Creek. At about 9 miles pass a sidetrail signed "Cathedral Lakes" and continue on the service road to the flowery little meadow of Monument 83, 10 miles, 6500 feet.

In the 1920s the U.S. Forest Service built the small log cabin on the highest point, which happens to lie in Canada. In 1953 the tower, tall enough to see over the foreign hill, was erected in America. The grave marker memorializes a pack mule that broke its leg and had to be shot.

From the lookout the now-true trail goes ¾ mile to join Boundary Trail No. 33, which descends 4½ miles along Chuchuwanteen (the American spelling of "Chuwanten") Creek to a campsite at the Frosty Creek crossing and a junction with trail No. 453, 4500 feet, 15 miles from Highway 3. Go right, upstream on Frosty Creek, to a camp ¼ mile past tiny Frosty Lake. The trail steepens and switchbacks to meadows of 6550-foot Frosty Pass, 21 miles, then drops 1 very steep mile to Castle Pass, 5451 feet, and a junction with the Pacific Crest Trail. Head north, passing water and a campsite in ½ mile. The Crest Trail descends gently above Route Creek, then Castle Creek, 3 miles to the border at Monument 78, then 7½ miles more along Castle Creek to Manning Park Headquarters.

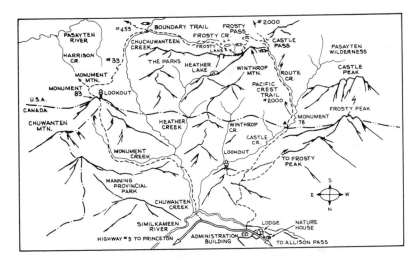

93 BILLY GOAT PASS– BURCH MOUNTAIN

Round trip 10 miles
Hiking time 5 hours
High point 7782 feet
Elevation gain 3082 feet
Hikable late June through
    October

One day
USGS Billy Goat Mountain

Hike to the edge of the Pasayten Wilderness, climb toward an old look-out site, and see miles and miles of broad valleys and open ridges. Carry plenty of water and start early before the sun gets hot. This is big-scale country, often with long stretches between points of scenic interest. For hikers, therefore, early summer is the best season, when flowers and snowfields add variety.

Drive north from Winthrop on the paved Chewack River road. In 7.5 miles cross the river and proceed up the west side of the valley. At 9 miles turn left on the Eightmile Creek road No. 5130 and follow it another 15 miles (the first 5 miles are paved, the last mile is steep and rough) to the road-end at a gravel parking lot, elevation 4800 feet.

Trail No. 502 is quite steep, passing a gated road to a mining claim, climbing 1800 feet in 2½ miles through an open forest to Billy Goat Pass, 6600 feet, on the border of Pasayten Wilderness.

Hike a few hundred feet over the pass and find the Burch Mountain trail No. 516 angling upward on the east (right-hand) side. This well-constructed trail was once used by horses to supply a lookout on top of Burch Mountain. At first the tread is lost in meadows but as the hillside

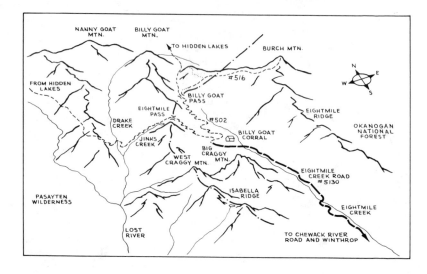

Big Craggy Peak from Burch Mountain trail

steepens the trail becomes distinct and, except for an occasional tree growing in the path, following it is no problem. The ascent is abrupt, quickly emerging to views southeast to Isabella Ridge and beyond to a horizon of 8000-foot peaks, the most dramatic being Big Craggy. Gaining some 600 feet in ¾ mile, the trail nearly reaches the ridge top, then contours around a high, rocky knoll to a broad saddle at 7200 feet. From there it switchbacks up to the 7782-foot summit of Burch Mountain 5 miles from the road-end. The lookout cabin has been gone many years, but the views are still there.

Old road: 392 383
New road: 51 5130

94 NORTH TWENTYMILE PEAK

Round trip 13 miles	Hikable June through October
Hiking time 7 hours	One day or backpack
High point 7464 feet	USGS Doe Mountain and Coleman
Elevation gain 4200 feet	Peak

Behold an infinity of forested ridges extending from Silver Star Mountain in the west to Canada north, Tiffany Mountain east, and beyond the Methow Valley south. So many are the trees that the summit has a fire lookout cabin with a real live lookout person (in season). In all the wild scene only a single road can be seen, along the Chewack River a vertical mile below. Ah, but the hand of man, if hidden, is everywhere busy, sawing and chopping. To be sure, no clearcuts give him away because the logging is selective, meaning he is selecting the beautiful, big, old Ponderosa pine and Douglas fir, leaving the small trees, which never will be allowed to grow old, big, and beautiful unless placed in protected wilderness.

Drive the North Cascades Highway to just west of Winthrop and turn north on West Chewack River road, which in 6.5 miles becomes road No. 51. At 17.6 miles from the North Cascades Highway turn right .6 mile on road No. 5010, then left 2 miles on road No. (5010)700 to the trailhead, elevation 3200 feet. Fill the canteens before starting, for this is the *eastern* North Cascades where the sun shines bright all day, except during thunderstorms.

Trail No. 560 starts on an abandoned logging road that yields to true trail with good tread, gaining 500–800 feet a mile. At 2 miles is the first and last water, at a campsite beside Honeymoon Creek. At about 5 miles the way attains the ridge crest and views that grow steadily in the last 1½ miles to the summit, 7464 feet.

An abandoned trail goes east 10 miles to Thirtymile Meadows and road No. 39. If the proposed Twentymile–Thirtymile Wilderness is not established, this trail likely will be reopened—for motorcycles. Barring that catastrophe, the first mile along the ridge from the summit is a marvel-

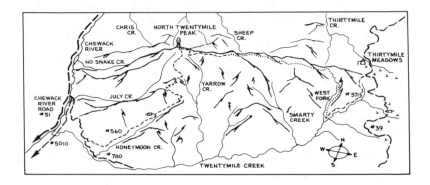

Lookout buildings on North Twentymile Peak

ous meadow stroll. One would love to camp here, if one could find (or carry) water. But one would not love to be here when lightning bolts are zapping prominently upright organisms.

Old road: 392   3715   371   370
New road: 51   5050   700   39

95 TIFFANY MOUNTAIN

**Round trip from Freezeout Pass
to the summit 6 miles
Hiking time 4 hours
High point 8242 feet
Elevation gain 1700 feet
Hikable July through September**

**One day
USGS Tiffany Mountain
One-way trip via Tiffany Lake
8 miles
Hiking time 5 hours**

A superb ridge walk to an 8242-foot summit with views west to distant peaks of the North Cascades, north into the Pasayten Wilderness, and east to farmlands of the Okanogan. The hike can be done as a round trip

Tiffany Mountain from Tiffany Meadows

or—by use of two cars or a non-hiking assistant to move the car—as a one-way trip to either of two alternate trailheads.

Drive north from Winthrop on the paved Chewack River road. At 7.5 miles, just before the paved road crosses the Chewack River, turn right on road No. 39. In less than 2 miles turn right again, still on road No. 39, which now follows Boulder Creek. In another 7 miles the road leaves Boulder Creek and goes up along Middle Bernhardt Creek. Continue 3 miles on very poor road to Freezeout Pass and the trailhead, elevation 6500 feet.

(To place a car at the first of the alternate trailheads, drive 4 more miles to Tiffany Lake trail, 6240 feet. For the second, drive beyond the lake trail 5 miles on road No. 39 to a junction, turn right 1 mile on road No. 38 to Lone Frank Pass, and go another 6 miles to the trailhead, 4990 feet, signed "Tiffany Lake trail." If you reach Salmon Meadows you've driven about 1 mile too far.)

From Freezeout Pass the trail climbs steadily 1½ miles through trees, then 1 mile above timberline, and begins a contour around the east side of the peak. Be sure to make the ½-mile (each way) sidetrip up grassy slopes to the unlimited views from the top of Tiffany Mountain, once the site of a fire lookout.

For the one-way trips, return to the trail and continue onward, descending through Whistler Pass to a 6800-foot junction, 3½ miles from Freezeout Pass, with the Tiffany Lake trail. Either go 4 miles to the road via 6480-foot Tiffany Lake or follow the open ridge above the North Fork Salmon Creek 2½ miles before dropping into trees and down to the road.

Old road:	370	391
New road:	39	38

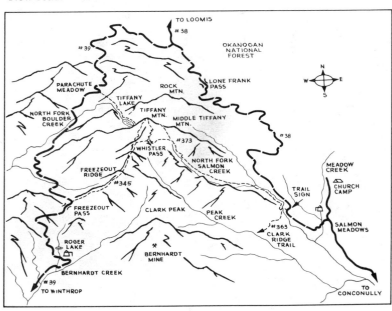

96 HORSESHOE BASIN (PASAYTEN)

Round trip to Sunny Pass 9 miles
Hiking time 6 hours
High point 7200 feet
Elevation gain 1200 feet

Hikable late June through
mid-October
One day or backpack
USGS Horseshoe Basin

At the northeast extremity of the Cascades is a tundra country so unlike the main range a visitor wonders if he hasn't somehow missed a turn and ended up in the Arctic. Meadows for miles and miles, rolling from broad basins to rounded summits of peaks above 8000 feet, with views south over forests to Tiffany Mountain, east to Chopaka Mountain and the Okanogan Highlands, north far into Canada, and west across the Pasayten Wilderness to glaciered, dream-hazy giants of the Cascade Crest.

Drive from Tonasket to Loomis and turn north. In 1.5 miles turn left at signs for Toats Coulee, cross the valley of Sinlahekin Creek, and start a long, steep climb up Toats Coulee on road No. 39. At 11 miles from Loomis is North Fork Campground and in another 5 miles a junction with a narrow, old, unnumbered road signed "Iron Gate." Turn right and drive 7 rough and steep miles to the road-end and trailhead, elevation 6000 feet, at the new Iron Gate Camp (no water) on the boundary of the Pasayten Wilderness.

The first ½ mile is downhill along the abandoned road to the old Iron Gate Camp (no water). The trail from here begins in small lodgepole pine (most of this region was burned off by a series of huge fires in the 1920s) on the old road to Tungsten Mine, which sold stock as recently as the early 1950s. The grade is nearly flat ½ mile to cool waters of a branch of Clutch Creek and then starts a moderate, steady ascent. At 3¼ miles the route opens out into patches of grass and flowers. After a brief steep bit, at 4 miles the way abruptly opens from trees to the flowery, stream-bubbling nook of Sunny Basin and splendid Sunny Camp, 6900 feet.

The trail climbs ½ mile to 7200-foot Sunny Pass—be prepared to gasp and rave. All around spreads the enormous meadowland of Horseshoe

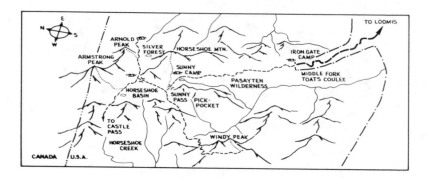

Louden Lake in Horseshoe Basin

Basin, demanding days of exploration. From the pass the Tungsten road drops left and the "pure" trail goes right, contouring gentle slopes of Horseshoe Mountain to grand basecamps in and near the wide flat of Horseshoe Pass, 7100 feet, 5¾ miles, and then contouring more glory to tiny Louden Lake, 6¾ miles (this lake dries up in late summer), and then on and on as described in Hike 97.

The roamings are unlimited. All the summits are easy flower walks— 7620-foot Pick Peak, 8000-foot Horseshoe Mountain, and 8076-foot Arnold Peak. The ridge north from 8106-foot Armstrong Peak has the added interest of monuments to mark the United States–Canada boundary. A more ambitious sidetrip is south from Sunny Pass 6 miles on the down-and-up trail to 8334-foot Windy Peak, highest in the area and once the site of a fire lookout. Don't omit a short walk east through Horseshoe Pass to the immense silver forest at the head of Long Draw.

97   BOUNDARY TRAIL

One-way trip (main route) from
  Iron Gate via Castle Pass to
  Harts Pass 94 miles
Allow 10 days or more
High point 7600 feet
Elevation gain 15,000 feet
Hikable July through September

USGS Horseshoe Basin,
  Bauerman Ridge, Remmel
  Mountain, Ashnola Pass,
  Ashnola Mountain, Tatoosh
  Buttes, Frosty Creek, Castle
  Peak

As the golden eagle flies, it's 40 miles from the east edge of the
Pasayten Wilderness to the Cascade Crest; as the backpacker walks it's
twice that far, with some distance still remaining to reach civilization.
Though the Pasayten country lacks the glaciers of more famous mountains west, and with few exceptions the peaks are rounded, unimpressive
to a climber, there is a magnificent vastness of high ridges, snowfields,
flower gardens, parklands, cold lakes, green forests, loud rivers. The
weather is better and summer arrives earlier than in windward ranges.
The trails are high much of the distance, often above 7000 feet, but are
mostly snowfree in early July, an ideal time for the trip.

Length of the route precludes a detailed description in these pages. In
any event the journey is for experienced wilderness travelers who have
the route-finding skills needed to plan and find their own way. The notes
below merely aim to stimulate the imagination.

Begin from the Iron Gate road-end (Hike 96) and walk to Horseshoe
Basin and Louden Lake (6¾ miles). With ups and downs, always in high-

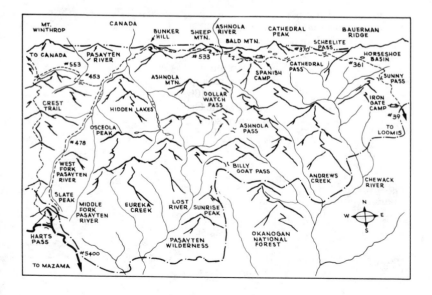

Boundary Trail and Remmel Mountain near Cathedral Pass

lands, the trail goes along Bauerman Ridge to Scheelite Pass (13¾ miles), the old buildings and garbage of Tungsten Mine (17¾ miles), and over Cathedral Pass to Cathedral Lakes (21¾ miles). The route this far makes a superb 4–7 day round trip from Iron Gate.

Continue west to Spanish Camp (26 miles) and the first descent to low elevation, at the Ashnola River (31½ miles). Climb high again, passing Sheep Mountain (34½ miles), Quartz Mountain (38 miles), and Bunker Hill (43¼ miles), then dropping to low forests of the Pasayten River (50½ miles).

Follow the Pasayten River upstream to the Harrison Creek trail, cross a high ridge to Chuchuwanteen Creek (60 miles), and ascend Frosty Creek past Frosty Lake to Frosty Pass (66 miles) and on to Castle Pass (66¾ miles). From here take the Pacific Crest Trail 27 miles south (Hike 100) to Harts Pass, ending a trip of some 94 miles.

(For a shorter alternate, hike up the Pasayten River to Three Forks and ascend the West Fork Pasayten to Harts Pass. Trails branch west from this valley route to reach the Cascade Crest at Woody Pass and Holman Pass.)

However, for the true and complete Boundary Trail, go west from Castle Pass on the Three Fools Trail (Hike 91), hike south to Ross Dam and cross Ross Lake to the Little Beaver, and traverse the North Cascades National Park via Whatcom and Hannegan Passes (Hike 10), concluding the epic journey at the Ruth Creek road.

Old road: 390
New road: 39

98 CHOPAKA MOUNTAIN

Round trip 4 miles
Hiking time 4 hours
High point 7882 feet
Elevation gain 1700 feet

Hikable mid-May through June,
 before cows arrive
One day
USGS Loomis and Horseshoe
 Basin

Stand on the absolute easternmost peak of the North Cascades. Look down a startling 6700-foot scarp to green pastures and orchards around Palmer Lake and meanders of the Similkameen River. Look east to the Okanogan Highlands, north into Canada and the beginnings of other ranges, and south over rolling forests of Toats Coulee Creek to Tiffany Mountain. And also look west across the Pasayten Wilderness to haze-dimmed, snowy summits of the Chelan Crest and Washington Pass. Aside from the geographical distinction of "farthest east," the special feature of the hike is the opportunity to wander alpine meadows as early as May, when windward ranges are so deep in snow that the coming of flowers seems an impossible dream.

Drive from Tonasket to Loomis and turn north. In 1.5 miles turn left at signs for Chopaka Lake and Toats Coulee, cross the valley of Sinlahekin Creek, ignore a road that goes right and uphill to Chopaka Lake, and start a long, steep climb up Toats Coulee on road No. 39. At 10 miles from Loomis, turn right 8 miles on the Ninemile Creek road (at this and all subsequent junctions follow "Chopaka Mountain" signs) to Cold Spring Campground, 6000 feet. The road generally is snowfree by Memorial Day; before then the way may be blocked by lingering snowfields, but if so this merely adds a mile or two to the hike.

Drive ¼ mile above Cold Spring to the road-end parking lot and campground (no water), elevation 6200 feet, with views west to Horseshoe Basin country. Hike a jeep track through spindly trees ½ mile. At 6600 feet, where the ruts start a sidehill contour northeast, find the first logical meadow opening and leave the track, climbing an obvious way toward the heights. The ascent winds amid clumps of alpine trees on

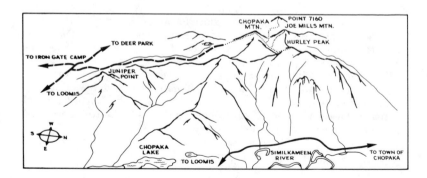

Chopaka Mountain

open ground that would be flower-glorious were it not devastated by cattle. However, a slope of frost-wedged boulders stops the hooves and marks the upper end of mud wallows and cow pies; the meadows now become genuine, clean, and natural. Emerge onto a broad plateau and amble a few more feet to the 7882-foot summit.

If another couple of hours are available, even better views can be had from Hurley Peak, a mile away. Drop north down a superb heather-and-flower meadow to a 7300-foot saddle and climb a gentle ridge to the 7820-foot top.

Old road: 390
New road: 39

99 MOUNT BONAPARTE

Round trip 9 miles
Hiking time 6 hours
High point 7258 feet
Elevation gain 2752 feet

Hikable mid-June through
October
One day
USGS Mt. Bonaparte

No, campers, we're not in the North Cascades here, but well to the east across the Okanogan Valley, in highlands that may be considered a suburb of the Selkirk Range. Two unique features of the mountain are the highest fire lookout in Eastern Washington and the original lookout building, constructed in 1914 of hand-hewn logs (see the ax marks) and now on the National Register of Historic Buildings.

Among the 20 miles of trail in the roadless area (proposed for wilderness status) around Mt. Bonaparte are three routes to the top, each with its own attractions. The South Side trail, 5½ miles long, starts at 4400 feet on road No. (3300)100 and gives views of Bonaparte Lake. Antoine trail, 6 miles, *presently* starts on private property so it is not recommended. The Myers Creek trail described here is the shortest and starts highest, but the way is dry and has no views until the summit.

Drive east from the north end of Tonasket on county road No. 9467, signed "Sitzmark Ski Area–Havillah." In 15.7 miles, just short of Havillah Church, turn right on a road signed "Lost Lake." Pavement ends in .9 mile; turn right on road No. 33. At 4.2 miles from the county road turn right on road No. (3300)300 (abbreviated on the sign to 300). Follow it 1.2 miles to the trailhead, elevation 4500 feet.

Mt. Bonaparte trail No. 306 starts on a logging road, crosses a creek, and climbs ¼ mile to a permanent roadblock (some cars drive this far). The trail continues to be a road, abandoned, through a reforested clearcut. Dodge several motorcycle trails, following the horse and foot prints straight ahead. At 1¼ miles is the end of logging and the start of virgin forest of lodgepole pine. The trail steepens to a junction at 2½ miles with the South Side trail. At 3¾ miles is a junction with the Antoine trail. Lodgepole pine yields to subalpine fir, which at 4½ miles yields to open

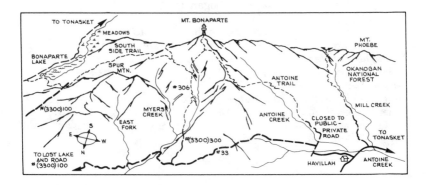

Old (1914) and new lookout buildings on Mount Bonaparte

meadows and all-around-the-compass views over forested hills to valley ranches. The summit of the Okanogan Highlands has been attained, 7258 feet.

Below the modern lookout tower is the 1914 lookout building, slightly bent out of shape by the weight of winter snow. The tower atop the cabin had to be removed years ago. In early days the lookout communicated by heliograph, an instrument that aimed a beam of sunlight and by means of a shutter transmitted Morse Code to a receiver as far away as 20–30 miles. On cloudy days and at night the lookout did not communicate—until telephone lines were installed in the 1930s. When the lines were broken by falling trees or limbs the lookout did not communicate—until the 1960s and the magic of radio.

Old road: 397   3902   3934
New road: 33   (3300)300   (3300)100

100   PACIFIC CREST TRAIL

One-way trip from Allison Pass to
  Stevens Pass about 185 miles
Hiking time 20–25 days
Elevation gain 30,000 feet
Hikable mid-July through
  September

North Cascades National Park
  backcountry use permit
  required

For rugged mountain scenery, the portion of the Pacific Crest National
Scenic Trail between the Canadian border and Stevens Pass is the most
spectacular long walking route in the nation. Undependable weather,
late-melting snow, and many ups and downs make it also one of the most
difficult and strenuous.

Few hikers have time to complete the trip in one season; most spread
their efforts over a period of years, doing the trail in short sections. Those

Upper Goat Lake near Holman Pass (Harvey Manning photo)

taking the whole trip at once generally prefer to start from the north, since pickup transportation at journey's end is easier to arrange at the south terminus. Though higher, the northern part of the trail lies in the rainshadow of great peaks to the west and thus gets less snow than the southern part; the north country and south country therefore open to travel simultaneously.

There is no legal way for a hiker to cross the Canadian–U.S. border on the Pacific Crest Trail. However, U.S. Forest Service wilderness permits for hiking in the Pasayten Wilderness on the U.S. side of the border were available until 1985, when they were no longer needed, at the visitors' center in Manning Provincial Park, Canada. Hikers must draw their own conclusion and decide whether or not to join the hundreds of hikers

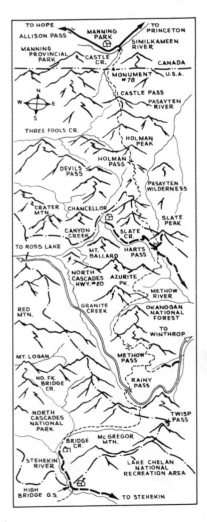

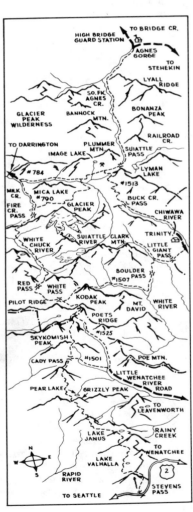

who hike across the border on this and the Monument 83 Trail (Hike 92).

Drive the Trans-Canada Highway to Manning Provincial Park and find the trailhead on an unmarked sideroad ½ mile east of the hotel-motel complex at Allison Pass. Hike 7½ miles up Castle Creek to the international boundary at Monument 78. Look east and west from the monument along the corridor cleared by boundary survey crews; in recent years the new growth has been cut or sprayed. Ascend Route Creek to Castle Pass, from which point south to Harts Pass the trail is almost continuously in meadowland, touching Hopkins Pass, climbing to Lakeview Ridge, crossing Woody Pass into Conie Basin and Rock Pass into Goat Lakes Basin, dropping to Holman Pass, swinging around Jim Mountain to Jim Pass, Foggy Pass, and Oregon Basin, crossing a shoulder of Tamarack Peak into Windy Basin, and from there continuing to Harts Pass as described in Hike 90. **Distance from Allison Pass to Harts Pass 40 miles, elevation gain about 8000 feet, hiking time 4 days.**

From Harts Pass the next road junction is at Rainy Pass. The trail contours around Tatie Peak to Grasshopper Pass (Hike 89), drops to Glacier Pass, drops more into the West Fork Methow River, climbs over Methow Pass, and contours high around Tower Mountain to Granite Pass and on to Cutthroat Pass and down to Rainy Pass (Hike 86). **Distance from Harts Pass to Rainy Pass 31 miles, elevation gain about 4400 feet, hiking time 4 days.**

The next segment is all downhill along Bridge Creek to the Stehekin River road. Walk east to the Rainy Lake–Bridge Creek trail and descend forest to the road at Bridge Creek Campground (Hike 78). Hike 5 miles down the Stehekin River road to High Bridge Campground. **Distance from Rainy Pass to High Bridge 16 miles, hiking time 2 days.**

The next stage is the longest, with a difficult choice between the alternatives of going east or west of Glacier Peak. From High Bridge climb the Agnes valley to Suiattle Pass (Hike 76). Continue to Glacier Peak Mines (Hike 37) on the slopes of Plummer Mountain and choose either the west-of-Glacier or east-of-Glacier alternate.

East-of Glacier alternate: Drop to Miners Creek, climb Middle Ridge, and continue to Buck Creek Pass (Hike 69). Descend Buck Creek to the old mining town of Trinity, walk the road to the Little Giant trail, cross Little Giant Pass (Hike 67) into the Napeequa valley, cross Boulder Pass (Hike 65) to the White River, and return via the White River trail to the Cascade Crest at Lower White Pass. **Distance from High Bridge to Lower White Pass 79 miles, elevation gain about 15,000 feet, hiking time 7 days.** The journey can be broken at either the Chiwawa River road or White River road.

West-of-Glacier alternate: Drop to the Suiattle River, climb the Vista Creek trail over ridges and down into Milk Creek (Hike 35), cross Fire Creek Pass to the White Chuck River (Hike 41), ascend the White Chuck to Red Pass, and continue via White Pass to Lower White Pass (Hike 63). **Distance from High Bridge to Lower White Pass 66 miles, elevation gain about 12,000 feet, hiking time 6 days.** The journey can be broken by trail exits to the Suiattle River road, White Chuck River road, or North Fork Sauk River road.

Pacific Crest Trail on side of Slate Peak. Silver Star Mountain in distance

The remainder of the way to Stevens Pass is comparatively level, wandering along the Cascade Crest with ups and downs, frequently alternating from east side to west side, mostly through open meadows of flowers or heather. From Lower White Pass (Hike 63) the trail stays high, dipping into forest only at Indian Pass and again at Cady Pass. From Cady Pass the route contours hillsides, traversing a mixture of forest and meadows past Pear Lake (Hike 57), climbing within a few hundred feet of Grizzly Peak, and proceeding onward to Lake Janus (Hike 59), Union Gap, Lake Valhalla (Hike 58), and finally Stevens Pass. **Distance from Lower White Pass to Stevens Pass 32 miles, elevation gain 5000 feet, hiking time 4 days.**

For details of mileages and campsites, see the Forest Service map and log of the Pacific Crest Trail, available free from any Forest Service office, or one of the guidebooks to route. From Harts Pass to Rainy Pass the signed camps are recommended, though not required.

STILL MORE HIKES IN THE NORTH CASCADES

This book covers the 100 miles from slopes of Mt. Baker to the scarp of Chopaka Mountain and the 90-odd miles from Stevens Pass to Canada. Companion volumes, *100 Hikes in the Alpine Lakes*, and *100 Hikes in the South Cascades and Olympics*, reach south. Another, *103 Hikes in Southwestern British Columbia*, follows the North Cascades over the border to their end. Shorter walks than those herein are described in *Trips and Trails 1: Family Camps, Short Hikes, and View Roads around the North Cascades*. The interface of Puget Sound lowlands and front ridges of the Cascades is treated in *Footsore 2 and 3: Walks and Hikes Around Puget Sound*. Approaches to and routes up peaks are the subject of *Cascade Alpine Guide*, a series of three volumes.

The 100 hikes have been selected to be representative of all the varied provinces of the North Cascades. However, it's a big country with hundreds of comparable trips. The books noted above describe many. Following is a sampling—some covered by the books, some not—that can be particularly recommended. The lack of detailed recipes may be compensated for by greater solitude.

NOOKSACK RIVER

Twin Sisters Mountain.

Silesia Creek from Canada: Reached from logging roads—lovely if brushy forest walk. Also accessible from Twin Lakes.

Bastille Ridge: Spectacular view of Coleman Glacier.

Middle Fork Nooksack to Park Butte: Glacier vistas and Mt. Baker views with sidetrip to Meadow Point.

Gold Run Pass: To beautiful gardens and Tomyhoi Lake.

Chilliwack River from Canada: Excellent forest walk from Chilliwack Lake.

Green Creek Trail to Elbow Lake.

Canyon Ridge: The loneliest trail in the vicinity, with many meadows and views.

Price Lake: Climbers' path to rock-milky lake under Price Glacier.

Easy Ridge: Abandoned trail to lookout site above Chilliwack River.

Ptarmigan Ridge: Snowy meadow walk to glaciers of Mt. Baker.

BAKER RIVER

South Fork Nooksack to Bell Pass: Trail over 3964-foot pass. An interesting route to Park Butte.

Elbow Lakes: 1½ miles on trail No. 679 and then cross-country to Lake Wiseman and Twin Sisters Mountain.

Dock Butte: See *Trips and Trails*.

Boulder Ridge: Forest trail climbing to edge of Boulder Glacier.

Swift Creek: Trail starts in meadows at Austin Pass and ends in forest near Baker Lake.

Anderson Lakes, Watson Lakes, and Anderson Butte: See *Trips and Trails*.

Baker River: Rain forest and beaver ponds on a low-elevation trail open in early spring.

Shadow of Sentinels Nature Trail: ½-mile walk. See *Trips and Trails*.

Blue Lake: ¾-mile walk. See *Trips and Trails*.

Slide Lake: Easy 1-mile hike from road No. 16. See the massive rockslide that dammed the lake.

SKAGIT RIVER– ROSS LAKE

Finney Peak: Short, abandoned trail to site of old lookout.

Sauk Mountain: See *Trips and Trails*.

Pyramid Lake: A faint trail in forest to lake under Pyramid Peak.

Diablo Lake trail: From Diablo Dam above cliffs to Ross Lake.

Ruby Creek: Magnificent river walk near North Cascades Highway.

Ruby Mountain: Abandoned trail, long climb, but spectacular views for the experienced hiker.

Perry Creek: Sidetrip on virtually vanished trail from Little Beaver into a hanging valley.

Silver Creek: Unmaintained valley trail on the west side of Ross Lake.

Panther Creek and Fourth of July Pass: 10-mile forest hike to view Snowfield and Eldorado Peaks.

Pierce Mountain Way: Alternate route up Sourdough Mountain.

McKay Ridge.

McAllister Creek: Dead-end trail from Thunder Creek.

Jack Mountain: Little-used trail starting from Ruby Pasture and going 6 miles to end amid meadows and views and camps. From here climbers continue to summit of Jack.

CASCADE RIVER

Marble Creek: See *Trips and Trails*.

Kindy Creek: Little-used trail providing access to Kindy Creek and Sonny Boy Lakes.

Trapper Lake: Rough trail to a deep cirque east of Cascade Pass.

NORTH FORK STILLAGUAMISH RIVER

Whitehorse Glacier via Lone Tree Pass; 2 miles of very steep trail to viewpoint, then 2 miles of straight-up blazed route to pass, then a climbers' route to the ice.

Mt. Higgins: Hike or drive Seapost Road from a mile west of Hazel to reach trailhead in 3 miles. Trail climbs past Myrtle Lake to abandoned lookout site.

SUIATTLE RIVER

Suiattle Mountain: From road No. 2640, 1 mile of unmaintained trail to Lake Tupso and White Creek road.

Tenas Creek to Boulder Lake: Long trail hike to wooded lake, also reached by bushwhack from Tenas Creek road.

Huckleberry Mountain: Old lookout site. Trail climbs 4800 feet in 7 miles. Big views. Good hiking in May to snowline.

Buck Creek: See *Trips and Trails*.

Sulphur Creek: See *Trips and Trails*.

Sulphur Mountain: Very steep trail to lookout site with commanding view of Suiattle River and Glacier Peak.

Canyon Lake and Totem Pass: A flower-covered ridge 5 miles from Image Lake.

Suiattle River to Suiattle Glacier: Magnificent forests. Trail is lost beyond Chocolate Creek. From there on the route is for the experienced only.

Bedal Basin: Steep miners' trail to a small meadow beneath Sloan Peak.

WHITE CHUCK RIVER

Mt. Pugh: Very long climb, the upper part usually steep snow.

Glacier Ridge: Shortcut to Pumice Cirque on a steep trail, partially maintained by a Boy Scout troop, past an old lookout site.

Crystal Lake: 1½ miles to a lake in a deep valley.

SOUTH FORK STILLAGUAMISH RIVER

Mt. Pilchuck: Popular hike to wide-view lookout (*Footsore 3*).

Mt. Forgotten: Forest trail to meadow views.

Big Four Glacier: See *Trips and Trails*.

Heather Lake: Very popular 2-mile hike to alpine lake (*Footsore 3*).

Lake 22: Very popular 2½-mile hike to alpine lake (*Footsore 3*).

Pinnacle Lake: 1½ miles of poor trail to beautiful lake with views (*Footsore 3*).

Meadow Mountain: Tiny meadows on wooded ridge from Tupso Lake.

Mallardy Ridge trail: 14 miles of unmaintained trail on wooded ridge.

Silver Gulch trail: 1½ miles on old miners' path to open ridges.

Marble Gulch: Plans are to rebuild this old miners' trail.

Martin Creek trail: Steep jeep trail to forested valley.

SOUTH FORK SAUK RIVER

76 Gulch: A route, no maintained trail, to old mines.

SKYKOMISH RIVER

Mt. Stickney: A route on logging roads and through bushes to high views (*Footsore 2*).

Sultan Basin: Short trail climbing beside waterfalls to Little and Big Greider Lakes (*Footsore 2*).

Mineral City–Silver Creek: Rich in mining history. The walk follows old logging roads.

Howard Creek: No trail, a bushwhacking climbers' route to Spire Mountain.

Troublesome Creek: Dead-end trail through the woods. See *Trips and Trails.*

North Fork Skykomish River: A long, forested, river-bottom approach to Crest Trail. Hike the trail now, before a logging road wipes it out.

Meadow Creek to Fortune Ponds, Peaches and Pear Lakes, Quartz Creek: Steep, long trail through virgin forest to Curry Gap.

LITTLE WENATCHEE RIVER

Dirty Face Peak: Dry trail to airy views of Lake Wenatchee.

Poe Mountain: Steep, easy trail to lookout site with big views.

Cockeye Creek trail: Over Poet Ridge to Panther Creek. Easy access to Poe Mountain from road No. 6504.

WHITE RIVER

Panther Creek: Long valley approach gives access to Ibex Creek canyon and Cougar Creek–Cockeye Creek.

White River: 14-mile valley approach to Crest Trail, noted for beautiful forest.

Indian Creek: 13-mile valley approach to Crest Trail.

Twin Lakes: Easy hike to popular mountain lakes.

Mt. David: A long 8 miles to a high lookout site.

CHIWAWA RIVER

Schaefer Lake: 5-mile climb to high country of beautiful Chiwawa Ridge. Difficult river crossing.

Leroy Creek: Steep trail to meadows and camps in a basin on the side of Mt. Maude, with access over the ridge to Ice Lakes.

Red Mountain: Old mining road, then trail, goes 7 miles from Buck Creek trail to high on Red Mountain. From trail-end a short, easy route leads over Red Mountain Pass and down to Spider Glacier.

Chiwawa Basin: The basin trail leaves the Red Mountain trail at basin entrance and winds through broad meadows, rejoining Red Mountain trail up high.

Phelps Ridge: A trail going from Red Mountain trail over the ridge and down to Phelps Creek trail at a point just above Leroy Creek.

Massie Lake: 6-mile trail from Chiwawa Basin up to Massie Lake and then up the ridge under Pass No Pass to join the Buck Creek trail.

Basalt Ridge: Long, dry climb, partly steep and brushy, to magnificent scenery.

Estes Butte: Steep and rocky trail to old lookout site. Few, if any, views.

Carne Mountain: High meadows along the Entiat Mountains—possible sidetrip to Ice Lakes.

ENTIAT RIVER

Duncan Hill: Former lookout with wide views of big peaks.

LAKE CHELAN–STEHEKIN RIVER

Domke Mountain: Sidetrail from Domke Lake trail climbs to old lookout site and views up Lake Chelan and Railroad Creek.

Holden Lake: 4-mile sidetrip from Railroad Creek to a lake in a hanging valley. Views of Mary Green Glacier on Bonanza Peak.

Flat Creek: Dead-end, 3⅓-mile trail into a scenic valley under the LeConte Glacier, giving access to a tough cross-country trip to the Ptarmigan Traverse.

Rainbow Lake: Popular trail to alpine lake.

Devore Creek–Company Creek loop: A long hike through beautiful alpine meadows.

Junction Mountain: Dead-end trail with views of Agnes and Stehekin valleys.

Prince Creek, Canoe Creek, Fish Creek: Long, steep access trails from Lake Chelan to the Chelan Summit.

Boulder Creek: To War Creek Pass and Chelan Summit.

Rainbow-McAlester loop: Long trail over a high pass.

McGregor Mountain: Long climb to long views from Lake Chelan to Glacier Peak.

TWISP RIVER

Scatter Lake: Very high alpine lake ringed by Lyall larch.

Hoodoo Pass: Into the heart of the Chelan Summit.

Fish Creek Pass: Long, easy hike up Buttmilk Creek to Chelan Summit.

War Creek: A much easier trail to War Creek Pass than the grueling approach from Stehekin.

Reynolds Creek: Joins the Boulder Creek trail.

North Creek: Steep, dry trail to a tiny mountain lake or down Cedar Creek to Early Winters.

Oval Creek: To small, wooded mountain lakes under the Chelan Crest.

Crater Creek trail to Crater Lake: High alpine lake under the Sawtooth Range.

Crater Creek trail to Martin Lakes: Beautiful alpine meadows and lakes.

Early Winters Creek

Silver Star: Hunters' camp reached by blazed route from Cedar Creek trail.

Rainy Lake: Easy hike from Rainy Pass (see *Trips and Trails*).

METHOW RIVER

Goat Peak: Short hike to a lookout (see *Trips and Trails*).

Wolf Creek: Long valley trail to Gardner Meadows, continuing to old mines and the summits of Gardner Mountain and Abernathy Peaks.

Setting Sun Mountain: Old lookout site on edge of Pasayten Wilderness.

Granite Creek

Panther Creek: Forest hike to Fourth of July Pass.

East Creek–Mebee Pass: Steep climb on old Indian-miners' route.

Mill Creek–Azurite Pass: Stiff climb beginning on an old mining road.

Canyon Creek: Forest walk on old narrow-gauge mining road to ghost town of Chancellor.

INDEX